PARADIGMS OF POWER

Styles of Master/Slave Relationships

PARADIGMS OF POWER

Styles of Master/Slave Relationships

Edited by Raven Kaldera

Alfred Press
Hubbardston, Massachusetts

Alfred Press
12 Simond Hill Road
Hubbardston, MA 01452

Paradigms of Power:
Styles of Master/Slave Relationships
© 2014 Raven Kaldera
ISBN 978-0-9828794-9-8

Printed in cooperation with
Lulu Enterprises, Inc.
860 Aviation Parkway, Suite 300
Morrisville, NC 27560

*Dedicated to my boys, Joshua and Brandon,
and to all my M/s friends who taught me
all the different ways a power dynamic
can be beautifully structured.*

Contents

Foreword: The Stories That Inspire Us
Raven Kaldera

When my alpha slaveboy and I first emerged from the woods with our nascent power dynamic relationship, in search of other kindred souls to commune with (or at least hang out with and talk about these subjects that no one else seemed to understand), it was well before the days of MAsT (Masters And slaves Together), or any M/s-focused conferences. We looked with dismay upon a demographic where everyone seemed to be either congregating in small sub-communities with one agreed-upon style of doing M/s (and if you hung out there, you were expected to conform to that style), or were solitary couples doing their own thing far away from community involvement. Some of the solitaries simply had no desire for M/s-focused community; others felt that they would not "fit in" to existing communities. When we probed further, we discovered that ninety per cent of that worry stemmed from the fact that they feared their particular style of M/s would not be acceptable to communities where other styles predominated.

At the same time, my slaveboy and I were making tentative forays into various M/s-oriented communities and testing the waters. We were fully prepared to pull back if the majority opinion turned against us, because we knew that our particular style (or mash-up of a number of unusual styles) did not in any way resemble the majority style in any of these communities. People scratched their heads when they saw us, and it did take a while for us to feel at home anywhere. However, in spite of everything, we managed to get to personally know enough people who could look beyond our "cultural" differences and form connections that we eventually felt like we belonged, at least in a few places.

Our experience—and the unhappy experiences of many people who reached out to tell us their fears and stories—made us curious about the actual makeup of this demographic when it came to styles of M/s relationship. There were plenty of assumptions in this vein by individuals who were the majority style in any given sub-community, but we were seeing and hearing something different. We wanted to learn about the imaginative diversity of this demographic, because we knew it existed.

We also knew that many BDSM practitioners had a rather limited view of M/s practitioners. We're often seen as rigid, prickly, reclusive, and unimaginative (because being controlling automatically means being unimaginative, right?), when the actuality is that we spend a great deal of time figuring out how to inspire each other on a daily basis, not just until the end of one scene. Finding practical, sustainable ways to reify a 24/7 power dynamic is not easy. You can't depend on constant arousal as you might with even a long-weekend sort of scene, because genitals are fickle and can desert you when you get a cold or the dog vomits on the floor. We wanted to see what stories M/s couples were whispering into each other's ears in order to keep that intensity flowing even in the face of turmoil and distress.

Just for the heck of it, I conducted a not-academically-rigorous-in-the-least survey of three M/s forums on the Internet site Fetlife, giving a list of possible M/s styles (including "other-please-describe" and "none of the above, we made up our own and it doesn't look like anything else") and asking people to label themselves. The results were surprising—the majority vote was with 1950s'-style, with "none of the above" coming in second, ageplay-focused third, and Leather fourth (with the rest distributed downward). The survey also gave me several new styles that I'd never heard of before, and some of them are in this book. At any rate, I realize that a larger survey conducted in a different place might yield entirely different results, but it was eye-opening to see so many styles described, and yet be clearly able to discern the power dynamic in each one.

That survey led to this book, but it's not just a writing buffet to display our fascinating differences. It's also here to inspire couples who are working out their M/s relationship and want to know their options. These styles are more than role-playing—every one of the couples who has written about them in this book has found a way to live them practically and usefully in the real world, perhaps disposing with the superfluous trappings but applying themselves to the philosophy. They are also more than just caricatures. They are sacred archetypes, stories that have been told over and over again until they have become part of the symbolic architecture of our culture, and our mind's eye. For many of us, they are the spice in our everyday M/s meal, and simultaneously the glue that holds everything together when trouble comes knocking.

Of course, no project is ever perfect. As you read through these essays, you'll notice that perhaps half of the couples whose relationships are delineated here employ more than one style in their day-to-day functioning. They have chosen to write about the style that is their main go-to, but they are not monolithic in their choices. In some cases, it was a little difficult to put them in one category. Relationships are not cookie-cutter things, and the ideal for a M/s relationship is to create something custom-built for the people in it. However, we felt that categories were useful anyway if only for reference purposes.

There's also the fact that this little book is not comprehensive. There are M/s styles out there—or at least versions of these styles— that are not represented in this book, if only because we were unable to find anyone who was willing or able to write articulately about them. For example, I sadly wasn't able to find essayists for Mommy/boy or Mommy/girl, Tamer/wild animal, Teacher/student, and others. (And yes, I've met people who use these styles and who are very definitely on the M/s section of the continuum.) Perhaps eventually this book can be expanded and reprinted; I'll look forward to that.

Enjoy your trip through our demographic. May it inspire, educate, and create smiles.

Raven Kaldera
HUBBARDSTON, MA
AUGUST 2014

Introduction: Diversity and Definitions
Sir Stephen

> *The beginning of wisdom is to call things by their right names.*
> –Chinese proverb

It may seem odd to begin a book about diversity in our Master/slave community by discussing definitions. However, we do have a desire to see these terms clearly defined, as evidenced by the repeated emergence of this question in seemingly endless discussion threads on numerous lifestyle forums. The topic also comes up within the confines of numerous off-line lifestyle groups and organizations. In opposition to this desire to define what in the world it is that we do stands the belief, firmly held by many, that the forms of our M/s relationships are simply too diverse and individualistic to be defined. Some take a line of reasoning beyond that, and voice a fear that defining the terms "Master", "slave", and "Master/slave relationship" is an effort to restrict the individualistic nature of such relationships.

Let's take a moment to examine this proposition. Look at this photograph:

A household salt shaker can be defined as a container that holds, and dispenses, ground salt through a set of small openings. Despite our ability to define what a salt shaker is, it does not limit the diversity of materials and styles in which a salt shaker can be imagined and created. If I ask someone to bring me a salt shaker and they hand me a chair, this is not evidence of their commitment to diversity, but rather a clear lack of understanding as to what I mean when I say "salt shaker", and what I mean when I say "chair". The fact that a salt shaker is not a chair, however, does not limit the diversity of salt shakers. So too with your M/s relationships—we can define them without limiting the diversity they can assume. However, we are confronted with a secondary issue when defining the terms "Master", "slave", and "Master/slave relationship", and that is the fact that these terms are used in multiple contexts, and within these contexts the definitions of the words will vary.

Hierarchically Structured Authority-Based Relationships

Hierarchically structured relationships require that one party in the relationship defers to someone else in the relationship for any one of a number of reasons. The individuals intentionally engage in creating a power imbalance. This imbalance might be limited, or extensive, depending upon the individuals involved, the circumstances in which they find themselves, and their end goal for their relationship. This deference might be non-consensual and short-term, as is the case when we are pulled over by the highway patrol for speeding. Or it may be extended out of respect for an individual's expertise in a particular area; or out of deference to their age; or because they have been awarded authority based upon their experience; or because we fear them physically or emotionally (this last being something that is typically indicative of an abusive relationship, which is not the form of relationship this book advocates or will explore). Some in the kinky communities may believe that we have a monopoly on such relationships, based upon the disparity inherent in hierarchically structured relationships and their attendant allocation of authority. However, hierarchical structure in relationships are not limited to kink.

We are exposed to this element in relationships at all stages of our lives and in all areas of our lives, vanilla or kinky. We can begin with the form of hierarchy that is common to us all—the parent/child relationship. Initially, of course, this relationship is non-consensual and the authority resides exclusively with the parents. Children rely, quite literally, upon their parents for their survival. They are wholly dependent and cannot obtain food, shelter or clothing on their own. However, as children grow, they fight to assert their own authority. Even before they can speak, children come to certain realizations—such as learning that crying yields food, relief from discomfort, or simply attention. As they begin to speak, they quickly learn the word "no", and use it to test the strength of the resolve of the adults around them.

As we grow, we are exposed over and over again to hierarchical relationships in which the roles of "authority figure" and "subordinate" are clearly defined, and in which our position in the hierarchy is explicit. Our educational experience is all about obedience to the teacher's instructions and demands. Our careers, if they are corporate, are about pleasing the boss or our clients, or both; in the military the hierarchical structure is much more explicit, and the power or authority we can exert is clearly defined by our rank, and so on.

So our "vanilla" relationships are almost always possessed of an authority-based dynamic: parent/child; teacher/student; principal/teacher; district supervisor/principal; boss/employee; customer/service employee; Father Superior/priest; Mother Superior/nun. As mentioned above, we defer to the police when pulled over; for that matter we defer to the TSA agent if we wish to board a plane. Hierarchy, authority, and subordination, are relationship elements that everyone has experienced and can understand.

The Matrix of Personality: Dominant/Dominance, Submissive/Submission

I am of the opinion that "dominant" and "submissive" are personality traits that exist within us all. Let us, for the moment, visualize a scale; at one end is 100% dominant and at the other is 100% submissive. Absent moderating external influences, we fall most comfortably somewhere along the spectrum. Where we fall helps us to identify as a dominant or submissive personality, or as someone right in the middle with no preponderance or preference for either. However, our default preference along the spectrum is not a constant in our lives. Individuals who live 100% of the time at one or the other absolute extreme end of the spectrum are most likely socially maladapted and suffering from some form of pathological disorder. (Time for a disclaimer—I have no training as a therapist or sociologist, but jeez, isn't this pretty obvious?)

For example, I consider myself to be possessed of a dominant personality. However, I do not express the same level of dominance with the armed highway patrol officer who pulls me over for speeding as I do with those in service to me. I do not express the same level of dominance towards my boss as I do towards those who report to me on a project. I make adjustments in my position along the D/s spectrum of behavior according to the power and authority I can legitimately and safely exercise within the context of any given situation.

Likewise, those who consider themselves to be submissive by nature will (or should) moderate their level of submissiveness according to the needs of the moment. A parent who is submissive in their relationship to their spouse or their lifestyle partner may need to express higher levels of dominance when it comes to getting the children to study rather than to play. Certainly there are those who are submissive in their home environment but who hold jobs outside the home requiring high-level leadership and management skills. I have come to the conclusion that "dominant" and "submissive" represents aspects of personality and behavior, and as such do not define a relationship format.

Relationships Based on Dominance and Submission (D/s)

On the other hand, dominant and submissive are part of the matrix of factors that lead us to decisions about the forms of relationships in which we do want to participate. The decision to assume the responsibility of command (or leadership) in one or more aspects of our kinky personal relationships—be that leadership in the form of topping, "parenting" (Leather Mommy or Daddy), trainer (of a pony or other pet), or as a Master—is just that; a decision independent of personality type. I know those with submissive personalities who enjoy topping, for instance. Likewise, the conscious decision to submit, whether it be as a bottom, adult "child" (Leather boy/boi or girl), or as a slave, can be made by those who are submissive in personality or by those who are dominant.

We have arrived, then, at the sometimes confusing difference between having a submissive personality and the decision to submit to the authority of another. Those who decide to actualize the submissive aspects of their personality in their personal relationships make a choice to submit. Submission requires a decision, and thus is inherently a part of us all. The desire to live in a hierarchical structure and take vows of obedience is not restricted to those who are submissive. Consider a Marine drill instructor. He (or she) is clearly not a timid, retiring, naturally submissive type. They can, and do, take control and assume responsibility within the limits of their authority. However, they have chosen to live within a community that demands obedience when confronted with orders from those who stand higher in the hierarchy. Marine drill instructors take orders from officers and they obey them; they submit to authority, for this is life they have chosen, even if they lack respect for a particular officer or disagree with a particular order.

Likewise, an individual with a powerful personality might choose to submit within one of our lifestyle relationship structures as a bottom, or as pony (or pet), or as a little, etc. Such individuals derive fulfillment from this conscious act of submission that exceeds their inclination towards dominance. It is also the case that those who move fluidly along the spectrum between dominant and submissive more readily take advantage of the option to switch. (For those who might not be familiar with the term, a switch is one who is comfortable in either the dominant or the submissive role and takes on one or the other as circumstances, or their mood, dictates.) The interaction of the dominant and submissive aspects of our personalities with the range of power exchange relationships available to us leads us to make the decisions about which form of relationship will be most fulfilling to us, and which role we choose to assume at any given time. In order to make the best possible choices, and offer ourselves the best chance of long-term success in those relationships, it is important to clearly define how to differentiate one from the other.

BDSM

BDSM is an acronym that, in the psychological literature, refers to Bondage, Discipline and Sado/Masochism. It is an umbrella term, encompassing a broad range of activities that are generally expressed in some form of physical or sexual interaction (although psychological elements can also be brought into play). These interactions tend to be episodic in nature. Participants in BDSM activities may or may not be involved in any form of relationship outside the agreed upon period of the BDSM activity. On the other hand, BDSM activities are found in a broad range of relationship formats, including relationships that are nominally egalitarian. It is not uncommon for those in an egalitarian relationship to occasionally indulge in rougher-than-usual sex play such as holding down their partner's hands, or to take a more dominant role and demand certain activities during sex.

As with the dominant and submissive aspects of our personalities, BDSM may be an element in our relationships—perhaps even a core element—but I don't believe it is accurate to describe a power exchange relationship as being a BDSM relationship. This is because BDSM is not necessarily a component in our M/s relationships. Although there is a high degree of cross-over, I personally know of numerous M/s relationships in which BDSM, or for that matter, any kind of sex, is not a defining element in the relationship.

One final note on BDSM: Some individuals now maintain that the DS in the middle of the acronym is meant to apply to dominant and submissive. This is becoming common usage in our community, but was not originally part of the acronym. And, as noted above, being dominant and submissive are really aspects of personality which we do not control via consent, although we do control our dominant or submissive behavior. Decisions based on our personalities and preferences, such as the decision to take control or the decision to submit in our personal relationships, for episodic activities or in support of long-term relationship goals, require that conscious decisions be made. I am not certain that it is beneficial to broaden out the application of the BDSM acronym, but I can't really see any harm in it either as long as we remain specific about the meanings we are ascribing to the acronym.

Context

> *England and America are two countries separated by a common language.*

> *–George Bernard Shaw*

It might also be said that the BDSM community and the M/s community are two communities separated by a set of common terms ... specifically the terms Master and slave. The assumption seems to be that, regardless of the kinky context in which we employ the terms Master and slave, they mean the same thing. In fact, countless hours have been spent in fruitless arguments about the fact that we cannot define what it means to be a Master or a slave because there is so much variation in the forms that M/s relationships can achieve.

Language and assumptions—they make for a bad combination. Take, for example, the word "engineer". It can mean an individual who drives a train, or an individual who has been trained in any one of a number of disciplines that may include chemical, electrical, civil, genetic, nuclear, systems, etc. The notion that when we use the word "engineer" it is automatically understood in the way in which we meant it cannot be assumed to be true. To avoid potential misunderstandings, it helps if we make known the context to which we apply the word when we use it. I don't think it would create an uproar within the general population, nor within the population of our alternative lifestyle communities, if we were that specific and that careful with our use of the word "engineer". However, when it is suggested that those of us in the alternative lifestyle communities can, and should, apply the same level of specificity to our use of the words "Master" and "slave", there is always an outcry.

Does the variability of meaning we can attach to the word "engineer" mean that we should abandon the attempt to define what it means in each individual specific context? Obviously not. I believe that much of the negative reaction to the attempt to achieve clarity about the definition and the use of the term "Master" results from the failure to clearly identify the context in which we are applying the term and the definition. I believe that there has been an unfortunately large amount of time and energy expended in heated debates that could have been easily resolved if we had employed the term "Master" a bit more cautiously, and with the understanding that when I say that I, or someone else is a Master, I do so within the context of BDSM dungeon play or within a Master/slave relationship. In each of these specific contexts the term will take on different shades of meaning, none of them being mutually exclusive, but all of them being correct once it is understood that we are actually talking about different disciplines that are unfortunately identified by the same term.

At Last … Master, slave, and M/s Relationship

Welcome to the Matrix.

It is out of this swirling matrix of aspects of personality (dominant and submissive), sexual preferences, kink/BDSM interests, fetishes and so on, that we begin to identify those relationship formats which will be most fulfilling to us. M/s is simply one of those formats. Let us begin with broader definitions and drill our way down to the specific definition of the term Master as it is applied within the Master/slave community.

In the broadest historical sense, we use this definition:

> *A Master is an individual who has acquired, and excelled at the application of, a specific set of knowledge, skills and abilities. Such individuals are frequently recognized for their accomplishments by their peers.*

Logically, the knowledge, skills and abilities so recognized are dependent upon the knowledge, skills and abilities needed to excel within the specific community in which the Master is operating. The body of knowledge required to attain a Master of Arts degree is different from that required to attain a Master of Science. It is also understood that while one academic will acknowledge the achievement represented by the acquisition of one degree or another, they are also clear that being a Master within one community does not qualify one to the title of Master within another community. A Master of Arts will not be expected to be able to design a bridge.

An individual acknowledged as a master in the dungeon for his or her skill with a flogger does not necessarily have an interest in assuming responsibility for control of another individual's life on a 24/7 basis. The requisite skills and abilities for each are different. The context in which the term is being applied is different. The word "Master" is correct in both contexts, but it has a unique meaning in each.

With those caveats in mind, I think it is fair to state that the Master/slave community is a subset of the extremely broad and varied kink community. However, the Master/slave community is differentiated by the creation of relationships that aspire toward an expression of the hierarchically structured dynamic that is as persistent as possible, up to and including the complete surrender of all aspects of the slave's will and life to the complete control of the Master. Within the context of this specific subset of the broader D/s community, we can arrive at a meaningful set of definitions for "Master", "slave", and "Master/slave Relationship".

A Master *is an individual who aspires to the complete control of another individual within a consensual, highly structured, and hierarchical relationship. A Master recognizes the responsibilities he or she assumes in taking such control. He or she strives to meet them by developing skills and abilities consistent with the fulfillment of his or her responsibilities as well as through the establishment of, and adherence to, personal standards of honor, integrity, ethical behavior, respect, loyalty, and courage.*

A slave *is an individual who aspires to complete obedience to another individual within a consensual, highly structured, and hierarchical relationship. A slave recognizes the responsibilities he or she assumes in striving to achieve this deep level of obedience. He or she strives to meet them by developing skills and abilities consistent with the fulfillment of his or her responsibilities as well as through the establishment of, and adherence to, personal standards of honor, integrity, ethical behavior, respect, loyalty, and courage.*

An M/s relationship *is that form of relationship in which consenting adults agree to establish a highly structured, hierarchical relationship that aspires towards the persistent (24/7) expression of complete control of one individual (the slave) by another (the Master). Within this context the Master and slave will tend to develop those policies, procedure, practices, rule, protocols, rituals, and ceremonies that best suit their needs and will uniquely define their particular relationship.*

With these definitions as a basis, we can see that (like the salt shakers) while the general nature of M/s relationships can be defined, there can also be extraordinary and virtually unlimited diversity in the forms that they will take. This diversity will be fueled, first and foremost, by the aforementioned policies, procedure, practices, rule, protocols, rituals, and ceremonies that best suit the unique needs of the individuals within that relationship. Your slave may appear naked at the door while mine appears in her household uniform. Your slave may sit on the floor, mine may use the furniture. Your slave may bow while mine curtseys. Each relationship will have its own uniquely diverse expression of what it means to be M/s.

Now, having established an understanding of what we can be said to have in common, it is the purpose of the rest of this book to explore what sets us apart one from another.

Leather

Living Leather
slave kelRat

I'm a slave in a Leather family, consisting of my Master, my two Leather brothers, and three other queer Leather people—a dyke couple who are friends of my Master, and the boy of one of my slave brothers. If that sounds a little crazy to you—and it might if you're either monogamous or you don't understand a household where not everyone is sexual with everyone else—then you might not be able to get your head around the place where Leather came from. It came out of the gay leather bars and the gay SM bar culture, and while it may have changed a lot between then and now, its origins look a lot more like our household than like the average married monogamous heterosexual couple who happen to also be Master and slave.

You want me to explain Leather? Understand that whatever I say will be disagreed with by someone, somewhere. Understand that there are many different definitions of Leather, from "wearing leather clothing and accoutrements while having kinky sex" to "being an honorable person while being Master and slave" to "whatever I decide it is". I'm in a somewhat more conservative camp. For me, being Leather means that the following concepts are a part of my identity and my lifestyle:

1. Leather is a specific subculture that crosses over both S/M and M/s. Some Leather people are only into S/M plus Leather culture; some are only into M/s plus Leather culture and some are into both. (I'm into both.) I've met some Leatherfolk who didn't practice S/M, but even they had rough sex that emphasized dominance and submission.

2. Leather, as a subculture, has rules and standards for its practitioners. These rules and standards may vary from group to group (and couple to couple), but in general if you discard too many of them, you may need to think very hard in a non-defensive way about whether you are actually *living* Leather or just playing with bits of it when it's convenient for you.

3. These rules and standards developed over time, from our respected forebears, and have become tradition, along with a number of

public and private rituals. A lot has been written (much of it fictional) about the "Old Guard" and whether they came up with any of these traditions. I'm not going to argue here about how many of the actual protocols came down from the Old Guard (if you want to know more, please read Guy Baldwin's essay "The Old Guard History, Origins, and Traditions" from his book *Ties That Bind*), but I can speak with surety that due to the military origins of Leather spirit, being part of a well-boundaried hierarchical society that judges its members by how they live up to specific standards is definitely one of the basic premises that *did* come down from the Old Guard, or at least once segment of the Old Guard. I'll go into that in a moment, but suffice it to say that those of us who practice these traditions and rituals feel that they are valuable enough to pass down to future generations.

As one more comment on Old Guard customs, I also recommend Joseph Bean's essay "Old Guard? If You Say So," which was first published in the VASM Scene Newsletter, and is available on the Internet. Here he talks about the two groups of early leathermen—one made up of correct, military-disciplined lovers of order, and one of rebellious bikers who loved to shock—who coexisted side by side in the bars until their lines finally blurred. This is the best description I've ever read about the differing "strands" that slowly wove themselves into the rope that is Leather, and how one person's historical recollections can be very different from that of another, depending on what communities they once belonged to.

4. If you commit to belonging to a Leather community somewhere, the respected senior members of that community do have the right to judge whether you are living up to those standards as they understand them. No one is required to belong to their local Leather community (or any other one) in order to consider themselves Leather, but if you cannot find a Leather community that you can bear to allow yourself to be judged by, think very hard about why that may be. Part of being Leather is being willing to be seen by one's peers and honored by them, but that also means they will tell you if you're not living up to these community standards.

That's part of having your back. Ideally, you should want to be held to high standards by your peers, just as you hold them to the same standards. It should make you proud to do so. Part of being Leather is *wanting* to be held to high standards by your community, and wanting to get it right.

5. Leather is hierarchical, and being OK with hierarchy is important, even if you're a Master. I hate to say it, but Leather is not for Masters who don't want to answer to anyone about anything. (Maybe they should pick a different style.) Slaves obviously answer to their Masters, but Masters should at least behave with a little extra deference to highly respected Masters in their communities, and in some cases, even (gasp!) very experienced and respected senior slaves. That's part of why we work so hard at making sure that people in our communities don't act like jerks—we don't want them sullying the respect we would otherwise intend to give them. The flip side of giving deference to elders is making sure that the "designated elders" are actually worthy of that deference. Does having community standards make a little more sense in that light?

6. Not all the rules have to do with protocols—walking a pace behind and to the left of one's Master, not initiating conversation with a Master if you are a slave, etc. Some of them—many of them, in fact—have to do with our moral character. *You don't lie. You don't steal. You treat everyone with basic courtesy, even if they piss you off. You don't spout gossip without checking your facts and making sure it's necessary to open your mouth. You treat subordinates with decency, not contempt and exploitation. You walk your talk; you're not a hypocrite. You make commitments and you keep them. You don't deliberately shock the outsiders. You act this way even when it's not convenient or comfortable, when you really just want to verbally gut-punch someone.* This is how we know that you're worthy to wear the leather that is our expression of this identity.

7. Community service is very important to being Leather. You can tell the Leatherfolk at the BDSM club at least partly because they are the ones who do the boring work of planning, spreading the word on, and sticking around throughout the fundraiser. This doesn't

mean that others don't contribute as well, but it does mean that service to whatever community to which one has committed is considered valuable and necessary to one's standing as Leather.

Some of the Old Guard-type rules feed my soul, giving me meaningful structure and a sense of reverence every time I follow a certain protocol or do a certain household ritual. That sense of reverence helps me to keep a more positive outlook on the more difficult aspects of my daily service, and as such it is especially important. It feeds me to be part of a community that holds me to a strict standard that I can achieve and rewards me for that, as opposed to the social standards I can't achieve because I am a pierced-up, tattooed, leather-wearing faggot pervert. It feeds me to be part of a community whose elders are actually worthy of respect, because it's been earned by their visible honor and commitment. It feeds me to follow protocols with history as well as power-exchange heat, linking me to the ones who came before and struggled against such odds.

On the other hand, there are a few rules and protocols that are carry-overs from an earlier time when Leather was the purview of an outcast few, guarding themselves against social and lawful backlash, and struggling to find family ties in the face of an overwhelmingly hostile society. I believe that we do need to lose some of those rules, including—to quote Guy Baldwin in the above-mentioned essay— "None of these rules are taught or explained to anyone except by innuendo, inference, or example."

Many of us Leatherfolk feel, for example, that educating others about Leather is not only a good way to make sure that our lifestyle doesn't die out, but is also nourishing to the character and soul of the educator. This means that we have to train newcomers, not just expect them to figure it out themselves. This latter method excluded those who lacked the social skills to intuit subtle and sometimes arcane protocols fast enough not to get kicked out. Some would say that this is a good enough reason to keep it mysterious, but as a Leather slave who is pretty darn dorky yet who believes that he is still a valuable part of his Leather family and community, I think we throw too many babies out of the bathwater there.

On top of this, we have the rule—which was definitely an original rule—that Leather Is For Gay Men. Some might argue that lesbians of the same era were copying gay men in their exploration of power-exchange protocols, but even with this expansion, it was still definitely a Queer Thing. Some older gay Leathermen still feel this way, which is off-putting to the hundreds (or perhaps thousands by now) of heterosexual couples who currently identify as Leather with all that implies. Certainly no gender combination has a monopoly on integrity, honor, or community service, but is there anything about Leather that is specifically Gay Sex and doesn't translate well to that kind of inclusion? I've seen one small struggle in our own Leather family. My Leather auntie Sasha is butch and has no problem with the Leather style, but her girl leesa is very much a femme, and found the military-edge protocols unfeminine. She felt that while she could show submission in whatever way that Sasha wanted—including standing on her head if that was the rule—her own femme self and feminine submission did not show through Leather uniform, movements, and style. Sasha found the idea of dressing her girl in a leather corset instead of a bar vest, and a tight leather miniskirt instead of chaps, quite sexy but contrasting entirely with her own Leather aesthetics, not to mention those of her local queer Leather community who might see leesa as "too het-BDSM-looking" or "not serious enough". The two of them have had to work out compromises, and it's a constant if minor struggle for them.

However, straight folk are turning to Leather in droves these days, it seems, and Leather is altering to accommodate them. (Similarly, younger people are poking into Leather and trying to see how much of it suits them and their relational aesthetics.) We queers raise our eyebrows when straight would-be Leatherfolk brag about having trained under "Old Guard Masters" who, of course, never used them sexually (if they are straight men) or made an exception for them (if they are women). It's kind of funny that for the first time, queerfolk have something that straight people want. I'm OK with that (although I still raise my eyebrows) but some older gay Leathermen feel like a disenfranchised Native American being exploited for their spirituality, and act accordingly. If you are Leather and straight, it's important to be respectful of the queers who created this lifestyle against all social odds. Learn about queer politics and struggles, and bother to attend and shell out at that AIDS fundraiser. Never say that queer issues aren't your issues. If you are Leather, they are your issues even if you are straight, because you have taken on queer lifestyle "ancestors", and it's part of how you honor them.

If you're interested in Leather, read up on it—and then expect that any Leather community you find will probably only use about two-thirds of the old rules (if that) and will probably have added several new ones. Part of learning Leather history, at least in overview, is to get an idea of where we came from so that you can understand where we are now. In addition, if you know something about the widely varying collection of Leather protocols, you can choose which you want to practice in your own household.

Leather isn't for everyone. If you don't resonate with what I've written so far, that's all right—there are plenty of other styles in this book, or you could just make up your own. But if you're going to identify as Leather, make an effort to actually do that. Don't just buy a bar vest and hat and slap the label on yourself. If so few of the traditions and rituals resonate with you that your lifestyle barely ever resembles traditional Leather, don't cling to the name just for the cachet. Figure out your own style, and educate people about that instead. While I love the idea of passing on Leather tradition, we do actually need more people doing M/s authentically and well more than we need an unending supply of Leatherfolk.

(Even if my Master looks wistfully at that latter idea.)

Mastery, Slavery, and Being Leather
Master Griffin of House Griffin

I established Castle Griffin in 2006 as an education-and-service-based Leather household, located in the DC Metro area. Our household's mission is to be an open and welcoming home to our friends and family in this lifestyle, and to provide opportunities for fellowship, laughter, service, learning, and personal growth.

Leather—to me and to my slave—has many facets. It is about putting all our passion into our play and our hot kinky sex. It is about wearing leather, for the look, the smell, and the feel; and our daily and event leathers make us feel good and sexy when wearing them. There is also a functional reason to put on leather. I own horses and wear leather to the barn; I used to ride motorcycles and wore leather for protection, and we fight in the SCA where we wear leather armor. Although the sexual passion, feel, and practicality are all part of it, there is more to "being Leather" than the physical leather we put on.

I have found that Leather also includes the spirituality of both owning our perverse selves and a continuing life of self-improvement and learning. This spirituality, for me, may be the most important aspect of the Leather lifestyle. In this community, I can be totally honest with who I am and not hide my twisted nature. By living honestly, I also live with pride and respect for myself and for others striving to live their truths. My community is made up of those whom I value and respect for how they live their lives and truths, and honesty is the most important trait I seek in my peers and friends.

My slave and I began our journeys separately, both of us engaging in private kink, BDSM, and D/s-based relationships to different degrees over the years. We began public kink and BDSM in the mid 1990's, and we met (in a non-kink setting) in 1998. We did not tell each other we were kinky then, though two years later we met again at a BDSM lifestyle bed-and-breakfast. Over the next few years, I watched the work and service slave Ann was doing for the community and different Leather families, and I liked what I saw in her work, dedication, service and integrity. In 2005 we began a Master/slave relationship and I decided to establish a Leather household. I found that our greatest resource is that our strengths complement each other. I tend to be the visionary and give direction to our journey, and slave Ann is strong at organization and planning. I have a good sense of humor, and my slave tells really bad puns. We know that as a couple and team we are able to do more for ourselves, our family and our community than we could do individually. I like knowing we have made a difference, even a little one, in people's lives.

Having a focus on education and service, we have found others who share that vision (or they have found us). I took on a live-in houseboy, Madra, in 2009. Madra found a young man as a partner, Rax, who moved into the house later that year. They both asked to join the household, and Rax became a junior Master. Two years later, Sir Rax was promoted to being a Master without the junior notation. Master Rax and slave Madra also moved out to their own place that year also, and they do a lot of work and lifestyle education with the local college group and young Kinklings in the area. Since I call my home The Castle, they are calling theirs The Fort. They have established their own Leather household, but remain under our Family structure. I believe in each household running its own affairs, but being part of a larger family unit gives it continuity, support, and unity. I do not tell Master Rax how to live his life or run his household—he's earned that right. However, when he seeks advice I try to give guidance as I can.

Education is our community service, and thus an important part of our family's Leather lifestyle. I started teaching kink and play topics in the late 1990's in North Carolina. (I was very active in the pony play world, as both a handler and as a pony, and I can be seen as *Red Hot Pony* in several issues of *Equus Eroticus*, and also in the documentary *Born In A Barn*.) As my relationships grew more towards power exchange and I settled into my mastery, my teaching focus shifted to self-development, personal growth, relationship building, and Master/slave education. Both my slave and I currently present and teach, both together and individually, on a variety of M/s topics.

I open our house to a variety of events and workshop several times a year. Our events usually develop from someone suggesting a topic and I mull it over a while, then give my slave her marching orders and stand back. Way back. Slave Ann is awesome at planning, contacting, coordinating and organizing the events. She brings any major decision to me, but she handles the little ones. I do not micromanage; I picked a smart, talented slave for a reason. I have her give me updates once a week and I can guide or change directions from there if I need or want to.

We enjoy all our events, but our favorite of all is our annual Orphans Christmas. Regardless of which, or any, of the holidays someone celebrates, Christmas can be a difficult time to be alone. As part of our Leather service, I open our house to anyone in the community who does not have a place to go and is alone for the holidays, whether due to physical or emotional distance. We offer a wonderful kinky, silly, happy Leather family who want folks to be a part of our family for the holidays. This is not a big production, just lifestyle folks getting together to celebrate *family*. Family is what brings us together. The intimate closeness of the household family, our Leather Family bond, or the connection we feel with the larger community.

Since venturing into the public kink world, we have continually sought out others who lived life in a way that matched our own. Both my slave and I have a military background and we strive to hold to a high standard of behavior. Becoming Leather was not a matter of finding the Leather community and joining it, of deciding to become like them. Rather, we found the community by finding folks who lived their lives to a standard we both had set for ourselves.

I have found that working on ourselves is the best way to improve our relationship and the family. Being a Master/slave couple is the basic foundation of our relationship. We fit in with our work, our bio families, neighbors, and outside interests, but we never drop the power exchange aspect of our relationship. Protocols are not dropped when in a vanilla public setting; some go stealth, but most continue as is. When the road has been rocky we do not back off from our relationship structure and protocols; in fact we adhere even tighter to our M/s and the structure it gives us. We work on the "us" part of the relationship, but it has been through the work on ourselves that we have made the greatest impact on the relationship.

We decided that slave Ann needed a mentor, and she picked our long-time friend Master Don. They met once or twice a month, sometimes weekly. I never asked what they discussed; I wanted to give her that time to work on whatever she needed without my influence. My slave also attended workshops, slave retreats, and slave circles (discussion groups for slaves only); she found places to improve her skills but came home talking more about how they affected her outlook and mindset.

My work on self-improvement included reading books and articles on a variety of topics. The set of books on Master/slave relationships by Dr. Bob Rubel has been especially good in giving me some insights and understanding about myself and how our relationship plays out. However, working on myself has recently lead me down a path of self-discovery I would have never dreamed would have such an impact on my mastery. I grew up riding horses, but never really got into training them. After being away from horses for twenty-five years, I bought a 4 year old mare and I jumped into learning all I could about training. As I learned about natural horsemanship and the relationship between horse and owner, I learned more about myself. I use my "barn time" to think about how to really lead, how to be observant, how I affect outcomes, and how I can understand better where my partner's (whether horse or slave) perception is coming from. As I learned to think about how my actions are perceived from the horse's point of view, I learned to use that at home with how my slave sees and reacts to my actions and words. I truly feel that becoming better at understanding my part in the interaction with the horse has made me a better Master and better partner to my slave.

There is a great deal of material going around at different events and conferences, as well as online, speaking about the history of Leather and the Lifestyle. While I value the history and those keeping it, I find my focus is on where we are now and our future. I have observed Leather families and households in our local community and across the nation while traveling and teaching. I have taken, used, modified and adapted protocols and rituals from them and made some of my own. Castle Griffin is not old, has not been around since the

1940s, and we can't (and would not) identify as "Old Guard". Our traditions have not been handed down from Master to Master for years now. Those things are not what define us as a part of the Leather community. Our actions do that.

We are just eight years old—a household still in its infancy in many ways. We have made a difference in our family, our local community and with events and individuals around the nation. I work daily to be a better person, leader, and Master. My slave works just as hard to be the best she can be as well. The power and authority I have with my slave is proportional to my ability to lead. My leadership, my slave's obedience, our service, and our actions are what make us Master/slave and our household a Leather household.

Listen to Your Leather Heart
Master Michael Shorten and his slave angie

Master Michael is a 47-year-old cis-male. He identifies as heterosexual and kinky, as someone attracted to S/M and kinky relationships—mainly of the "authority transfer" type. He's had kinky fantasies since he can remember being sexual, but he didn't come out as kinky till the mid-1990s. It was then that he first started attending demos and weekends at the old Leather Rose in Chicago, and he's been hooked ever since.

Slave angie is a 46 year old cis-female. She identifies as queer and kinky. She has been active in the BDSM community since 2003, but she's been reading (and having fantasies to) books like "Story of O" since she was a teenager. She experimented some before meeting Master Michael, and then they began their M/s relationship.

We both are active in the Leather/kink community. Michael is a co-founder of the Chicago Leathermen's Group, a discussion group for Leather and Leather-curious men. He's a community member of the Chicago Hellfire Club's McAdory Committee. Michael is a full member and former president of Chicago Leather Club, as well as a full member of LRA Chicago, and co-director of MAsT: Greater Chicago. He's an associate of Corn Haulers L&L, Atons of Minneapolis and Leather Hearts Clan of Dallas. Slave angie is a full member and officer of the Chicago Leather Club. Angie is member of MAsT: Greater Chicago. She is a former Board Director for the LRA Chicago, a pansexual dungeon social club, and she volunteers as a bootblack at many local events.

Together, we are honored to hold the titles of Illinois Master/slave 2013, Great Lakes Master/slave 2013 and International Master/slave 2014.

Master Michael: My slave and I live in a 24/7 Master/slave relationship. We define the "power exchange" as an authority transfer—she's given me total authority over her life. We've been together for over 10 years. To the vanilla world, our M/s relationship looks like a loving, respectful, and supportive relationship, and she has a pretty necklace that she wears all the time. Inside the kink/Leather world, we look like a loving, respectful and supportive relationship, but one where the collar around her neck has much more meaning than just pretty jewelry.

Our relationship inside the kink/Leather world looks like what I learned from folks, what I took away from classes, examples and—most importantly—experiences that we've shared together. It's based on authority, respect for each other, responsibilities to one another and the relationship, her service and duty to me, my service and duty to the relationship and our Leather.

Now what does that "look like"? Well, that's probably something I could write a book about, but I'll try to summarize. The authority part may not be easy to spot, but although angie can (and does) operate on her own, she does it within a set of protocols and expectations that I've communicated to her. So you'll see her go about her business in a way that may seem pretty average, when she is actually working within a set of my guidelines. There are times when she will come to me to ask about specifics, but this is done quietly and smoothly, without drawing attention to them.

The respect part—I hope—simply shows in how we interact with each other. We laugh and play a lot and we don't take ourselves seriously (too much), but we also don't hide that she belongs to me. I don't treat her badly and I'm not shy about valuing her—whether it's her input to a conversation or her activities with me or our community. The service and duty from her to me, and from me to the relationship, hopefully shows in what we do—as she takes care of me, so I take care of the relationship. Our Leather... well, that's how we play and fuck, that's our circle of friends, and that's our service back to the community.

My story starts back to when I was a little "kinkling" looking for the things that made me hard and interested me. Out of the straight people that I knew, there were a few who acted and played differently. After a while, I learned they identified as "Leather". These straight people had friends in the gay, lesbian and trans* communities here in Chicago. A couple of them were associated with a (now closed) back-patch Leather club called "Leather United Chicago". The men and women in these circles wore hot leather, and those who identified as Tops/Dominants/Masters acted in ways that I found attractive and worth emulating. Their knowledge and skills were equally matched in strength by the bonds I saw between them. It was something that spoke to me.

In 2001, a couple of these folks attempted to restart Leather United Chicago, but instead they formed the Chicago Leather Club. I wanted to be a part of what I saw as a greater whole with these folks. I had formed friendships, but it was at that point that I went through some serious life issues and had to pull back. It wasn't until 2008 that I was in a place where I could pledge to be a full member.

In those early times, I was also part of the Leather Rose (which became LRA-Chicago) a social BDSM dungeon. It always had the reputation for being seedy, edgy and "leather". The Leather-identified folks that I'd mentioned earlier played at the LRA, so that also became a home for me. This was my place to play, where I learned my skills and where I saw the differences between those who identified and lived as "Leather" and the kink/BDSM people. I also had the opportunity to go to the Chicago leather bars Cellblock and Touché, and went frequently during International Mr. Leather. I saw these straight people interact with and be accepted by gay, lesbian and trans* people, although their numbers were few. I saw how they played in those spaces—with passion, with intent, and sometimes with a spirituality that I was attracted to. I also played in those spaces. Through my M/s relationship, through the S/M connection, through the trust and bond I have with my slave, and through being open to experiences, I've discovered that spiritual side.

Over the last decade, I've formed my own bonds and connections to the gay, lesbian and trans* Leather communities by being an active member in the Chicago Leather/kink community and by being an active ally. I watched, listened, learned, and emulated the things that I admired and felt kinship for: Hard, rough, outward sexuality; dedication to my sexual and lifestyle choices; loyalty and brother/sisterhood to my fellow club members and the club members of other Leather clubs with the same feeling I held for those I connected with at the Leather Rose/LRA-Chicago; and a belief that I was a part of a community where I had a place, a duty and a purpose.

I call myself Leather because those people with whom I have formed these bonds call themselves Leather. They cross a wide swath of communities. I identify with them, and they identify with the ways that I feel. I've learned from people I admire, from people that turned me on, and from people that I felt/feel a bond with. My definition of Leather is very consistent with their definition.

I have also struggled with my definition of Leather, with whether I had a place in the Leather community, and what that place was. Not too long ago, I thought pursuing "het Leather" history was what I needed to do. That earned me a harsh rebuke which gave me pause and got me to thinking ... to where I came back to see Leather as Leather. I'm straight. I'm Leather. Leather is Leather—some are pioneers, some are old settlers, and some are new settlers.

My definition of Leather, stated later on, is what I hold to for myself. How we, as a Leather tribe, as a kink subculture, as a niche of the niche, choose to define ourselves, how we choose to evolve, how it evolves whether we personally choose that or not ... this I can't say. My story is my own, and how I pursue this journey is only my personal reflection of that.

slave angie: I had started off in the kink community playing with others, but I had never seen anything about "Leather" until I met Master. I had been invited to join him at a dinner which would feature an "exchange of colors" between the Chicago Leather Club (CLC) and the Knights of Leather from Minneapolis. When I saw this happen, when I saw the brotherhood and how much these people felt it there, I also felt something.

It sat in me for awhile, because as Master and I started our relationship, we were focused on ourselves, making our home, merging our families, figuring out what this all meant. Master had taken a break from the community and so I let it go as well. After a while, I started to ask Master about it. I had kept watching CLC on the website, and I wanted to know more. We talked about Leather and he said "It's hard to explain, you have to find what it means to you." He said that our interpretations, how Leather speaks to us may not end up being the same. He said he wasn't going to make me get involved if it didn't speak to me.

So eventually, when Master decided to pledge to CLC, I didn't know if I should join with him. But then it occurred to me that pledging was the only way I would know. So I went in with him, and I found that what I wanted to do was contribute to the community in a worthwhile way. I did that as part of my pledge project and I was welcomed and supported. That gave me the courage to get more involved, and I did—by getting involved in our local playspace, the LRA Chicago, and by becoming a bootblack.

I met two wonderful people through CLC—Daddy T and Nat. They made a huge impact on me in learning about Leather and my place in it. They had a way of mentoring me without making me feel like I was doing it wrong, and that it was OK to make mistakes and then learn to do better. Working my butt off as part of the LRA board, I learned how to stand on my two feet and stick up for myself within the Leather community. I learned that I did have a voice.

Through bootblacking, I gained a love of leather (both the community and the material), of the preservation of the items, and of the history. I had started my bootblacking by doing Master's leathers, and learning how to do that from other bootblacks got me interested in doing it on my own. I was inspired by watching bootblacks at the LRA Chicago, like Riley, Rachel, Leslie Anderson and Pony (IMsBB 2009). I liked it because it was service, it was hotness, it was art. I came to love bootblacking because of the connection with the person in the chair. I love the experience, the look on their face. I learned about the common ground between Leather people.

And that was how I got started in Leather.

Master Michael: Our definition of leather is simply stated:

It's about how we fuck. It is about the circle of friends and chosen family that we would do anything for. It's about earning and having our place in a greater whole.

To define each of these three parts is huge and difficult, and it's wrapped up in where we both came from, how we see the world, and how we want to be seen.

A huge contrasting definition, of course, is the idea that there is one true Leather way of doing things (from "Ye Olde Guarde" traditions handed down by the "Council of Elders") versus the idea that Leather is whatever one wants it to be. It's tradition and mysterious rituals versus sexual radicalism and sexual outlaws. The idea that a couple of people can write books that somehow codify what a Leather person is and what Leather is all about is up against the refutations of these books by gay leathermen, lesbian leatherwomen and trans* leatherfolks who were there then and are here now.

There is also the idea that Leather is about "honor, duty, trustworthiness" ... and that's a contrast to a lot of what I hear it was about in "Ye Olde Dayes" where Leather was about how hard and macho someone looked and fucked while living in the shadows and dark bars. A lot of that history gets mixed up, I believe, with concepts stemming from brotherhoods/sisterhoods forming out of GLBT motorcycle clubs and sex clubs. For those club members, their colors and their club were their family, and it was important (and possibly life-saving) to stick by them no matter what. The places and people they were fucking were their safety net.

Today, however, we have to face the fact that a root element of Leather—the need for Leather clubs and bars as a safety net and surrogate family—is fading with the assimilation and integration of Leather into the more mainstream kink world. People far smarter than myself have been speaking out about this, and I encourage the reader to seek them out—Master Skip Chasey, Hardy Haberman, Guy Baldwin, and Laura Antoniou are the ones that first come to mind. Look for keynote speeches and articles—this is a topic that consumes much of the Leather world on a regular basis. It's a question of "To be or not to be"... and what it will mean "to be".

Leather feeds my need for a structured relationship where everything is tightly coupled together, where we have defined roles and responsibilities that can still be explored to find new things. It feeds my need for living in the extremes and on the edge. It brings a mindfulness and awareness to the relationship, and allows us to explore spiritual places—places where those roles and the nature of who we are open up to us as we explore and grow in our roles. Within this relationship, I feel that it is vastly bigger than just the sum of myself and my slave, and that gives me comfort.

Leather feeds my soul in those moments of sexual ecstasy, where people join in a dance or work that goes to the extremes and explores physical, mental, emotional, and spiritual places. Leather and my Leather club are made up of the people I trust, to whom I can go to with anything, who have my back as I have theirs. Having a place within a greater Leather community, knowing who I am and how I relate to others in terms of being a member of a backpatch Leather club, knowing that I have earned my place, knowing that I have a good reputation … this gives me comfort and a sense of security. I feel as part of a greater whole and I like that.

However, we have found that each M/s relationship is unique, just as Leather is unique to each person who identifies that way, so it is hard for me to ascribe specific rules/protocols/rituals to Leather specifically. We identify with Leather; does that make our rules/protocols/rituals Leather? I think that out of everyone I know, Master Robert Rubel probably answers this far better than I could with his Protocol books, in terms of general knowledge and general protocols, even though I don't follow many of his recommendations, such as having a contract. These are the three guidelines I have for my relationship:

+ Because of the way we define our leather, there are some protocols related to the leathers we wear.

+ We are both to be involved in the community and our club.

+ We are to be dedicated to supporting leather events.

Wait… scratch all that. Yes, I'm leaving that in, but as I've been chewing on this for several days, I started going back to what my elders/mentors taught me and it hit me—there was a *huge* lesson that I see echoed in my leather brothers and sisters. I've told this story before: When angie and I first got together, we decided to "throw out the rulebook". What that meant to us was to drop the preconceptions, drop the baggage, don't rate or judge ourselves by other relationships and what we saw around us.

This was how I was taught by the leather people who I learned from. Find your own path. Listen to your own heart. Find the beat of a different drummer and follow it … but do it with respect for the person you are with. Honor their role and their heart. Do it from the heart and look for the deeper, spiritual meaning from it; look for where it touches your heart and their heart. Don't do these things from ego, or a one-way street, but foster, mentor, raise each other up.

So to that end, all of my rules, protocols and rituals stem from those lessons. That's not to say I don't see these echoed in other types of M/s relationships, but when you add in how we define our leather, and then add in the lessons I learned, and then the direction we took on our own—finding our own way without the idea that a specific approach, or even a specific definition (aside from just the large umbrella Master/slave and leather labels) would define us or guide us. I guess that's the spirit of Leather, or at least the Leather I was taught.

However, there are a few definite ideas that I would recommend to those who are interested in a Leather form of M/s:

✦ **Get involved in Leather community. Volunteer. Support. Show interest, not replacement.** Leather is a journey of inner heart, as much as it is a family/fellowship between those you hold dear—your chosen family, or your club, or your circle. Follow that journey. Get involved in your local/regional Leather community. Volunteer. Pitch in. Learn from those you are working with, from those you share time with. Then live #2. And, while you're doing this…

✦ **"Sit down, shut the fuck up and listen."** A lesson I learned in the military, reinforced in the Leather world. A Leather journey is sexual, spiritual and one of self. There are many who walk to their own rhythm, and I have learned so much by just listening, observing and being present in the moment with them. It's also how I've earned my way to being accepted by other communities and individuals. I'm grateful that those people have called me friend and family, and it's mainly by implementing that one lesson. It shows that I am here to be a part of the community, not here to replace or appropriate.

✦ **Walk to the beat of your different drummer.** Remember that there is no official or "right way" or "one true way" to do Leather traditions, aside from "Follow your own path". The traditions of your region, your locality, your club, your family—those are yours to investigate and explore to see if they speak to you and complement your path. Honor them, but don't be beholden to them. If they speak to you, then use them! If not, invent your own.

✦ **Don't rewrite history. Don't accept rewritten history. Learn Leather history, then go forth and make your own by living your life.** If someone says "I learned from Ye Olde Guarde so what I say is the Truth." take pause. Most of the elders who were really active in the 70s and 80s don't proclaim the "Old Guard" or "Council of Elders" to be their guide—you'll hear them talk about their heart, their sex and their spirituality. They will share lessons, but with the same breath encourage you to find your own path. I'm not going to rewrite Leather history, I'm going to make my own history... and I've learned to recognize when someone is doing the latter. Those are the kind of people I would tell someone new to find, befriend and listen to.

✦ **One final rule that I encourage M/s couples to consider: Fuck radically.** However you define fucking, do it to break the rules. Do it to explore yourselves. Do it to open up those doors. Do it because nobody should tell you how to get off, and do it so that you and the people involved come out better, more fulfilled, and closer to who they are meant to be.

Spiritual Leather
slave Kathleen

Writing about myself is always the hard part. I am currently 44 years old and born under the sun sign Sagittarius. (No, that wasn't a pick-up line! That piece of information actually comes into play a little later.) I am a second generation Angelino from Los Angeles, California; being born in the same hospital as my mother. Despite growing up in the porn capital of the world (the San Fernando Valley), I was incredibly sheltered as a child. My parents raised my younger sister and myself Catholic, and I attended Catholic school from pre-kindergarten to my first year in college. (I can hear the "*Ohhhh*, one of those!" from here. Yes. I was a very good girl.)

OK, well, maybe I was a little naughty. I began reading "anonymous" authored books about pain, sex, domination and submission when I was sixteen years old. (Yes, I read the *Story of O.*) All these books and my vivid imagination fueled my fantasies and masturbation for many years, although I kept it all a secret. In high school I was labeled a brat by my friends and taunted by several guy friends to try to keep me in line. After school one day, one of these guy friends and I got into our usual banter except this time he slapped my face. In the moment I acted outraged but later I was secretly pleased, turned on and scared. Let me be clear: I wasn't scared because he hit me. I was scared because deep inside it unlocked something that I couldn't put back into the box completely.

In my twenties, I had a relationship with a very loving man. We were very monogamous and vanilla. For those who saw *The Secretary*, do you remember when Lee was trying to get her boyfriend to spank her? Yes, that was my life. Every now and again kink was brought up— he introduced me to the *Sleeping Beauty* series, but they turned him off. For me, well, it just fanned the smoldering desire I had. Eventually I found my way onto the internet and into chat rooms, and suddenly I was not alone. I was not a freak, I was not broken. There were other people, real people, who had similar desires and fantasies and, and, and... That was my head exploding. Over five years the internet led me to my first Mistress, numerous play sessions, and a new boyfriend who was a self-proclaimed Dominant! It finally also led me to real-time people literally in my neighborhood. My first play party was three blocks away from where I lived, and I did everything a newbie should not do that night. Luckily I left with only the bruises I wanted.

By this time it was 2002, and I now had a community. I attended munches and classes and parties. BDSM was no longer a secret box hidden somewhere behind my clit; it was real. 2002 was also the year I met Master Skip, who introduced me to a whole new side of my fetishes. Yes, my first introduction to Leather was through Master Skip Chasey and slave pug. I was initially attending a class on caning, although that was hardly what I noticed. This man spoke about something more than just delivery of a stroke or where to hit. I can't even remember the exact words, just the emotion. There was something more here than just "hit and fuck". I was so compelled that I forced myself past my shyness to speak to Master Skip. I just had to know what was this thing that he called Spiritual Leather.

Fortunately for me, Master Skip was more than generous with his time, and answered my questions. By the end of the conversation, he had mentioned the Metropolitan Community Church and P.L.A.Y. (People of Leather Among You). I started attending these monthly meetings and began to develop a sense of community around this common concept of Spiritual Leather. There was a beauty to SM found in catharsis; it was radical spirituality and radical sexuality combined. Butchmanns and South West Leather Conference were my initiations into a community who integrated BDSM with spirituality and with Leather, and somehow it fed my soul.

Leather, for me, is a spiritual thing. I love the core ideals of honor, integrity, trust, and service; not to mention the leather boots. I am a boot pig. I love worshipping boots, licking boots, letting boots fuck me, everything hot and nasty fun about boots. (Until Mister Kel changed my perspective to being more about who was actually wearing the boots, and then I began to practice adoration of *His* boots.) Yes, Leather is about the actual items you wear, because it should mean something to you regarding whether you bought it, or it was presented to you. Leather is the vestments of the Master and the magical skin slaves wear to makes us feel safe and empowered in our slavery. Finally,

Leather, for me, is family. In that same vein of it being sacred, my "church community" as others have said, the others who behave, and believe in Leather, like I do. Master Skip Chasey once said "Blood is thicker than water; but Leather is thicker than blood." Leather is hot sex, the fabric that binds us together, the fetish that allows us to worship at the boot of another while that boot is on my face.

I know that for some, leather is fetish-wear with no attachments of behavior. I know that some people wear leather as a uniform because they are bikers or part of a club. Right now there is a big struggle to figure out what Leather means to people, because the once-clear waters of masculine-identified-gay-male-SM are completely muddied by everyone else who felt drawn to Leather as well.

Over the last fourteen years, I have been in and out of D/s and M/s relationships. I discovered what I like, what I don't, and what I am petrified of (and still do anyway). In 2009 I ran for and won the Ms. Southern California Leatherwoman title, which allowed me to be of service in an amazing way to the womens' Leather community. I am a founding member of the Los Angeles MAsT Chapter and co-lead the D/s poly group in Los Angeles for a couple of years. I am lucky enough to be a presenter, and have taught classes regarding relationships, energy, biting, and "littles".

I met Mister Kel in the winter of 2009. He had just relocated to Los Angeles from Virginia, and we were at the same dungeon party when he asked me about myself. At the time, I was currently dating a man who was cheating on his wife. Mister Kel bluntly called me on integrity issue of being polyamorous and still being involved with a cheater. Needless to say, I was a bit taken back. No one ever called me out on anything. Who did he think he was?

It turns out he knew a thing or two about rough childhoods. He began as a baby butch in the early 80's in Hollywood. Raised amongst queens, gay leather and lesbians in the street of Hollywood and West Hollywood, he marched in Gay Pride parades, and during the AIDS epidemic buried a lot of good people. He was a construction worker and heavily involved in building and participating in the development of unions. For me, this speaks of his sense of what is right and what is wrong, and standing up for those rights. He eventually ended up on the East Coast, at which time he was introduced to ethical BDSM and M/s dynamics. His style of M/s is high-protocol Leather. Boots are more than just things to put on your feet or have polished. Stations of status are integrated into everything, including separate slave dishes and other kitchen utensils. He has the expectation of total obedience, and we do not have a romantic relationship.

We ended up having a two-hour conversation at that dungeon, and then another hour conversation in my car. I felt compelled to tell him the truth. He "saw" me. He saw the desire to be a slave with a worthy Master; he saw past the physical and straight into my soul.

Two weeks later I was released from a mental facility rehab hospital, and the person I was in a M/s/Daddy/girl relationship broke up with me via email … at work. He said he couldn't leave his wife, and that he would have nothing more to do with me. My whole world collapsed. Honestly, I was incredibly fragile and simply did not know how to handle such a betrayal. I was extremely suicidal. Mister Kel came over two days later and brought me food for dinner. Actually, what he said was "I am bringing you dinner," which in a girl's head is Thai food or at least a pizza. What he brought was ingredients for me to cook. *Cook?* And yet, I pad-footed into the kitchen and got busy. He recognized that I was in crisis, and over the next week, we agreed to do a Master Guardian relationship for ninety days. The time eventually lengthened to a hundred days even, and at midnight on day 101 he removed the collar I had worn. It was at this moment that I said "I would do this for real with you."

He quietly contemplated what I had said, and then told me that I had served well. In his mind, our time was over and he wouldn't hear of anything but a friendship for at least three months. I smile now, because in that first month I was miserable and we both struggled to not be who we were to each other. Texts went out saying "Hey, you!" and "Hi, stranger!" as we both tried to figure out what to call each other, because calling him Kel or me Kathleen was just too foreign. All this frustration and angst came to a head one evening when we were out to dinner with my leather sister. I was in "get stuff done" mode and being cheeky. He reached over the table to correct me and I immediately complied. The next day I called Kel and told him we had to talk. I told him that though the physical collar had been removed, the emotional one had not, and I was still fully in obedience to him because I was abiding by his timeline. Shortly after that conversation, we began our journey once again. Nine months after that he collared me.

We have had our ups and our downs, and as I write this, I am not wearing his collar. We've had to step back from the M/s dynamic at this time. Happily, we are still in a relationship and living together, and have hopes that our M/s dynamic will return.

However, I am still part of the Leather community. After years of seeking, I finally found a way to combine spirituality and sex. Well, to be specific, I discovered a way to integrate radical spirituality with radical sex. I adore having rules and structure and a way to express my service heart. Despite the amount of debate on social networks, the beauty about being in the lifestyle is that you really can carve out your own niche and make it work for you, and overall, have that be accepted by large portions of the community. I love this lifestyle, and specifically the Leather lifestyle because for me it is home. I found real family that loves me, who will nurture me and smack me up with a 2x4 if necessary if I am wandering off the path too much.

MK and I love it because it allows us to integrate what vanilla society calls bad and transform it into a beautiful relationship. He has control issues and can be demanding. He's very gender traditionalist (i.e., women cook and clean, men take out garbage and lift heavy things). He's a sadist and I am a masochist. All these elements of who we are do not exist as beautiful explorations in the vanilla world, and to some degree how we operate our M/s Leather path does not even exist in the regular BDSM world. But our world does exist and thrive in the M/s spiritual Leather universe.

For us the emphasis on the physical leather is important. Leather is sacred and is treated as such; therefore, boots are cleaned and shined, and other leather items such as vests are also treated with much respect. I am expected to know the hanky code, as Mister Kel will flag at certain events or conferences. As mentioned before, Mister Kel prefers a more high-protocol environment, especially when socializing. If you were someone observing us, you would see that I was walking on his right slightly behind him, or standing just to his left and slightly behind him. I'm usually not speaking unless told to, and I am not allowed to speak to anyone unless permission is granted from Master. In our everyday life, everything I do is a reflection of status. There is no privacy, even when using the toilet. I ask for permission before eating, taking meds, and sleeping.

In regards to public high protocols in Leather-oriented groups: Besides the standing to his left and slightly behind, someone has to get permission give me a hug. They must ask my Master before they can speak to me. I found high protocol forced me to be more aware of the little things—the tone of my voice, being observant of his needs while still being engaged with others, how I answer him (i.e. Master, Yes Master vs a simple Yes Sir). As a Leather Master, he has protocols as well, but much of it is being more conscious and aware in that public space. He too must be attentive to his tone, and take care in how he addresses other Masters and their slaves. Master Kel also "uniforms up" for events or conferences. His attention to dress detail includes his leathers—boots, vest, gloves, etc.

In addition to all these rituals or protocols, I am also expected to maintain my spiritual practice, which means constant introspection, meditation, and doing the hard internal work of improving myself. I am to protect the property at all times, which means working on integrating all of me (including my spirituality), and researching and honing my own spiritual gifts.

All this structure equates security for me. I function better as a human being when there are clear rules and structures. It's soothing to me. It's also soothing to me to be in a high-protocol environment because the focus is solely on Master. Though there are days when I despise the rules, the reminders of our stations are comforting to me because it reinforces our dynamic every day.

I wouldn't recommend jumping feet first into either M/s or Leather. Both areas require so much research and observation and patience. This is not about cookie-cutter rules or expectations, you first need to figure out what you truly want. What would feed your soul? Why do an authority exchange? Have you cleaned out your own closet (childhood issues, insecurities, etc.) in preparation for being responsible for another human being (Master) or turning over your entire life to another person (slave)? What is leather for you? How will leather and M/s integrate in your life? There are lots of aspects to consider, and that will take time.

Everything is an Experiment:
M/s from a Queer Leather Perspective
Sinclair Sexsmith

"Draw the top five memorable scenes we've had." "Clean the refrigerator." "Take Daddy on a date of your choice." "Organize and clean our sex toys."

These are some examples of week-long protocol from my newest game with my boy. I'm calling the game "52 protocol stars" because of the form: each protocol item is written on a small strip of paper which is folded into a star shape, and the rules are that boy pulls one of them out of a small wooden box once a week, during our usual check-in time, and that's his task for the week.

Technically, it was a winter solstice present in 2013, but it is also an experiment. I use the "experiment" concept all the time, especially in my power dynamic, but also in creating steps toward my own goals, and in my art and creation. It is a Tantric principle handed down through my lineage from Swami Rama and Rudolph Ballentine, which states, "Everything is an experiment. Conduct the experiment, and collect the data."

So that is what I do. I apply a modified version of the scientific method for experimentation, asking questions like, What is the challenge I am addressing? What is my goal or ideal outcome, what am I aiming for? What is the methodology? It could be a protocol, a scene, or a request. What is the procedure? The procedure could be a simple request, a command, an additional training area, or a topic to remember for the next check-in. And then, after actually conducting the experiment, I "collect the data" by reflecting on what happened, asking, What were the variables? What could have made it different— better, worse, or just not the same? Do any of those things need to change? How is my mood, my body, my clarity? How is our connection, our power dynamic? How is his well-being, his mood, his body? Did it get in the way of things, or did it integrate smoothly into our lives?

Using this data as a foundation, and our backgrounds in feminist, queer, and leather sexualities as guiding principles, we set forth to play within the power structure we have set up.

Though I have been kinky since I started exploring sex in my early teens, my involvement in the Leather culture came later. I primarily have gone into the leather and kink worlds to gain skills to take home and use in my own bedroom, or to occasionally participate in the thrill of public play. But since seriously prioritizing a power dynamic in my relationships, my interest in the Leather culture has shifted from being one of the many communities I take part in to being one of the places in which I and my relationships am most centered.

Leather culture means so much to me. I love being in a lineage, knowing that I am able to do what I do and play how I play with the rights and privileges that I have because people before me fought and learned and shared and enhanced the community with knowledge and experiences. I am enthralled by being part of communities of sexual outlaws, and I thrive in them. Queer Leather is not gay Leather or lesbian/women's Leather, but built upon and incorporating both of those cultures and histories. Queer Leather takes the radical politics of women's leather and the sexual outlaw of gay Leather, and both throws gender out and invites gender celebrations. In queer Leather, ideally (though of course not always), gender roles and essentialist gender differences are deconstructed, and radical gender explorations are encouraged and supported.

What I love about doing M/s in a queer Leather context is that the M/s roles are not gender-based or gender-presumed. This is essential for my experience of M/s, as I would never associate power dynamics with any particular kind of gender expression or role. In addition, all sexual expressions and possibilities are active. My own sexed body holds none of the requirements of what role I do or don't fit into: I can be a person assigned female at birth, currently living in my home-grown body with no serious alterations, and expect to be a Master, Sir, Dominant, and Daddy. There is nothing incongruous about my own gender expression and my power expression. Similarly, my boy's gender, while different from mine, is also masculine-based, but in a very different way. He is a trans boy, but not a trans man. His boy-ness is one of the most appealing things about his gender expression to me, as thriving as a Daddy myself is a very important role both in my power dynamic and gender expression.

I spent a lot of time turned off by M/s and decidedly thinking it did not apply to me, because I did not see it applied in conscious, queer ways where gender and sexuality were deconstructed and the power dynamic had more to do with the individuals and less with cultural structures of power. It took examining extensive power dynamic and M/s theory and fiction from queer writers—like John Preston, Guy Baldwin, Mollena Williams, Lee Harrington, Patrick Mulcahey, Raven Kaldera, and Joshua Tenpenny—before I was able to see myself taking part in this particular flavor of power. Now that I've been able to settle into it, I am surprised I didn't see it sooner—but it is clear that it wasn't until now that I was really ready to embrace it and explore it to this depth. I'm grateful for the many queer Leather folks who shared their stories with me, as each one has enabled me to understand myself and my desires so much deeper and clearer.

Rife and I have been together just over two years. We spent the first year and a half as long-distance lovers, but we have since moved in together and are living full-time in a state of 24/7 total power exchange we define as M/s. We both had experience with D/s prior to our relationship together, but we'd never before been involved in M/s. I had a nagging feeling through the D/s I've experienced in the past that somehow, I wanted … more. He's told me he felt the same. I suspected I would be more comfortable, and feel more like myself, by deepening the power dynamic and taking on more of an "owner" role. I wanted my reach to go farther, to encompass … more. More than sexytime play in the bedroom, more of his free will and life and choices, more of my own precise desires.

I'm still pretty uncomfortable with the titles of "master" and "slave." The social justice activist in me is uncertain of using terms which have such oppressive and racial histories, and I am unclear how to engage with that as a white person who is working on my own white privilege and internalized racism. But those terms also have a rich history in the Leather worlds, and as my boy and I also both have one boot firmly planted there, we do occasionally use them in deeply intimate moments with each other.

Political correctness aside, we do usually use the shorthand of "M/s" when discussing the type of power dynamic we live in. When he addresses me directly, he usually calls me Sir or Daddy. When I address him, I use his name, or I use boy, or some other sort of sweetheart nickname. Our contract uses the terms "Dominant" and "boy," not Master and slave, but also clarifies: "In addition to being the boy's Dominant, the Dominant is also his Daddy, Top, and Owner. The boy serves as the Dominant's property, submissive, bottom, and toy for the Dominant's pleasure."

In the nearly ten years I explored power dynamics in my intimate relationships before he came along, I never knew I was interested in a path of mastery. Perhaps I wasn't, until very recently. Regardless, it is clear now that what I want is more than dominance over certain areas of my submissive's life: I want all-encompassing commitment, surrender, trust, transparency, and possession.

Rife and I spend a lot of time talking and theorizing and writing about the differences between D/s and M/s. It's clear that the Leather, fetish, BDSM, and kink communities have many applications and uses for all of those terms, so it's difficult to pinpoint where one ends and the other begins. I don't think there's one singular accurate definition—I think we all figure out the ways of using these words that work for us, in the context of the communities that we know and in which we are invested. Raven Kaldera and Joshua Tenpenny's writings on M/s have certainly influenced me significantly, as have Andrea Zanin and Mollena Williams, so many of their concepts have folded into my own methodologies and frameworks. I still feel new to this field of study, but it holds more promise for me than I have felt in other aspects of the leather, fetish, BDSM, and kink communities. I love figuring out the nuance of usage, the precise terms and conditions of my power, and intentionally building a partnership that feels based in equality with specific agreements, rules, protocol, and areas of growth.

Our M/s dynamic operates with the intention of the boy giving over access to every aspect of their body, mind, will, and time to their Dominant (that would be me). The flip side of that is that our power dynamic operates with the Dominant continuously seeking ways to use the access that is granted for the betterment not only of the relationship, but for both of us individually.

I tend to believe that, as a broad-sweeping generalization, the biggest difference between D/s and M/s is a) the ownership and possession fetish and b) the exhaustiveness of the Dominant's control. While D/s does often play with *acts* of ownership and possession, usually the control is not as extensive as an M/s dynamic. Usually it is non-exhaustive, meaning there are still aspects of their life that the s-type does not prefer or allow the D-type to control.

Early on, while rife and I were co-creating our first complete contract, he wrote a section on "Requests and Limits," where he detailed what boundaries he wanted in our dynamic. It became an extensive thought experiment for him, asking himself what—if any—aspects of himself he would not want me to have access to. He did come up with a few things, such as me making requests that "would strongly negatively impact the boy's self-care rituals over the long term, including limited long-term access to food, air, water, rest, hygiene, exercise, emotional support, time outdoors, and time to draw and meditate." But while he has come up with dozens of examples of things that he would be willing to do, should I request them, most of them I cannot imagine actually desiring from him, and I would be very unlikely to make requests of him, especially taxing ones, that wouldn't fulfill some deep desire in me. Perhaps some requests would be purely for amusement, or to experiment how far my power goes ... but that doesn't currently feel necessary. Perhaps there is some unforeseen reason I would want something from him that would interfere with his long-term self-care of, say, access to adequate rest—I don't want to rule out the possibility!—but I don't currently know what that would be. So his limitations, even when he was allowed them, didn't limit me much.

Years ago, I found my way to Guy Baldwin's book *Slavecraft* after one of Mollena Williams' workshops, and the "prime directive" concept has always stuck with me: that a slave's primary action should be protecting and respecting the Master's property, up to and including from the Master themself. This too is deeply integrated into how I operate as a Dominant, and how the boy operates under my power. I always aim to make my decisions based on the best well-being of both of us possible, and I do want his input on what he believes that well-being is. He's insightful, self-aware, and incredibly observant—of course I want to know what his brilliant brain is thinking.

What I realized, after all of those thought experiments of what he would or wouldn't do and what I would or wouldn't ask for, was that ultimately, *everything* was on the table. He would do literally *anything* I could possibly desire him to do for me. That is a concept that is both mind-boggling, heart-wrenching, and deeply honoring. It is my purpose in this dynamic to live up to it: to be worthy of it. Not just to deem myself worthy of it and go forth, but to daily earn that kind of devotion and beautiful submission.

This is how we created it, and how it works.

We started out with a 10-page contract that had a lot of caveats and details. The contract began in a mimicked legal document style, with sections like I. Participants; II. Purpose; III. Terms. It made me hard to read the combination of power and sexiness with official-sounding statements. I love words; I loved the process of co-creating the structure that the boy and I would live within. It made my mind all swimmy and my heart feel heavy and pump hard, and my stomach rattled with butterflies to attempt to define and name what we were trying to do with each other. A part of the Terms in our contract speaks to what we aimed to do: "This document serves as a map of the boy's submission, a non-exhaustive reminder of what the Dominant can have, and what they want and expect from the boy ongoing. It serves as the boy's explicit stating of permission and consent, and as the Dominant's guide for requests and use."

It was indeed a map of his submission and a reminder of what I have—but it also became a guide for what feels best to me to do in order to feel worthy of the power he gives freely over to me. Not because he complains—on the contrary, it's because I am still getting used to being seated in this kind of power, and I want to ensure that I use it well, both for myself and for him.

After we finished writing the long contract, I began penning an appendix with the title "Noblesse Oblige." I noticed that much of the contract dictated what the boy was supposed to do and how he was supposed to behave, and started asking myself what *my* side of the contract is or should be. What responsibilities come with having this kind of power? How am I to use my power? What do I need to be aware of, and keep in mind? What obligations do I have? So I began collecting the answers.

There came a point when it was more laborious to list the areas of my control than it was to list the few exceptions to my reach. This was after we began living together and were no longer navigating airports, pining, and other partners and their accompanying needs and responsibilities, and it turned the contract on its head. It became simpler, and my control over him became farther reaching and more extensive. The "simplified version" of the contract includes my obligations, his rules, our commitments to each other, and the most important points of the other long document—and it is just one page long. These sections of our agreements, rules, protocol, and training areas, are based on what is now in our distilled contract.

Agreements

The agreements we've made are broad and sometimes all-encompassing. I go back to them frequently, often keeping this brief list written up in the back of my writing notebooks. If I am having a day where I'm struggling with making requests or giving orders, or if I'm feeling less like I'm in charge or adequately standing in my power, I ask myself, am I living up to these agreements? Am I operating from these agreements?

The first agreements is: The Dominant owns the boy. This reminds me that he is bound to me by our mutual agreements, that I am responsible to some degree for his well-being under my care, that I am in charge of him, that I can do with him what I wish (as I could with any of my possessions).

The second, and perhaps my favorite, is: The Dominant actively seeks out ways the boy can add pleasure and value to our lives. I go back to this frequently and ask myself how I'm doing with this one. Is there some *other* way I could be actively seeking out ways he would add pleasure or value? What could he be doing for me, for us? My imagination is the only limitation here, and I want to think big, to vision beyond what I have ever thought is possible, and to bring him my ideas on a silver platter to see how we can play with them together.

The third I've already touched on, which states: The Dominant will act with the Dominant's and the boy's best interests in mind. This seems like duh obvious to me, but it is this agreement that keeps me from freaking out about the vast endlessness of my own power. If I am operating with our best interests in mind, I won't go ask him to commit acts of self-harm or to do things that go against his long-term self-care.

The next agreement addresses the ways that we have agreed we will operate around fuck-ups: The Dominant will not punish for mistakes. The boy can correct mistakes, and the Dominant will reflect on why instructions were inadequate. There is a strong discipline and punishment fetish in the BDSM and kink worlds, and I have always been under the impression that punishment was an important part of "training" or of any D/s dynamic, but the more I look into M/s, the more examples I have from practitioners who don't believe in punishment at all. I certainly know from things like animal behaviorists and psychologists that punishments of the negative reinforcement kind just don't work. But as we were writing our rules, and as we experiment with more and more protocols, I had to ask: What happens if mistakes are made? What happens if something I request doesn't get done? What do I do? What do *we* do? This agreement lays out where we start, when something happens.

If he intentionally disobeys me, well, we have an entirely different problem. And, this doesn't include the faux-punishments of BDSM play, where he is "in trouble" for doing something I've either explicitly told him not to do (for example, moving his hands from the wall) or for something I've just randomly decided to punish him for (for example, for being dirty and touching himself).

The next agreements dictate what the boy agrees to, including: The boy will respect the Dominant's property, which is our phrasing of the "prime directive" concept.

The next agreement states, The boy will execute the Dominant's preferences to the best of their ability. "Preferences" has been something that has come up a lot in our years together—in our creation of protocol, and now significantly more with our creation of a household together. My *preferences* drive our dynamic. In some ways, I believe that the path of mastery is a path of cultivating my personal preferences and putting them out into the world, vulnerable as they may be to reveal. He often asks what I would like, how I prefer to have things be, which type of spoon is my favorite, or how I want things to be arranged, and I often don't know off the top of my head. So I make note of it, and watch it for a while, and ask myself what honestly I would most prefer. What are the options, I ask myself. What annoys me? What would make things easier?

The final agreement on our list, at least for now, is: The boy will do *anything* the Dominant requests. This was a carry-over from our first long contract, and I still remember the notes we had in that document about this sentence. It had some caveats in the long contract, many footnotes and ifs and buts, but at this point, it has been distilled. Assuming that all those other agreements are kept to, the boy's job is to do anything I ask.

Rules

We did detail a few rules, as we were writing things down. These are more about the way we should conduct ourselves in this dynamic, and the over-arching philosophies that drive us.

- ✦ Identity reminds us to remember to whom you belong, or whom you own, and to know who and what you are for them.

- ✦ Transparency dictates that the boy not to deliberately withhold anything from the Dominant, always answer direct questions truthfully, proactively tell the Dominant if you've slipped or failed. It also reminds me, the Dominant, to explain my logic or what is behind my decisions when requested, and to keep him informed of what is going on in my inner world.

- ✦ Connection is deeply important to me. If we start falling away from each other, our dynamic and the energy between us will wither. Our rule about connection reminds us both to keep the energy exchange strong, and to keep ourselves as available as possible to each other.

✦ Obedience is primarily a rule for the boy, and as it is one of his primary fetishes, it dictates that he do anything the Dominant asks, to the best of his ability, with a minimum of hesitation, critique, and judgment.

✦ There can be significant hurdles with ego and pride on the path of mastery and servitude, and as such, we have a Humility rule. That dictates to the boy to: know that the Dominant is in charge, always; know your place is for service and submission; show respect and honor those you've ascribed higher authority to; work on minimizing ego and pride, especially as it might interfere with your service & submission; trust that the Dominant knows what's best for you; and respect the Dominant's property as a steward of it. From the Dominant's perspective, Humility reminds me to own up to my mistakes, and to acknowledge and honor my own humanity, which to me means the aspects of me that are fully human, and thus flawed. I cannot be held to superhuman standards, and while many fantasy Dominants are practically perfect and

✦ Our last rule, Access, dictates that the Dominant has access to the boy's mind, body, will, and time. Please note the deliberate use of the word *access* and not *responsibility*. The boy's mind, body, will, and time are not the Dominant's responsibility, and thus I am not "in charge" of them exactly. I am however granted access to them, to know what is going on within them, and to use them at my discretion for the above mentioned purposes.

Our Access Rule is the one I think of when people say to me, "But isn't being a 24/7 Dominant so much *work*? So much responsibility?" The short answer is: No. If it is, then I'm probably not doing it well, or right. There is some responsibility of taking care of another person, yes, of course, but there is also quite a bit of responsibility within a committed partnership of any kind. Just because I have access to the boy's every ability doesn't mean I am required to tell him what to do every minute of every day. Sure, having control over his time is sometimes a lot of fun, and gets us both hot, but it is also sometimes a drag and distracting from the things I need to get done—like my writing, or other work. So it is my responsibility to access him, as a tool, when I need him, and to let him go in self-sufficiency when I do not.

Protocol

The rules are simple, and somewhat overarching meta-concepts from which we should conduct our lives and partnership. But the protocol ... well, that's where the fun is. Our protocol dictates our day-to-day. The boy has a wide variety of protocols—probably hundreds, if you include the detailed executions of my preferences. Some are specific and time-based, some are more general. Most of the protocol in the original long contract are no longer relevant or acted upon, because our circumstances are so different now than when we wrote them. But many of them are still applicable and used, such as: *Wear a collar; Use the Dominant's appropriate titles; Check-in weekly.*

The current, active protocol is specified on a living document, which changes frequently—sometimes weekly. Currently, it is a large piece of cardboard propped up on the altar with about a dozen short sentences. Some of those protocols include: Shave your pubic hair when showering or every other day; serve the Dominant a glass of water first thing in the morning, last thing at night, and at meals; respect the bedtime and morning alarms; create and accomplish three Most Important Tasks daily.

Check-Ins

Each week, we do a check-in, with the possibility of setting up further protocol to experiment with. This is how we keep our M/s smooth, functional, and refreshed; this is also how we deal with conflicts that come up, and how we come back together to restart things. The check-ins include a reflection on any amazing things and challenging things that happened in the past week, and a look at our schedules and obligations for the coming week. Sometimes, we set week-long goals for ourselves—to write a certain word count, this many hours of work, this many hours of exercise, more experimenting with this kind of sex, that kind of thing. Sometimes we set intentions, prayers, or wishes. Sometimes we pull altar items down and ignite them for a little extra support and focus with our growth. Then we move on to experiments, and training areas. Check in experiments are often focused around the boy's or the Dominant's training areas.

Training Areas

When we wrote the long contract, we distilled many of my favorite ways that the boy serves me into specific areas of training. We have since added one more—houseboy—now that we share a living space.

Rife's Leatherboy training area includes traditional high leather protocol, leather care, cigar service, toy care, and toy creation. The Sexual training area includes learning as much as possible about the Dominant's bodily pleasure, which includes things like massage, sexual touch, and dirty talk. To be an excellent Houseboy for me, he focuses on service around the household—our pets, cleaning, and projects. As an Assistant, the boy focuses on service around my work, which includes public events, readings, and a use for his excellent tech and design skills. His Faggot training area includes more sexual talents, like cock sucking, fisting, butt plugs, and ass play, but also includes other aspects of masculinity, culture, and gay male history. We used to call it "prized possession," but now I tend to shorthand it with Trophy, and that area of training includes spiritual practices, grooming, exercise, diet, and dress. Mostly, the Trophy category is about discovering my preferences and clearly communicating them, and finding a way for my desires to enhance his own personal tendencies as best as possible. The last training areas is another sexual one, this time Submission: to receive pain, praise, humiliation, commands, and to provide service as part of his position of submission.

This is a non-exhaustive list (as the original long contract points out), and most of the areas include "And other specificities TBD by the Dominant." I love that we still have a lot of room for growth possible, but that we also have a significant amount of definition and places to jump off of already outlined.

Frequently, I use his training areas as ways for us to play, and to form more experiments. When I was creating the "52 protocol stars," I went to his training areas for ideas and made sure to have at least five different protocols for each of the areas.

The Dominant—that would be me—is not exempt from training areas, but I don't have a set in our agreed-upon contract. Lately, I've had three work areas and three personal areas of focus, which would be my equivalent. The biggest one is to seek to be better at Mastery, which, first and foremost, includes complete mastery of *my own self*, which breaks down further into most aspects of my conduct in the world. There are certainly many areas of my life which are running fairly smoothly and need minimum triage and only semi-ordinary maintenance, but many others I am still attempting to fold into my daily life and get running smoothly.

The largest influences on the way rife and I have structured our power dynamic have been the principles of feminism, the queer communities and theories of deep acceptance of our own bodily impulses, and the traditional "old guard" leather traditions. While there are pieces of every one of these communities that don't personally fit us or our day to day lives, we also find deep value in the learnings of each of them, and have both been formed by all of the concepts and people that I believe are the best places to find liberation.

The structures, check-ins, and personal areas of growth and interconnectivity feel extremely vulnerable to share, because they are so special to me, precious, and I hold them dearly in a protected place inside me. I put them forward with hopes that others will connect with some pieces that they find useful or interesting, and be able to discard the parts that won't personally work for you. It is, as is everything, a work in progress, and everything is subject to change, but this is what currently works to keep us close and connected, in a power dynamic that enhances both of our lives, and makes us better people in all of our interactions.

1950's Style

The Modern-Day 1950's M/s Household
Mrs. Darling

I. The Home Built on Love

It is nearing the end of an almost-summer day. With only two weeks until school is out for the greatly anticipated summer break, the children are abuzz with a frivolity that only this time of year can create. A boy and a girl are playing outside a tidy home in the early evening light. The home could be any one of thousands nearby; a white wrap-around porch laced with wooden rocking chairs invite visitors to stay a spell. Vibrant annuals recently planted by the lady of the household line the front flower bed, and an American flag flowing in the lazy breeze evokes a moment of patriotism from the passers-by walking in the neighborhood.

The two children, homework complete and checked as always by Mom, have been riding bikes and coloring with chalk for an hour in the yard under Mother's watchful eye. Smiling at her children, Mom sets the broom against the brick home and takes a break from sweeping the driveway to help the kids draw a hopscotch board. She is careful to stay clean, already having done her hair and makeup, changing from her errand clothes into a light summer dress that shows off her hourglass figure, hoping to please her husband upon his arrival. The three play a game of hopscotch together, laughing, talking, and enjoying each other's company. Nobody stops to check an email or search something on a Smartphone. This moment is just about family and togetherness.

At long last, Dad's car turns around the corner. The woman's heart lifts, glad for her husband's arrival. She sends the kids in to wash their hands and faces for dinner, and waits in the twilight to greet the head of her household.

As he steps from his car, white starched shirt unbuttoned at the top, tie long removed and sleeves rolled, she steps forward and greets him with a smile and a kiss. Exchanging pleasantries, she takes his briefcase and he leads her into the family home; the home they have created each in their own contribution, creating a synergy that only exists when two parts create something magical by coming together. As husband and wife they walk in the door, smells of the roast finishing in the oven wafting in the most comforting way, and you hear hollers of "Daddy!" coming from the other room. Kissing his little lady on the cheek (and giving a playful swat on the behind), the husband leaves his wife to plate up the hot meal while he goes to enjoy the lights of his life: his children.

The four sit down together as they do most every evening. Dad rightfully perched at the head of the table, children on each side, and Mom constantly popping up to fetch an additional napkin or second helpings of this or that. No TV is playing; no fancy tablets are out, just a tight-knit group sharing their day. Mom allows Dad to guide the conversation. If he wants to talk about work, she listens attentively, offering suggestions or laughing at shared workplace humor. She encourages the children to pass along stories from their day so Dad can cheer for their accomplishments or advise with struggles. It is a conversation as natural as breathing, a conversation driven by the love and care for the other members of this little family.

Once bellies are full and plates are cleared, it is bath and bedtime for the children. Walking out of each child's room and closing the doors tight, having said "sweet dreams" and tucking in tight the littlest ones of the house, the husband and wife find themselves alone in the quiet of a house built on love.

The wife approaches her husband and stands in front of him waiting, as always, to have him take the lead. The husband kisses his wife deeply for the first time that night, one hand gripping the back of her hair, creating heat through both of their bodies. His hand caresses the curvy body that belongs to him, feeling the top of her garter belt, wondering what she will be wearing underneath her demure appearance, aching to find out. Breaking her lips away, he guides her by his handful of hair, bringing the woman to her knees in front of him. She takes a moment to hug his body tight, showing gratitude to the man who gives his all for his household.

Letting go and looking up to the face of the man she adores, a rich and honest smile crosses her face as she speaks plainly, "Hello, Master," ... and their night together begins.

Who We Are

I am a woman (a wife, a mother, a slave) living happily, and gratefully, in a "modern day 1950's Master/slave household". What is described above may seem to some like an impossible dream. To some it is an idealized version that could never be achieved, or that is entirely impractical in today's day and age. To others. this may read as a feminist's nightmare, or a fool's dream, idolizing a decade rife with less-than-ideal social constructs, or an entirely dull way of living. I hope that in sharing the inner workings of our 1950's dynamic I can help to clear up some misunderstandings about this particular M/s structure.

This is not to say that I think everybody reading this will then run out to buy a copy of Emily Post's Etiquette and learn to set victory rolls before going to bed. We live our life not only with the understanding that this isn't for everybody, but thankful that this is not the only way of living any more. How dreadfully monotonous that would be! Everybody has to find their own path in life. This is simply ours.

The "Old Us"

My husband (referenced here as MR, short for Master Ryder) and I began living in the 1950's M/s style at the end of what we refer to as our "old marriage". We had a fairly typical start in our relationship. We met at our mutual workplace, and that spark was ignited almost at once. It led to dating and living together, and eventually marriage. Shortly into our marriage, we both realized we were pretty miserable. We were working long days, focused on our individual careers, barely having time to eat take out at the end of a 12-hour workday. The power struggle was a constant burden. Who would walk the dogs every morning? Who would be in charge of dinner? Who would pay what bills? Who had the harder day and deserved the back rub? Exhausted yet? We were too.

Here is an example of what we used to sound like "before".

(Calling each other as leaving work:)
MR: Hey babe, I am leaving work. What's for dinner tonight?

Me: I don't really know. I was going to go to the grocery store on my lunch break, but I got busy and couldn't. Do you have time to stop and get something?

MR: I guess. I am stuck in traffic right now though. Can you?

Me: If I have to. My heels are killing me and I just want to go home and change. Should we get takeout instead?

MR: We've eaten out every night this week.

Me: Well what do you want me to do about that? I have been working late on this project and my job is important too. *You* could have picked something up on your lunch. you know.

MR: (*Sigh*) I wasn't implying anything. Takeout is fine. What sounds good?

Me: (*Sigh*) Sorry. *Again.* I don't really care. Whatever you want.

MR: OK, I can get Chinese.

Me: Well, I had Chinese for lunch.

MR: Well, you said it didn't matter. What do *you* want?

Me: What about pizza?

MR: Sure. What toppings?

Me: You pick.

MR: You know I want mushroom and you don't.

Me: Then why are you even asking me? Get the mushrooms. I guess I can pick them off. *Again.*

MR: (*Sigh*) OK, I'll call in the order. See you at home.

After the ten-minute petty debate, we were annoyed with each other, both of us in our own way feeling like our voices weren't heard, eating garbage food, exhausted from the day, just wanting to roll over in bed and sleep as fast as possible. It was a constant battle, and it was killing our marriage. However, please don't mistake us as saying that living as Master/slave was the savior of the relationship. What helped most was the tools we acquired in marriage counseling. Facing divorce and wanting to try and salvage that genuine spark and love we felt for each other, we sought out professional help. But during the work that took place there, we learned to openly and honestly communicate how we wished to see our ideal marriage. When we realized that it looked like this, we learned to work together towards that goal, and our modern 1950's household was born.

Now we have more years together as 1950's M/s than we lived as the "old us". We cannot imagine ever wanting to live another way. The M/s power structure has simplified our lives more than we had ever dreamt possible, and the freedom that comes with living how you see fit despite what society says about that lifestyle keeps us working together to grow in a dynamic that is so strong, nothing could bring us asunder.

II. What Exactly is Modern 1950's M/s?

The 1950's style of living Master/slave varies with whomever you are speaking, and across the board people will pick and choose things from that decade to bring into their modern 1950's home. Ways of incorporating the decade into an M/s dynamic typically fall under two categories: the look of the decade and relationship functions/power structure of the decade. Many modern 1950's M/s homes incorporate a bit of both of these categories into their life, taking what they like and leaving the rest behind.

The Look of 1950's M/s

Many people enjoy the styling of the 1950's. Clothing such as colorful aprons, garter belts, bullet bras, vintage dresses, and petticoats for women; men in suits, shirts with cufflinks and pleated pants are all common. They also seek out other vintage regalia, including furniture, music, and accessories.

Also important to the 1950's family is that you represent your outward appearance in a positive way both in and out of the home. Whether wearing modern or vintage clothing, a 1950's slave would never leave the home without their "face on", hair neat, and often in a skirt or dress. Children in the home wear clothes that are clean and well fitting, and the Master wears clothes that are pressed and stylish.

1950's M/s Power Structure

The root of the modern-day 1950's M/s couple is the power exchange that exists in the relationship. While many "kinky" 1950's homes incorporate other elements of BDSM (such as discipline, sadism and masochism) it is entirely possible to live 1950's M/s and only participate in the power exchange dynamic.

The 1950's Master/slave seats the man as the Head of Household (HoH) and Master; the woman in the dynamic as the homemaker, and slave. This is most often a full time way of life. The man is *at all times* ruling over the home and wife. The woman is *at all times* tending to her home and family, being submissive to her husband.

It is important at this point to address some questions that often come up. Can the man be the homemaker and the woman the breadwinner? Can both people work in a 1950's household? My answer would be that you can genuinely take what works for you about this lifestyle and make it your own. If you just love listening to Elvis and making icebox pie, and that's it, then do it! A male slave and female Master in this way of living is often referred to as a "reverse 1950's household". Many women worked outside of the home in the 1950's. In fact, being a "household worker" was only the fourth most common job for women in the 1950's according to the US Census Bureau. A similar style would just be seating one person as the main decision maker (and they will often be the main income earner); and the other as the secondary partner. In sharing my experience going forward, I will be talking about the traditional 1950's household with the man out working and leading; and the woman staying at home and serving.

The Master is the king of his castle and expects to be treated as such. He takes on the burden of making the ultimate decisions, enforcing rules, and disciplining his family. Usually working outside of the home, he is committed to ensuring the financial health of the family and its future. The Head of Household assigns tasks amongst the rest of his family and creates a set of standards that he expects his wife to follow. He may also take on the job of training his slave to be his vision of the "ideal" housewife. This Master is a gentleman at his core, and prides himself on being a man of old-fashioned values: honorable, honest, well-mannered, and even-tempered.

The slave is to see the Master as the main decision-maker. Part of her job as a housewife is to make her husband's life as plush and comfortable as possible when he is home, and to live every moment of her day considering "What would Master have me be doing right now?" This woman puts her family's needs above her own, but this is not a life of self-sacrificial misery. She takes pleasure in doting upon her husband and children, finds fulfillment in domestic duties, and feels grateful to have a husband that supports her staying in the home. This slave is a true lady—poised and graceful, even-tempered and patient with her children and husband, kind to others and humble about her chosen place in her home.

Why Say "Modern" 1950's Household?

It is 64 years since 1950. More than half a century has passed. And while the decade has plenty to learn from and admire (think Elvis and Marilyn, women everywhere in beautifully colored dresses instead of sweatshirts and jeans, American made cars, and polite children saying "ma'am" and "sir"), there *are* some things we've learned over the past six decades.

A "modern" 1950's household knows:

❖ A brainless, spineless, cake-toting, apron-wearing Stepford Wife isn't sexy, or practical. (This isn't accounting for those that have a kink for the Stepford Wife specifically. That certainly exists, and is one way of living.) For the most part, the modern 1950's housewife should be a *smart, sleek counterpart* to her husband. Not only can she cook a killer meal on a dime, but she can be a positive influence on her husband. The days of the woman being seen but not heard are gone. This is a woman that a man *wants* to hear; a woman who has a *value* in the home.

❖ Segregation and racism are disgusting. No person is any better than another based on race. 1955 was the year of Rosa Parks, and Martin Luther King Jr. was coming on the scene. We all need to work together and continue to end racism worldwide.

❖ Feminism, and specifically the women's liberation movement of the late 1960's, is something to be celebrated. Women are, and should be, an equal gender. I am personally grateful for both having a right to live this lifestyle, and also that other women have the same right to live another way. This lifestyle isn't "setting the woman's rights movement back 50 years", as I have heard over and over again. I am making a conscious choice to live the life I choose, without shame or societal pressure preventing me from doing so. And that *is* feminism. My life. My equal choice.

❖ Families come in all shapes and sizes now, and that's a *good* thing. Some families are headed by grandparents, some by a single parent, some women have powerful careers and their spouse stays home, some have two dads, some have two moms and a dad. Et cetera. How boring would life be otherwise? Not only boring, but I want other homes to serve as an example of different ways of life for my children.

As long as a household is full of happiness and love, it's considered good in my book. Our house is one way, not the *only* way.

What it is Not

Many times when people bring up the 1950's household, they use the terms "Taken In Hand", "Domestic Discipline" and "1950's Household" interchangeably. Anybody who participates in one of the lifestyles will gladly clarify to the best of their knowledge the inherent differences.

"Taken in Hand" (TiH) has substantially less information available than Domestic Discipline. It refers to a similar household power structure as 1950's M/s. Taken In Hand seems to have a few concepts that are universal: it is a monogamous, married couple who puts the male in the place of power. He in turn places his wife and the relationship as the priority, making decisions in her and the relationships best interest first. 1950's M/s can be non-monogamous, and certainly can function with non-married partners. The Master may make choices in his own best interest at times, and doesn't have to justify his ultimate decision making to his slave. In an M/s dynamic there is often an incorporation of S/M scenes, as well as protocols and rituals in the relationship, including the wearing of a slave collar of some fashion. 1950's M/s may incorporate a more extreme or kinky sexual relationship, and may use discipline in an erotic way. None of these things are a part of a purely TiH relationship. Many TiH couples find the idea of BDSM either unfamiliar or extreme.

Domestic Discipline (DD)—or sometimes Christian Domestic Discipline (CDD)—appears to incorporate the S/M side of the M/s dynamic at first glance, but the differences become clear upon inspection. Again, the man is seated as the head of the household and main decision maker, with the woman as the submissive partner. There is often, but not always, a calling to this lifestyle from the Christian belief that the man is intended to lead the family based on biblical writings.

Domestic Discipline is the act of the HoH disciplining his wife for misbehavior, most frequently through spanking (you can easily find pages and pages of information regarding the "proper" way to spank in a DD marriage) and also through activities like "corner time". There are two types of spankings involved. One is a spanking for infractions, and the other is "maintenance spanking", which is given in specific intervals to remind a woman of her place in the home. It is also suggested that the husband positively reinforce the wife for good behavior.

The difference in DD and a 1950's M/s household is that DD and CDD practitioners vehemently deny there being any erotic nature to the discipline. DD is corporal punishment within a marriage. Domestic discipliners insist they are not in any way interested in BDSM, and that it is only for disciplinary measures.

III. The Functioning of the 1950's Couple

The actual functioning of the modern 1950's M/s household is incredibly basic. Master is in charge of the financial health of the household (often the only income earner) and the decision maker/leader of the home. The slave is responsible for virtually everything else, unless requested otherwise by Master.

So the day becomes simply divided. Who cooks? Homemaker, unless the HoH enjoys cooking and chooses to do so. Who runs the errands? The homemaker, unless the HoH decides to do it himself. And on and on and on.

The Good Wife's Guide: Potential Protocol

One of the most hotly debated topics when the 1950's household is researched is that of *The Good Wife's Guide*. It is posted all over the internet as an article from *Housekeeping Monthly*, claiming that it was being printed in May of 1955. It has now been called a hoax, insisting that no such article existed. Some claim that it is actually from an old home economics textbook of which no copies exist anymore. Incredibly controversial and with a bit of an urban legend history, *The Good Wife's Guide* is still raising eyebrows and voices.

Regardless of when it was first printed or whether it is a good example of an actual home in the 1950's, I feel like it is an outstanding example of the modern 1950's Master/slave guide. It would be hard to discuss the rules and protocols of this lifestyle without bringing this into the discussion. It is a perfect example of how our home is run on a day to day basis, and I will expand on why I feel it is applicable to this specific lifestyle. My additions will be between.

The Good Wife's Guide

1. Have dinner ready. Plan ahead, even the night before, to have a delicious meal ready, for his return. This is a way of letting him know that you have been thinking about him and are concerned about his needs. Most men are hungry when they come home and the prospect of a good meal (especially his favorite dish) is part of the warm welcome needed.

It has been said before: the way to a man's heart is through his stomach. If your partner is going to be off working all day, a simple way to show your thanks is to have a homemade, nutritious meal waiting upon arrival. Over time, learn your Master's preferences in food tastes, and until then, ask. Pay attention to details. Ask yourself, "How can I make his life better?" Focus on other meals too. Prepare breakfast happily each morning and make a to-go lunch for Master to bring to work.

2. Prepare yourself. Take 15 minutes to rest so you'll be refreshed when he arrives. Touch up your make-up, put a ribbon in your hair and be fresh looking. He has just been with a lot of work-weary people.

A slave is likely Master's favorite person in the world. Remembering that, present yourself to him in a way that is visually pleasing. Be seen as the feminine, sexual being that you are, not a schlumpy homemaker in messy sweat pants. Many homemakers overestimate how much time it actually takes to do the daily tasks. While a pot of water comes to a boil on the stove, you can change into a dress, brush your teeth, and fix your hair and makeup. Throw on an apron to protect your look and you'll be back at the stove in no time.

3. Be a little gay and a little more interesting for him. His boring day may need a lift and one of your duties is to provide it.

The HoH spends all day at a business, with business associates, talking about business. When he comes home, be in a great mood and have a wide range of topics to talk about. (Remember? No Stepford wives here.) Whether it is a funny story about the kids to make him smile or a bit of news he missed through the day, contribute to the conversation.

4. Clear away the clutter. Make one last trip through the main part of the house just before your husband arrives.

Just do it. You would be shocked at what fifteen minutes of continuous picking up can accomplish.

5. Gather up schoolbooks, toys, paper etc. and then run a dust cloth over the tables.

It is all about time management. If you have had a productive day, this should take minimal time and effort.

6. Over the cooler months of the year, you should prepare and light a fire for him to unwind by. Your husband will feel he has reached a haven of rest and order, and it will give you a lift too. After all, catering for his comfort will provide you with immense personal satisfaction.

This is of course based on personal preference/availability. If one has a fireplace one can light a fire, but this can also be clearing his favorite chair where he likes to sit and talk to the children about their day, or lighting a favorite scented candle of his. The key is to create a ritual that works for you, and that shows Master you are dedicated to creating a haven for him to come home to. And we can't bristle at the whole "taking personal satisfaction in his comfort". After all, we are slaves. If you are living as Master/slave, and doing kind things for your Master doesn't bring you delight, you may either have chosen the wrong calling or the wrong Master. Be happy to make him happy, and don't be ashamed of that.

7. Prepare the children. Take a few minutes to wash the children's hands and faces (if they are small), comb their hair and, if necessary, change their clothes. They are little treasures and he would like to see them playing the part. Minimize all noise. At the time of his arrival, eliminate all noise of the washer, dryer, or vacuum. Try to encourage the children to be quiet.

The kids have to get cleaned up at some point before dinner. Why not have it be before Dad gets home? What would a man think, after working all day to make money to provide things like soap and clothes and water, if he comes home to a wife who doesn't even bother to keep the kids well groomed? And what is that teaching the children about the importance of personal hygiene?

8. Be happy to see him.

Even if not in the greatest of moods, having Master home at the end of a hard day should make life a little happier.

9. Greet him with a warm smile and show sincerity in your desire to please him.

Living as Master/slave, it may also be protocol to greet him kneeling if possible and remove his shoes. If the children are there, a wife can stand with proper posture and a welcoming smile, and greet him kneeling when the children go to bed.

10. Listen to him. You may have a dozen important things to tell him, but the moment of his arrival is not the time. Let him talk first—remember, his topics of conversation are more important than yours.

This is one of the most discussed and disliked parts of this list by 21st century wives. The reality is that it is often true, even if it is unsavory to admit. Unless a child has done something incredible or there is a time-pressing decision for the HoH to make, his issues likely are more important. And instead of this being an insult to the homemaker, you can choose to see it as a compliment. Master sees his slave as an intelligent woman capable of contributing to important conversation.

I can't tell you how many times over dinner MR has said, "There is this client I am trying to help. The situation is ...." and he and I would spend the meal discussing it. I'd offer a new viewpoint or suggest trying things a way he'd not considered. Lo and behold, the next day he would come home and scoop me in his arms, covering me in kisses and thanking me for the help. My suggestion, or something that came out of the conversation, saved the deal and resulted in thousands of dollars in commission.

A housewife's voice matters. If I had, that night, chosen the topic of conversation and began with, "Ugh, I had such a bad day, let me tell you about what happened at the dry cleaners,." I would have had a quiet Master still focused mentally on a work problem, a slave frustrated for not being heard, and a potential loss in income. A slave who knows when to speak and when to listen can be an invaluable asset to a Master.

11. Make the evening his. Never complain if he comes home late or goes out to dinner, or other places of entertainment without you. Instead, try to understand his world of strain and pressure and his very real need to be at home and relax.

Try to see his being late or going out alone as an opportunity for you to do something you enjoy. If he is going to be late, spend some time doing something fun with the children; maybe teach them how to make a new dessert from scratch or do a seasonal craft project. If you will not be serving Master dinner, make the kids' favorite meal that he usually doesn't favor. If he is going to be out late, pamper yourself with a hot bath and facial mask, or catch up on some TV programming the HoH doesn't enjoy. Learn to make lemons into lemonade.

12. Your goal: Try to make sure your home is a place of peace, order and tranquility where your husband can renew himself in body and spirit.

And further, as a slave, learn what makes that for your specific Master.

13. Don't greet him with complaints and problems.

No man or woman alive wants to be barraged with problems the moment they return from work. Choose a more appropriate time to approach your husband with issues.

14. Don't complain if he's late home for dinner or even if he stays out all night. Count this as minor compared to what he might have gone through that day.

Another controversial one. This may reference a time when men commonly "slept at the office", but many feel it is a way of saying "Don't complain if your husband keeps a mistress".

This boils down to picking a worthwhile and trustworthy partner and Master. Could MR be gone overnight without explanation? Sure. He can, in theory, do anything he wants as the Master of the household. Has he ever? No. Because it would cause me fear for his safety, and give me uncertainty regarding our relationship, and that is not the kind of HoH he is. If he did, though, I still wouldn't complain, I'd simply ask him about it in an open-minded and respectful way.

15. Make him comfortable. Have him lean back in a comfortable chair or have him lie down in the bedroom. Have a cool or warm drink ready for him.

This is solid advice and again very specific to the HoH. Find a ritual that works in your home. Some breadwinners like to have thirty minutes of alone time to unwind before being expected to join the family. After all, he has been working all day. Some prefer to have his family greet him and fill his night with love and affection. It's about personal preference here on how he wants to be greeted.

16. Arrange his pillow and offer to take off his shoes. Speak in a low, soothing and pleasant voice.

Lovely example of a 1950's M/s ritual. By kneeling to remove his shoes and adjusting your tone to be feminine and light, you are showing him that you are enthusiastic about serving him that night.

17. Don't ask him questions about his actions or question his judgment or integrity. Remember, he is the master of the house and as such will always exercise his will with fairness and truthfulness. You have no right to question him.

Here is the first time that the power exchange is seriously addressed. It is this faith in the HoH that will make your days feel carefree. Once you trust in your Master's ability to reliably make decisions based on what is fair and right for all involved, it is easy to live in the freedom of decision-free 1950's M/s. A quality HoH should be living a life of integrity. Listen to him, even if you don't understand exactly why he is making that choice.

A homemaker should be allowed to contribute to the household decisions if only by suggestions and by providing accurate information. If the husband doesn't know all of the details surrounding (for example) a child in trouble at school, he cannot properly determine the consequences. A wife should speak honestly to her husband, but she should also pay close attention to make sure that she presents that information. Always wait until an appropriate time and place (never insult or question Master in mixed company or in public) and ask permission to speak freely before just launching in with an unrequested opinion. It shows him the respect he has earned as the Head of the Household, and you catch more flies with honey. A slave is much more likely to be heard if speaking in a courteous manner.

18. A good wife always knows her place.

Insert the word "slave" for "wife" above, and this is an appropriate rule for any Master/slave dynamic. Living Master/slave is about seating a person and his or her needs above your own. As a good wife I do know "my place". It is as my husband's counterpart, the yin to his yang, his grateful servant, his charming wife, poised and graceful, eternally dedicated to his home.

The Good Husband's Guide (?)

I have heard this question before as a seething charge against the unfairness of *The Good Wife's Guide*. "Oh, well, here is all of the stuff a woman should do. What should the man do? Where is *The Good Husband's Guide?*" I actually think this is a good question. Not that a Master needs a slave wagging a finger and telling him what to do, but I think on the whole in the BDSM community there are more readily available resources for submissives or slaves to learn "proper" behavior, so why not create a counterpart for the above list? A reference guide for the Gentleman Master, if you will.

In asking "What makes a great 1950's Head of Household/Master?" MR and I have compiled a list of some ideas to consider. Every M/s couple should come to a mutual agreement on what is important or not, so don't feel as if this is a comprehensive list or mandatory requirements. For me, for us, for many other modern 1950's couples that we associate with, here are the most common attributes.

The Good Husband's Guide

1. As Head of Household, your day doesn't end the moment you leave the office. You are, as your title states, the "head of a household". You must lead that home in the right direction. You may have important decisions to make. You may have to enforce discipline for your wife or children. You may have to problem solve issues in the home. You may not have to do any of those things, but there *are* obligations within the home as well as at work.

2. Be career oriented. Take the freedom that come in having a homemaker tend to menial tasks and use it as an opportunity to focus on and enhance your career. Be self-motivated and push yourself to move to the next level, qualify for bonuses, and excel at a career you and your family can be proud of.

3. Graciously accept and encourage good service. A simple "thank you" when given a cold drink, a hand resting on the head of your slave kneeling to you, or a "The house looks great today, I am proud of you" can positively motivate your homemaker for days.

4. If there is a problem in the home (a messy area, dinner late, misbehaving children) address the issue promptly, but there is no need to be an irate tyrant. There are times when things aren't done because of extenuating circumstances such as a sick child or a flat tire preventing a timely meal, *not* because of direct disobedience. Learn to discern the reason for a problem, discipline when appropriate, and also show mercy when appropriate.

5. Provide swift and fair punishment when appropriate to all members of the household, and allow it to serve as atonement. Never hold grudges or bring up past problems once they have been resolved. Showing forgiveness and absolution are important lessons to those who you lead in the home.

6. Act as a gentleman should. Treating your lady like a queen encourages her to treat you like a king. Hold her hand. Open doors. Pull her chair out. Help her with tasks requiring strength. Be well groomed and appropriately dressed. Speak politely to everybody, be it the waitress serving dinner or your boss. Don't speak vulgarly or release bodily functions in public. Don't ogle other women. Periodically give tokens of affection such as flowers or a card. These things do not make you a "wuss"; nor do they make you any less of a Master. They make you a gentleman.

7. Be the living example of a good person for your children. Live a life based in honor, pride, respect, and morals. Show your sons how they should treat a potential partner. Show your daughters what kind of high standard they should expect out of a life mate.

8. Participate in your children's lives. No adult ever looks back on his or her childhood and thinks about how much they wished they had a specific toy. Instead they think back and wish they had more time with their family. Since your time is more often spent at the office than at home, the children you are raising up need special attention from you when you are home and available. Consider implementing a weekly family night that is technology-free as a chance to remain close. Periodically have special father/son days or father/daughter days to get together with each child and show them that you are always available to them. You directly impact

both the quality of their childhood and also what quality of person they will become as adults.

9. Your homemaker is not a mind reader. Give her specific tasks with specific deadlines, outlining the expectations you have for the home.

10. Inspect what you expect. If you do give her a task, check in on the task to be sure it is being handled. A good wife shouldn't have to be micromanaged, but does need to be checked up on periodically. Give positive reinforcement along the way to encourage her for a job well done.

11. The financial production may be your responsibility, but you have the choice to assign the keeping of the books however you see fit. Many HoH ask their homemakers to tend to the monthly budget and bills, and may only focus on long term planning, such as investment strategies and retirement plans. Structure it however you see fit, utilizing each person's strengths, and again inspect what you expect. The most important thing is that each person is on the same page, understanding who is responsible for what.

12. Just because you aren't obligated to perform a household task, doesn't mean you *can't* do it. Many HoH enjoy running the grill, or offer to take the trash to the curb on garbage day. Don't feel like in order to be a "manly man" you can't do *any* domestic duties. Your housewife should be prepared to manage the entire home and child-rearing obligations, but if you want to join in and help, don't let ego prevent you from doing so. You are still the Master of your home if you choose to help fold socks with your wife at the end of the day.

13. Be respectful in mixed company. Unless public humiliation is a part of your M/s dynamic that is agreed upon by all parties involved, save reprimanding your wife for an infraction for an appropriate time and place. It is awkward for everybody involved to bring private issues into the public. Quietly let your wife know she needs to adjust her attitude or behavior to save you both from future embarrassment, and then handle the issue at home.

14. Present a united front with your wife in front of the children. While you may be the final word in the household and everybody knows it, don't undo the word of "Mom" in front of the children. She has a difficult job every day in the home, and the children need to see their mother as an authority figure too. If you and your wife disagree on an issue with the children, discuss it in private and present the decision as a united parenting force.

15. Recognize that your homemaker may become worn and weary with her job just as you may become with yours, and encourage her to take time away. Homemakers don't get the benefit of paid vacation time or sick days, there is no lunch break during the day, and if she is being efficient, she won't have much time for a rest. If as Master you see your homemaker wearing thin, encourage her to go to the salon or take lunch with friends as a day off. A woman dedicated to service may not take the initiative to request time away, so you may need to pay attention and require her to step away for a break.

16. As the ultimate decision maker, you need to make choices based on the ultimate good of the family. These are not always easy choices or well-received decisions, but nobody ever said leading a home was easy. Be prepared to stand your ground and enforce your rules.

17. Honest communication leads the home in the right direction. Your homemaker and children look to you as the ultimate authority, and that is based on their trust in you always doing what is right. By speaking with them in a candid and honest way, they can maintain their faith in you as the rightful Head of Household.

18. Be a man deserving of the title Master in your home.

IV. For the Love of the Modern 1950's Lifestyle

The beauty of this lifestyle is really the simplicity of it. It makes living as life partners cut and dry, and removes so much of the negotiation that goes along with many 21st century relationships. By defining the roles in the function of the home with such a basic line— Master/HoH/Man is responsible for the financial well-being and decision making of the home, slave/homemaker/woman is responsible for the functioning of virtually everything else—the days become lighthearted and easy.

Remember the weary conversation about dinner from our "old marriage"? Now I can easily focus solely on serving my husband and Master. In our 1950's M/s marriage, I keep a list of available meals for the week on the refrigerator. As Master leaves in the morning for work, he can simply pick from the list and say, "I'd like grilled chicken for dinner". And that is it. The discussion is done. No back and forth. No puzzling over who is contributing to what part of the day. He makes decisions. I follow his choices. He makes sure I have money to run the home. I make sure to be frugal with the household finances. Simple.

MR in particular loves having a wife that shows herself as prim and proper to the outside world, and only he knows about the naughty, kinky slave waiting underneath the dress and apron. We have a dirty little secret together, and that adds so much excitement to the day. As Master of the household, he can't wait to come home at the end of the work day now. MR also wholeheartedly enjoys being the boss. He feels like he has always been a natural leader, so why not be able to lead his home? He is living life his way, by his rules, and not making any apologies for it. He is the man he always imagined being, married to the wife he always hoped to find.

My very favorite aspect of this life is the freedom that comes in being a 1950's slave. It may seem like a life chained to dirty diapers, never-ending laundry, and constantly thinking of others first, but in reality I am so loved and cherished that the mundane tasks hardly seem like payment enough for the freedom in being ruled by a Master. I feel like a precious piece of glass that needs to be handled carefully, always protected by my husband, and set on a pedestal to be admired by all. I no longer worry about money. I no longer stress about major decisions. I can spend my time doing activities I love: my hobbies, honing my domestic abilities, enjoying the children, doing volunteer work, or participating in local women's clubs. And of course, serving my husband, showing him how thankful I am for him providing for us. And I, like MR, am being the woman I have always wanted to be. Some people are natural leaders. I am a natural follower. And that's ok.

V. But What About the Children!

One of the most hotly debated issues regarding this lifestyle is what kind of impact it will have on the children that are involved in the home. What will the kids take in subconsciously when they see Dad being the sole breadwinner year in and year out? How will the children be impacted by a friend questioning, "Yeah, I know your mom is a *mom*, but what does she *do*?"

Parenting is tough. Nobody will deny that. All we do as 1950's M/s parents is raise our children in the very best way we know how. Kids thrive on stability, on consistency, on having parents who are actively involved in their lives, and on being brought up in a nurturing, loving home, so we provide this for our children.

As a direct result of living this "alternative lifestyle", we as parents are probably more hyper-aware of not putting our children in a specific box labeled "male" and "female". Just because this is how their parents live does not mean this is how our children will want to live. Both our boy and girl are taught to set a table and put away laundry. Both are taught how to change a flat tire and will spend time around other adults of both genders that have important careers. Both children will be taught manners and etiquette—not necessarily "this is what a gentleman does" or "this is what a lady does", but instead "this is what a respectful person does." We will show them everything we can in life. We want to enrich their experience, not shelter it.

Our children do see a pretty specific style of living, but really, don't all children? We expose them to other ways of life in every regard, including persons of varied religions, economic brackets, career paths, ethnicities, disabilities, and relationship dynamics. We teach them how to be accepting of differences, to embrace the beautiful diversity that is people on Earth, to enjoy learning about other people's individual walk in life, to empathize with the struggles of mankind, and to get really thrilled about choosing their very own path one day.

We hope that they will learn from being raised around our marriage dynamic:

❖ Being polite and knowing proper etiquette is important.

❖ Treat your partner with love and care.

❖ There is a joy that comes in doing something kindhearted for your partner.

❖ Be whoever you want to be. Set your standards for living high.

❖ Everybody lives differently. To each his own. Don't judge others based on how you want to live.

❖ The partnership of a committed couple needs to be the household priority. Put that relationship first, because without a strong helm guiding, the ship can easily drift off course.

VI. Sounds Peachy Keen? Right On, Daddy-O!

To the person who is considering this M/s style, I would invite you to do your own research into what sparks your interest about the 1950's household. Focus on that and build from there. Toss out what you have no interest in, and don't regret it for a minute. There is no right and wrong in this, only what is right for a particular couple.

❖ *On the note of finances*: Many people with whom I speak desire this lifestyle, but feel they are unable to work it because of financial reasons. The question is often brought up of the possibility of having both husband and wife working. Of course this is possible, and as mentioned previously, there were plenty of women in the actual 1950's who worked. But if you are curious about having the homemaker in the home full-time, start working towards that goal and try to figure out a way to make it happen. When we first decided to live on one income, we took a step back and asked ourselves what was worth the sacrifice to have me home. We went from two cars to one, which also decreased gas and insurance. Factor in being able to make scratch food three times a day instead of dining out. Saving on daycare expenses. Saving on work clothes for the woman. There are endless numbers of ways to decrease expenses if you get really serious about it.

Try an experiment for six months. Only live off of the Head of Household's income, and try to stash away as much of the slave's income as possible. Make it a challenge in your home to see who can decrease expenses the most. Shop insurance rates. Negotiate cell phone plans. Rent a movie instead of going out to one. You may be surprised how close you can get to living on one income. And if in the end if one can't quit and you *do* need two incomes, at least you are saving money. A couple can certainly both work and seat the Master as head of a 1950's household. Embrace it and make it work for you.

❖ *For the M/s couple*: Consider a written contract. Many D/s or M/s couples have a written contract and I think it works swimmingly for the 1950's dynamic. Because as the goal is to simplify life, to avoid a Master micro-managing his slave, having a written guideline for how he expects the running of his home as well as potential disciplinary actions creates a simple reference for the homemaker. Putting things in black and white takes the guesswork out and gives a great running guide for the home.

❖ *For the HoH (from MR)*: Let the responsibility drive you to be the best man you can be. If you are the type to crumble under pressure, this may not be the lifestyle for you. You have tough decisions to make; make them with confidence. Run a home the way you see fit, and be proud for doing so. And communicate, communicate, communicate. It may not seem "alpha male" to talk about your feelings, but this is a Master/slave dynamic so the backbone, like that of other M/s relationships, is to communicate, and listen to your slave. There is nothing wrong with expressing yourself to your partner, and she will likely tell you exactly how to lead her in the most effective way possible.

❖ *For the homemaker*: Don't let societal pressure stop you from wanting to do this. Find joy in subservience. If it fulfills you to iron your husband's clothes the way he likes, damn it, then *do it*. Just because others may not understand or agree with your lifestyle doesn't mean you shouldn't do what feels right or natural. It is no different from somebody having convictions regarding their chosen religion or their right to have a career and family. You may run into naysayers, but at the end of the day you need to look into the mirror and like who you see.

And finally, as it is in all M/s dynamics, have fun. If you aren't, then *change something*. Our fun may seem like a drag from today's standards, all about old-fashioned values and board games on a Saturday night and the little wifey cross-stitching on the floor at her husband's knee, but to us, it's a gas. And at night ... when the lights go out in the home and the kids are tucked in...

Well, you never really do know what goes on in somebody else's bedroom, do you?

The Victorians

The Victorian M/s Household
Sir Stephen

When I give workshops on topics related to being a Master, I try to present my ideas in a neat and orderly manner, and to convey the lessons learned in ways that will be beneficial to those who are listening. However, I would be lying if I said that the process as I lived it was neat and orderly. It was not. Life is messy, and it took me a long time and lots of trial and error to reach this point in my life where I am comfortable saying that I understand who I am as a Master, as well as what it is that I hope yet to achieve for myself, and for those in service to me.

Had I known at the beginning of my journey what I know now, I would definitely have begun by trying to identify a model, or a mix of models, upon which I wished to base my household's development. The types of models I am referring to are ones that are readily available to us all—the military, cloistered communities, corporations, educational institutions, prisons, and others. Each of these forms of hierarchical community has a history that stretches back for years—sometimes for hundreds, or even thousands, of years.

We all have some experience within some these communities. Even if we were not in the military as adults, we were in the educational system as children, and many of us have had some experience of the corporate structure as adults. For some of us, one or more of these structural models will resonate with us as we encounter them in our non-scene lives, and not just for their primary purpose. On some primal level, they resonate with that part of us that is striving to build a Master/slave relationship.

Those of us lucky enough to have had such a powerful, direct experience within a structured community and have it resonate with the Master within us, can move into M/s with a clear vision of the model we are hoping to follow. (There are also those lucky few who grew up in a home with servants, and are familiar with the concept of hierarchy within their home environment.) However, for those of us who have not had that kind of experience, we generally begin our journey as Masters a little less clearly focused. That is not to say that we are less motivated, or less determined to be successful, but we may be somewhat at a loss as to the direction in which we should move and the forms we should adopt.

Fortunately, if we learn early in our journey to examine the potential within such models, we open ourselves up to a great deal of useful information. Each of these communities has left a record of what they do, how they do it, and why. For those of us trying to create structured relationships, the wealth of knowledge available from these models is invaluable. One example might be books of military codes, training, protocols, etc. In addition to the books written by the military for the military, there are thousands of books written *about* the military, both contemporary and historical. There are books written about monastic orders, and thousands of books written about corporate structures. If we are able to find a model that resonates with us, much else that we wish to accomplish falls into place, such as:

- Definitions of concepts within the context of the model such as honor, courage, respect, courtesy, loyalty, etc.
- Codes of conduct
- Codes of dress
- Instructions for the creation and maintenance of hierarchically structured relationships, that apply both in our M/s Households or in our communities
- Protocols
- Rituals

The advantage of acknowledging that in creating our consensual M/s relationships and households we are creating something new and unique is that we are not limited to historical accuracy, even when we choose to implement some elements of a specific historical model in our relationship structures. And so it was for me. I found myself collecting more and more material—movies and recordings of TV shows—that revolved around the fictionalized reproduction of Victorian, Edwardian, and early 20th Century English Manor houses. Included in this collection were:

- **Remains of the Day**—I recommend you watch this film twice. The first time, relish the story. The second time, with the story already absorbed, you can focus on the quality of the service taking place throughout the film.

ॐ **Gosford Park**—As with Remains of the Day, watch it twice. Wait for the oft-quoted line about anticipatory service:

> What gift do you think a good servant has that separates them from the others? It's the gift of anticipation And I'm a good servant. I'm better than good, I'm the best; I'm the perfect servant. I know when they'll be hungry, and the food is ready. I know when they'll be tired, and the bed is turned down. I know it before they know it themselves.

ॐ **Upstairs Downstairs**—Watch it, watch it, and then watch it again. There is so much to learn here about service, about what it means to be a Master, about structure, about etiquette, about Leadership and Management ... plus the soap opera story is wonderful.

ॐ **Manor House**—As with the others there is much to learn here, but what is most interesting is that this was an experiment in which a collection of 20th century volunteers attempted to learn and live the roles of Lord and Lady of the Manor, as well as the servants. Their transformations, trials, and tribulations add up to an interesting commentary on those above stairs and those below.

ॐ **Downton Abbey**—Although the focus is much more on the lives of those above stairs, this is still quite instructional.

ॐ **Jeeves and Wooster**—If you are in the mood for a comedic look at service, this should fill the bill. Although there are wonderful moments of service woven into the comedy, it is a little bit dangerous for slaves to be allowed to view this, as it encourages subtle forms of smart-assery.

The upshot of my interest in these films and TV shows was that I realized that I had a love of things Victorian and the management style displayed in the Victorian Manor house. It was a macro-management style that assumed for intelligent and capable individuals both as Master and as servant. This historical model became the cohesive element that brought into clear focus how I wanted to organize and run my M/s Household. And how excited I was when I found examples in the historical reality of Victorian life and literature of how service was viewed, and how *closely it resembled* my own image of what my M/s dynamic would incorporate! For example, note this quote from *The Butler's Remembrancer* (not a work of fiction, but advice from someone who had lived a life of service in Victorian England):

> *Such of my readers as may be now candidates for gentlemen's service must consider that it is a way of life wholly different from any that they have been accustomed to; comprising comforts, privileges and pleasures, which are to be met with in but few situations; and, on the other hand, difficulties, trials of temper, and self-denials, beyond what you might be called on to bear in some other state of life. When you go into service, all the ways in which you may have been indulged at home must be given up; and you will find it equally to your comfort and profit to have none but those of your employers, as far as they may be consistent with justice and moral government. Reflect that when you once engage yourself in a situation, neither your time nor your abilities are any longer your own, but your employers', and they have consequently a claim on them whenever they may be required.*
>
> *Some persons speak of servants as if they were so far beneath them as to be unworthy of notice; but this adds nothing to their own respectability, and only betrays their ignorance and pride. There is no degradation in being a menial worker except as you fail in the duties of one; there is no disgrace in wearing livery unless you bring reproach on it by your behavior. I have never been ashamed of being in livery but when I have seen other servants disgrace it.*
>
> —Onesimus, *The Footman's Directory*
> *and Butler's Remembrancer*

Or this quote from The Complete Servant (1825) by Samuel and Sarah Adams:

> *Young persons, on their first entering into service, should endeavour to divest themselves of former habits, and devote themselves to the control of those whom they engage to serve. They*

will probably find everything different from what they have been accustomed to at home, or in common life; and as their mode of living will be greatly altered, if not wholly changed, so must their minds and manners. They should endeavour to discard every low habit and way of thinking, if such they have; and there will be set before them, by those of superior rank, and cultivated understanding, the best modes of conduct and the most approved behaviour, they will wisely take advantage of the opportunity which Providence fortunately presents to them, to cultivate their minds and improve their principles.

It struck me how both quotes advised those about to enter into service to put aside their old lives and habits, then to adapt themselves to the best of their ability to the modes of behavior expected by the Lord of the Manor. It also struck me how both advise that the Lord of the Manor should be an individual possessing such qualities as would make him or her worthy of the loyalty, obedience, work and commitment offered by those applying to be in service. To me, this was the stuff of M/s—it spoke to the essence of the dynamic that exists between Master and slave, and the difficulty of turning from the path we have known to strike out in an entirely new and uncharted realm. Although this might be a place difficult to imagine, it contains within it the promise of the most profound fulfillment.

It is important to remember that, as demanding as a life in service could be, it was entered into by consent, just as slaves enter into our M/s relationships today. Our slaves, like the Victorian servants, must be willing to alter their mode of living to suite their Master and strive to live up to the highest standards of obedience and service. We Masters strive to live up to the lofty expectations of our slaves, just as the best of the Victorian Masters made the attempt in their households.

The Victorian households had a clearly defined hierarchy both above stairs and below. As it is presented both in the literature of the time and in the books and movies of our era, when it was done correctly, those both above and below stairs lived with the expectation that adherence to their roles and fulfillment of their responsibilities would result in personal rewards, harmony in the Household, and the betterment of the world.

So what attracted me to the Victorian model for my Household? Ultimately it was that which was sustainable—the management style and the efforts to live up to the agreed-upon codes of conduct by both Master and slave in the most exemplary way. However, there is still the fantasy ... the Manor House, the clothing, the staff of servants. I dream the dream of myself as landed gentry in a town like Cape May, New Jersey, a town that relishes Victorian recreations ... owning a Bed and Breakfast. I fantasize about the fulfillment to be found in living Upstairs with a staff of dedicated servants (in my case, slaves) below. I imagine all of us dressed in proper Victorian garb, free to walk about the town; my servants bowing when they see me and with the freedom to address me publicly and privately as "Sir" without a sideways glance from our neighbors or the passersby on the street.

Sigh. Perhaps someday.

The Naughty Victorians

Sir John of Cawdor and slave girl yoni

The Victorian Era was noted for a return to "proper behavior", with social norms and protocols intended to show one's social standing. It is the symbolic nature of this lifestyle that just fits with who I am, and what I want from my slave-girls. When you study relationships during that era, you see many commonalities with other M/s lifestyles that are reflected here, such as knowing looks, special hand signals, earrings, dress, etc. The Victorian-inspired slave knows her place—she knows she is a slave, yet also knows she is highly valued.

What I find noteworthy is the history and the relational structure from the era. Victorian era families were patriarchal. They encouraged hard work, responsibility, and social deference. Men were considered superior to women, but a woman's thoughts and opinions were respected. Let's start to examine this more closely.

I'm a fan of the Myers-Briggs system of personality types, and I come up an ENFJ on that system—extroverted, intuitive, feeling, and judging. This means that I draw energy from both structure and my partners, and in some contexts, from other people. I find a great deal of energy in play and obedience, and having a slave who understands my Victorian values allows me to feed off of her energy. Having more than one slave allows me to be a Victorian patriarch, which gives me a great sense of responsibility for the well-being and behavior of my slaves. As the patriarch, their behavior is a reflection of me.

Our M/s relationship feeds on obedience without hesitation. This means that my core values of honesty, listening on a deep level, and a deep self-respect are my moderators, and I expect the same from my slave girls. This may also be a given in other lifestyles, but the difference here is reflected in our cultural codes of dress and deportment. Lace and the necklaces and earrings of that era replace leather boots and clothing; Victorian deportment replaces leather protocols. It can be demonstrated in the way my slave-girls carry themselves. Posture and carriage were important to Victorian ladies, and they were trained to carry themselves well, to have poise, and to gesture gently and elegantly. My slave-girls know to carry themselves with pride and to keep their heads up—never to look down at the ground. In some M/s dynamics, the slave is never to look her Master in the eyes without permission, but I demand that my slaves look me in the eye at all times—it is the window to their souls and their slave-hearts. It also shows that I respect my slave-girls. I value them and treasure them, as Victorian men valued and treasured their wives. Yoni walks proudly in her service to me. She walks beside me, giving me easy access to her body and her mind. She can walk on either side of me, having the appearance of equality, and in most cases she is actually treated as my equal. Her humanity and slave-heart grant her that right and position, and the length and quality of her slave-service is acknowledged. Her demeanor is a gift to me ... and to herself.

The key to all of this is subtlety. I want to see a quiet manner that proudly says, "I am Owned by my Master, Sir John of Cawdor." My own gentlemanly manners, grace, and style should be reflected for all to see, and this will encourage her to be able to handle almost anything, vanilla or not. Victorian women were proud and demure at the same time. They were deferential to their husbands—who could be seen as the master of the house, as he always had the final word—and yet they were not afraid to speak their minds. They knew their place, but they knew they had certain rights. My slaves are allowed speak freely to me in private by using a special phrase to get my attention, as long as they remain respectful. I, in turn, will listen and take what they say to heart. I do have the final say, but I take into consideration their feelings, needs and desires. I hold these almost equal to my own needs and desires.

A Victorian M/s lifestyle, like the Victorian era, is bound with strict rules and protocol. Meekness and modesty were considered beautiful virtues in Victorian times, and this is seen in the deference a slave pays to her Master. Victorian girls were trained to prepare themselves for a life dedicated to home and family, and a Victorian-style slave is trained to dedicate herself to her Master. She never offers her hand to another man without her Master's approval. She will not speak to another man without permission, and she will not allow herself to be touched. She adheres strictly to the rules of etiquette and protocol as dictated by her Master, as well as by her Victorian training.

Our etiquette rules help to define our structure. A Victorian gentleman tipped his hat to ladies in greeting, opened doors, and walked on the outside of a lady. I always open the car door for my slave-girls, and they know to wait until I come around to do this. I also open doors when we enter and exit a building. I do not use humiliation, as that devalues my slave as a treasure. Her pride and feelings of self-worth are highly valued. My Victorian-style slave is a treasure to be cherished and prized, to be shown off as a sign of status. To humiliate or debase her is to devalue her worth, and my own in showing her off.

In discussing any intimate relationship, we must also touch upon also the matter of romance and love. I know other Masters who do not allow love to interfere with their M/s dynamic, as they feel that to show love to a slave takes away their power. However, like the Victorians, love and romance are very important in our M/s relationship. I will send flowers and cards to my slave-girl yoni's work and home, reminding her of her value to me.

Bound in their strict codes of etiquette, the Victorians had to use modes of dress to express themselves, including fans, gloves, and handkerchiefs. I am very aware of my slave-girl's dress; I have her wear certain earrings or dress in a certain color for work. These are ways to express my control and her obedience and devotion in a subtle way which has great meaning to us. Grooming was also of great importance to the Victorians; a Victorian woman usually wore her hair in a chignon or a bun, and paid attention to the details of her clothing. Departing a bit from the rules of the era, my slave usually wears her long hair loose, although I will occasionally have her wear braids. However, her dress must always be carefully thought out; even when it is deliberately provocative, it must be in a mode which I call "elegantly slutty".

Our cultural dynamic draws its elegance from another era, but we do live in this one, and we modify it to "pass" easily. We are not trying for flashiness and "look at us"; only those who are in the know can discern who and what we are. We wish to blend in in all contexts. We hide in plain sight.

We are, as our tattoos say, *Anam Cara*—Irish Gaelic for "Soul Friends".

Nobility and Fealty

Fealty as a Model for M/s
Unbennes, owner of caeth

Why M/s?

We had been together for twenty-nine years, we were a bit kinky, and had been through some pretty severe bumps. I found an old unlabeled journal of his, and opened it to see what it was. The entry was from fifteen years ago, wistfully saying that he wished I would own him. So I showed him what I had found, and asked if he still wanted that. He fell to his knees with an exuberant "Yes!" and then we spent the next year trying to figure out what it meant.

All I really knew about Master/slave relationships at that time was that caeth needed it, and that I needed him. I had a fantasy of what it meant that I didn't like; coming from a history of abuse, I did not want to become an abuser. Early on in our marriage, we had explored the idea of weekend "contracts" to give structure and safeguards to our D/s play. My fearful fantasy of M/s was that the safeguards would be set aside, that I would have to be barking commands at him, dishing out impact play more severe than I could handle, and would have to give constant kinky sex. It wasn't based on any exposure to a real M/s relationship, but on the imagery of the overculture—hints in movies, Betty Page playing cards, and cartoons in Playboy. He had a fantasy of what it meant, too, but reality trumped the fantasies—for which I, for one, am grateful.

Our "jobs" within the relationship are not much different now than before we brought M/s into our relationship, but our "headspaces" are. A lot of what I thought of as my "dark side" has been aired out, and has turned out not to be as evil as I feared. Being honest about what we are has helped both of us.

We are complicated human beings, and therefore interact with one another in a number of different complementary and even archetypal pairings. We have always worked together as artist/engineer, designer/builder, drawing-sculpting/math-whiz-musician, and maiden/dragon. With M/s, we also include Goddess-priestess/priest-acolyte, sovereign lady-queen-liege/bondsman-courtier-vassal, Greek lady/educated slave, and lady dragon-tamer/dragon.

I'll include a little bit about the Greek part and the dragon-taming toward the end, but the focus of this article is on the sovereign lady to bondsman and liege to vassal aspect, since it is probably the single most influential archetypal pairing we use. *Unbennes* and *caeth* are the Welsh words for "queen, tyrant" and "slave, bondsman".

Why Fealty?

Just as popular conceptions of M/s are distorted by fantasy, the popular image of feudal society is influenced by modern distortions. Some are romantic and lovely, like the paintings of John Waterhouse; others are silly, like the film *The Court Jester* or the more recent (and very far in left field) television series *Merlin*. And while John Waterhouse's paintings are beautiful, caeth is not a fighter. His service to me is more like that of a squire, bard and court wizard all rolled into one.

Fealty is a relationship of mutual obligation, founded on an unequal balance of power. It was the backbone of feudal society, in which class stratification was seen as "the will of God". It is possible to have a network of obligations based on a hierarchy of fealty. A knight might be in fealty to his duke, who is in fealty to the king. In exchange for a grant of lands, the king might call upon the duke to provide a number of knights, and the duke would send the knights to fight under the king. If the duke and the king have a dispute, the knight would be expected to support the duke. In M/s, if a master is active in their local community, they might send their slave to serve at an event, even if they can't attend the event personally, and the slave would still be seen as belonging to the master, not the event organizers.

As for me, I had long admired the leadership of certain strong women in history. As a child, Eleanor of Aquitaine and Joan of Arc were influential role models. Later, as I studied folklore and history, Maeve of Connacht, Boudicca of the Iceni, Elizabeth I of England and Gráinne Ní Mháille came to resonate for me. I look to their better qualities as inspiration for how to exert my own authority. For his part, caeth was inspired by Howard Pyle's books *King Arthur and his Noble Knights* and *Robin Hood*, the aforementioned *The Court Jester*, as well as Kenneth Graeme's *The Reluctant Dragon*. Later, he studied mediæval history, and got his B.A. in Mediæval Studies.

We met through the Society for Creative Anachronism, so the first thing we knew that we had in common was a love of things mediæval. When we got married, our wedding had mediæval trappings. We did not have any contracts for the relationship other than our wedding vows[1], which had unconscious elements of D/s in them. Those vows, of course, still stand, but we chose to add the layer of the Oath of Fealty when we settled into our M/s.

Since we were active again in the SCA when we came to ownership, sovereign and bondsman was a flavor of energy we were immersed in a good deal of the time. We have strongly developed and reasonably well-matched senses of honor and loyalty, so doing an Oath of Fealty was more meaningful for us than writing a M/s contract or doing a collaring ceremony. We don't live entirely mediævally, but many of the chivalric virtues are core values for us, and we think that they make a reasonable guide for behavior. We didn't look at history and then apply it to our relationship; we looked at our relationship and noticed that it reflects history.

Oath of Fealty as "Contract"

This is the core of our Oath of Fealty, shared in February of 2008 on the 30th anniversary of the day we met, almost a year into ownership:

> **Unbennes:** *I am your Mistress, you are my slave. I am Owner, you are owned. I command, you obey.*

caeth: *You are my Mistress, i am Your slave. You are Owner, i am owned. You command, i obey.*

Unbennes: *Will you swear fealty to Me and accept my mark?*

caeth: *Here do i swear, by mouth and hand, fealty and service to You, Mistress (Unbennes), to speak and to be silent, to come and to go, to play and to create, to do and to let be, to reveal my heart and my mind, to live or to die by Your command. Upon my honor, so say i, (caeth). i am Your bondman, i am your slave, Mistress, i am your man.*

Unbennes: *This do I hear and accept, and for My part do I swear, by mouth and hand, fealty and command to you, my slave (caeth) to be silent and to speak, to go and to come back, to play and to create, to do and to let be, to reveal my heart and my mind, to protect and defend you and our household. Upon my honor, so say I, your Mistress (Unbennes). I am your Bondholder, I am your Owner, slave, I am your Mistress. In token of these vows, come now, and accept My mark, to be permanently inscribed over your heart.*

caeth: *As You will, Mistress, so i will, and i gladly accept the mark of Your Ownership to bear on my body, and in my heart, for the rest of my days.*

My caeth and I had been discussing the idea of his tattoo over the course of about twenty-five years, with me using temporary tattoo paints to put it on his chest from time to time, but we had not talked about it in the eight years before we came to M/s. Once the M/s was chosen, the idea resurfaced as one potent for both of us, and he got the tattoo as an adjunct to the Oath.

Historically, oaths of fealty read somewhat like real estate contracts, spelling out the terms between the parties involved. The oath of fealty above differs only a little from the common points of some of the oaths of fealty used in the Middle Ages, and differs less yet from the oath of fealty sworn between peers and the crown in the Society for a Creative Anachronism.

Ours does not include the fine detail that some historic oaths had, but does cover a few points of vital importance to us. It has elements that express the agreements we had come to in the ten months we had been figuring out how we were going to conduct the M/s in our relationship.

Elements of "traditional" consensual slavery are woven through the oaths. "To speak and to be silent" and "to reveal my heart and my mind" refers to the transparency I require of him. "To come and to go" refers to the fact that he prioritizes me over others, so that if I call him, he will close off what he is doing with others and come to me. "To play and to create" means that I can command him to accompany me to events, and to play music, and to build furniture, or whatever else I ask of him.

"To do and to let be" indicates that he will not only do things for me, he will back off if I want to do them myself, and he will refrain from doing things I don't want done. "To live or to die by Your command" is a promise not to commit suicide. Living is sometimes a hard thing to do when feeling suicidal, but being people of honor, the oath adds weight to the living side of the balance. My promise to caeth to refrain from taking my own life is not part of this oath because I made that promise years before. At that time, he did not feel he could honestly reciprocate. I am relieved that the promise is now mutual.

In accepting his fealty, I was also accepting responsibility for his well-being. "To go and to come back" in my vow is there to address his fear of abandonment, which at the time was stronger than it should have been. That and the "to protect and defend" were reassuring to both of us. I see protecting us as my job, to the point where I was the one who walked toward the next town and left him to read aloud to the children when our car engine burnt out on the highway, and for that matter, I'm the one who goes to check on suspicious noises. I'm also better trained in fighting. "To play and to create" in my promise means that I will engage in joint projects with him, which strengthen our relationship.

The Virtues of Chivalry and Noblesse Oblige as Values for the Relationship

As a child, my German grandmother instilled in me a strong sense of *noblesse oblige*. She made it clear that we were better than people who were "common", and because we were better, we owed it to those poor "common" people to be charitable—financially, in kind, and in our expectations of them. Her European values were mixed up with my American love of freedom and equality, and it wasn't until recently that I understood the contradiction. Even though I believed myself to be egalitarian (which, philosophically, I still am), caeth recognized the underlying sense of dominance and superiority, tempered by *noblesse oblige*, in my personality.

There are many different lists of the "chivalric virtues", ranging from the qualities extolled in "The Song of Roland" written in the 12th century, to modern lists compiled and interpreted by members of the SCA and other recreation/reenactment groups.[2] My own list is a concatenation of several, with my personal spin on making them applicable to modern life.

Some of the obvious virtues are *honesty, loyalty, justice, courage, perseverance, prudence, reason, discipline*, and *courtesy* (which I usually call politeness). Most people would agree that these are the qualities of a decent person. They don't tend to think of them as particularly "knightly", yet there they are in period texts. My caeth values them too, though he may rank their relative importance differently than I do. We have them internalized, so we need not give them a lot of attention.

A few of the virtues seem "soft", such as *mercy* (which I see as kin to compassion), *gallantry* (protecting the less fortunate), *largesse* (generosity), *humility* (modesty), and *chastity* (having sex only with those one is supposed to). People who sneer at them are people I prefer to exclude from my life.

Humility is not the same thing as humiliation, though the words share their roots. Humility is having a realistic sense of one's place in the world, and a sense of one's foibles as well as one's strengths. Humility comes from within; humiliation is imposed from outside. Since part of the abuse I endured included humiliation, I choose to exclude it from my life now.

For us, *chastity* means that we do not go off and have flings in order to hurt each other. If flings happen, they require care to see to it that nobody is harmed. As his owner, I do not require permission from him, but I am certainly considerate of his feelings. As my property, he does require permission from me, though he has yet to make the request since our coming to ownership. While we do not hold to the notion of courtly love being aimed at an inappropriate recipient, like Lancelot's love of Guinevere (which amounts to what is nowadays called "emotional cheating"), caeth does have the general sense that service to women fulfills him, but he is especially fulfilled by service to me.

Service is a large theme in both M/s and the codes of chivalry—service to one's liege, service to the defenseless, orphans, widows, women generally, and so on. I do sometimes chafe at the constraints placed on the liege—things like waiting to be served rather than pouring my own drink—but since this is consensual, I can declare that I will do certain things for myself. The services that I most appreciate receiving from him often involve the use of skills which he has but I lack.

In fealty and in M/s, *obedience* is to those who hold one's oath, not to just any dominant. My caeth obeys me before he follows the instructions of his employers, because he is my slave, not theirs. In accepting his fealty and giving him my protection, I allow him to abide by their instructions to a reasonable extent.

Some of the chivalric qualities make little sense to the modern ear, but parsing them helps to makes sense of them. *Prowess* is usually thought of as meaning to fight well, but has been expanded by us to mean competence in general. We both appreciate competence. *Grace* is both a manner of movement, and thoughtfulness about the implications of actions, which prevents mis-steps. Extended into *graciousness*, it implies kindness and perhaps a minor sacrifice of convenience for the greater good.

Nobility also implies the will to do what is right rather than what is convenient. It includes the sense of obligation to see to the needs of those over whom one has authority. Related to that is *franchise*, which means not just "having a vote" but being in a position to manage one's obligations, and an acknowledgement of one's privileged status. This one was difficult for me to embrace, due to my philosophical egalitarianism and former denial of my dominant nature. My caeth has a limited level of *franchise*, partly because our relationship is consensual, and partly because I delegate back to him certain rights and responsibilities (such as keeping silent even to me about confidential information regarding his employment), and he has both the wherewithal and the mandate to fulfill them.

Fortitude means strength, and generally refers not only to physical but to mental strength, such as keeping one's head in the face of disaster, and holding complicated mental structures in mind. Related to fortitude is *hope*, because giving up on caring for one another is not an option. Holding out hope is another obligation of authority. Also related to fortitude is *wisdom*. Where fortitude is mental strength, wisdom is the ability to look through the complicated structures, recognize which parts are most important, and figure out what to do with them.

Faith in the Middle Ages was assumed to be primarily faith in God, but also trust and trustworthiness. Our faith is in each other. We have developed trust over the years and had it bruised from time to time, but have emerged more deeply bonded than ever. *Honor*, to me, means honesty in action. It is the fulfillment of one's obligations and the acknowledgement of rightness in others.

In our relationship, some of the virtues belong more naturally to me than to him. *Mercy, largesse, nobility* and, to a great extent, *franchise* are primarily the prerogative of the person in authority. The virtues that belong more to him are *modesty, service* and *obedience*. He is by nature more *diligent* and *perseverant* than I am.

Chivalry is a word which has been co-opted and diluted by some, who define it as being about holding open doors and pushing in chairs. Some use "chivalry" to try to excuse perpetuating "traditional" gender roles. Yet even the aforementioned "Song of Roland" included in the code "to eschew unfairness, meanness and deceit." While sexism was taken for granted as "God's will" back then, I see no point in perpetuating its unfairness.

How This Works in Daily Life

I said previously that we do not give a lot of attention to the virtues that we have internalized, but though we don't give them much direct thought, they do inform our world view. Aside from the oath of fealty, we spent a good deal of time in our first year of M/s "thinking on paper", the result of which is called our "Dragon Taming Manual". We do not refer to it as constantly as we did when we were assembling it, but we do review it a couple of times a year in order to see what still rings true and what may need to be thrown out. Of the forty-three pages we had when we first finished it (if an evolving document could ever be said to be finished), we have only thrown out about two.

The manual begins with the oath, and addresses what our expectations were going in and how they have evolved, our processes for communication, my rules for him, what he is allowed to expect of me, a bit about archetypes, and what constitutes "slave maintenance", including assertion of control, authority, touch and sex, creative projects, music and dance, and a good deal of miscellaneous musing. While not couched in mediaeval terms, a good deal of it covers aspects of the chivalric virtues, including the relationship between transparency and honesty. The manual builds upon our oaths, clarifying how we go about fulfilling them.

My caeth is a multi-talented craftsman and sees that as an aspect of his role as bondsman. His talents are at my disposal and his service to me includes the creation of objects. When I was doing illumination but my calligraphy was less than adequate, he took up calligraphy and got very good at it. Later, I made an idle comment about wanting a chainmaille parrying glove for my rapier fencing, and he chose to learn how to make chainmaille. He likes to make things, likes the mediaeval period and likes to feel useful.

When I was still fencing, caeth acted somewhat as my squire, carrying my gear to and from the fencing field, watching my bouts, holding a parasol over me when I was resting, and ascertaining that I had water. When camping, he took on the bulk of the setup and teardown work, prepared meals and did the dishes.

My caeth enjoys giving me anticipatory service. He brings me lattes in bed each morning, carries packages or bags when I'm shopping, and sometimes my purse too. While I think of it more as politeness than specifically chivalry, he does open doors for me unless he is laden.

He likes to kneel before me as I am seated. He likes that I face and handle our interactions with outside authority. I like that I can ask for his counsel and know that it will be wise.

Other Archetypes We Use: A Greek Model

In ancient Greece, slaves were ubiquitous and served a huge number of functions. While some were abject—digging ditches and scrubbing floors—there was no great distinction made between craftsmen and slaves, and skilled craftsmen were highly valued. Additionally, there were higher-status slaves whose purpose it was to teach the children of the household before they went elsewhere to academy.

My caeth is highly educated, highly skilled, and appreciates being valued. (Humiliation is *not* one of his kinks.) The concept of the valued and skilled slave serving the Lady of the house appeals to caeth immensely. My interest in Greek mythology, particularly the stories revolving around Aphrodite, Persephone, and Hecate, has given me enough familiarity with the model of the skilled slave that I appreciate it as well. My caeth's skills run from things the Greeks would recognize, such as cooking and massage, to things they could not conceive of, such as computer architecture.

Other Archetypes We Use: Lady and Dragon

My caeth and I also relate as a dragon and the Lady who tamed him. His identity as "dragon" fits both the description in *The Reluctant Dragon*[3] ("…a peaceable sort of beast enough … enjoying the cool of the evening in a poetical sort of way") and in Starhawk's analysis of group dynamics in *Truth or Dare*[4], where the role of "dragon" is seen as a *defender of boundaries*. He does not like to have very many people visit our lair, er, home. As a somewhat reclusive dragon, he appreciates that I insulate him from social demands he might find excessive.

He shares with traditional imagery of dragons both the fierce temperament and the hair-splitting wiliness that exposes muddy thinking, like Smaug in *The Hobbit*. This keeps me on my toes, since he is even more of a stickler for exact and clear wording than I am. Dragons are also renowned for their wisdom and scholarship; caeth is an excellent scholar, and enjoys bringing to bear his aptitude for research both when I express a wish for it, and to satisfy his own curiosities.

My dragon is generally slow to anger, but can be quite intimidating when he finally loses his temper. Since we have come to ownership, my fortitude in facing his anger has become stronger. Often when he is angry, it isn't at me, so I can elicit information and begin thinking of solutions while he is still steaming. When he is angry at me, the situation is tense, but I ask him questions to find out why he is angry so that I can rectify it if possible. When he is angry but I feel justified, he has to make peace with the situation as it is.

Like other dragons, caeth has his "hoard". He collects fancy kitchen appliances, woodworking equipment (though the lathe is mine), books, tools generally, coffers bursting with coins (mostly those collectable state quarters), and dragon-themed things from figurines to jewelry to a tea towel from Wales. He would love to think of me as his treasure, except that he ultimately bows before his Queen.

Of course, our relationship is just about us. Whatever we do may or may not work for anyone else. I think that being honest with and true to yourself and your partner is the best approach to any relationship.

Notes:

[1] My caeth's vow to me was this: "My beloved, I come this day to share a promise with thee to love thee, respect thee, and grow with thee; to strive always to be to thee husband, lover and companion; to share with thee all my sorrows and joys, my thoughts and my life; to care for thee, comfort thee, and support thee as best I can; and, as we face the world from this day forward, to share with thee all of my resources, both material and immaterial, so long as though shalt do the same."

My vows to him were: "Mine beloved, I have come to affirm and share this promise I have made thee in my soul: that ever shall I strive to share both the joys and burdens of life with thee, to share my love, my strength, my beauty, and all my life with thee. I will stand beside thee throughout all our days. This promise does not deny that sometimes I can be weak or cold, for that is human, but always will I try to be otherwise. I love thee with my mind, my body and my soul."

[2] More information may be found at:
http://castrorum.blogspot.com/2009/12/chivalry.html
http://www.lordsandladies.org/knights-code-of-chivalry.htm
http://middlewiki.midrealm.org/index.php/ChivalricVirtues
http://www.21stcenturychivalry.com/The_Code_of_Chivalry.html

[3] The text of *The Reluctant Dragon* can be found in Chapter 7 of Kenneth Graeme's Dream Days which is online at http://www.online-literature.com/grahame/dream-days/7/

[4] Chapter 10 of *Truth or Dare* goes into the "roles" that may be filled in group dynamics. Healthy groups have balance between them. (HarperOne; Reprint edition, December 27, 1989, ISBN-10: 0062508164 ISBN-13: 978-0062508164)

It's Good To Be The King

LuckyAlbatross

"It's good to be the king."

The first and foremost element of identifying my style of Master/slave with a monarchy is simply that the king is king. There is no equivocation in that state. There is no quibbling or bartering or appeal to somehow compromise the absoluteness of his place in the world. Authority of the king may be justified by religious direction, and may be upheld through gaining favor of his subjects—but the king is simply the king. His kingdom remains whole and contained within itself and none can be higher.

The simple elegance of this state is enough to be appealing to me as someone who has always naturally been inclined towards the extremes, someone who has always sought the quickest, cleanest, straightest line of absolute truth in understanding.

He is king. Always and in all ways.

I am no historical scholar. I have a vague notion, the more I learn of different kingdoms' formations as a way to protect the people from outside invaders, and the uprising and perhaps inevitable chipping away of monarchical authority through cabinets and parliaments, that I will continue to enrich the sense of my own slavery through monarchy. But suffice it to say that the base element of knowing he is king and nothing will diminish that alignment of authority from him to me is what brings me fulfillment.

"I'd ask to reserve the right to change my mind, but I don't have the right to begin with."

Often people confuse slavery and subjugation with weakness. They are in the lesser position when it comes to enabling activity. Yet, to be objectifying, is a racecar any slower because the key is held by another? Is a bomb any less a threat because it can't light its own fuse?

The power held within slaves can be, and usually is, mighty. It built monuments and maintained the kingdoms. In our modern consensual context, slaves can be even more powerful with education, life skills, and the freedom to walk amongst other free people with no external notice of their station at all—or any limitations imposed by society based on their status. But power must be directed before it can be used most efficiently and productively. This authority is what the king claims without compromise. And the king claims everything—marriage, religion, food, and clothing. No matter how strong or capable and wise a slave may be, it is the king who authorizes their lives and orders it to their vision.

For the slave, this righteousness of the king is the right order. The king bears the responsibility for invading forces, for hunger when there is famine. By giving him authority, I know my place better. I may advise, I may request, and I may beg, but at the end of the day, the king's consent is what I am given (or not), and that frees me to know I am always acting within the right of my sovereign.

He does expect me to use his authority for the betterment of his kingdom. I may be his slave, but even slaves are advisors, workers, guardians, and warriors. If he expects me to take care of his kingdom as he goes off to travel, then I must be able to maintain what's best until his return.

"A wrong king is still a king."

It would be idiotic to think, despite the great enormity of responsibility and wealth (not necessarily literal economy) that a king has within his kingdom and under his authority, that kings are always right. One of the best elements of monarchy is that the king has every right—even the right to be wrong. The king needs no justification for his authority; it exists by his mere status as king. If he uses that authority in a way that doesn't work out, it in no way negates that status. The king remains king and the subjects remain within the accepted kingdom of subjugation. As the slave has no right even to their own body, the king has every right, even to their own foolishness.

The king may take, the king may be selfish, the king may be whimsical, the king may be base, the king may be crude, the king may be whatever the king expresses at any time, merely by right of being king. While we may wish to impose a judgment on what the best qualities of a king would be, and our own "kings" may almost always rise to or even above that judgment, we can never forget that our judgments are empty in the face of their absolute authority.

"The king has every privilege except that of being at ease."

One of the unique elements of my slavery is that of being kept in the basement, quite literally; I am a slave living in a basement room with no windows. I am welcome with my Master's family, and often invited to share his bed both carnally and platonically, but that is a privilege for me, and my place is in my basement quarters, as he chooses it to be.

Do not let the basement with no windows be taken too darkly—it's got a fluffy queen-sized bed with a huge wardrobe, internet access, carpet, and I'm allowed to decorate however I please. Hardly dank and dreary quarters. But the main purpose for this is because my Master is married, with children. His queen's place is in bed with him. They have the family and the house and the genetics of his line to consider and maintain. While they are indeed married in the modern way of love and romance as well, it is a marriage and family with all the everyday hardships and responsibilities. I am the concubine, kept literally away in my own apartment for amusement. He may come to visit as he likes, or not.

I am created for his comfort, through his will. I have the privilege of being his confidant. As his absolute slave, the king may be secure and free to know there are no repercussions for whatever he chooses with me. As his consensual slave and concubine, the king knows I am fulfilling myself by obeying and being kept where and how he pleases. I provide a place of distraction, of pleasure, of freedom from some of the overall load. As his marriage is also gifted with pleasure, his ownership is also laden with responsibility. While everyone looks to the king for absolute guidance, he knows he can trust his slave for absolute acceptance.

ANCIENT ECHOES

Roman Slave~Advisor

Ancilla

Our relationship is somewhat based on the ideas of the more benign forms of Roman slavery. This is all my Master's thought process in describing us, as I am much more like a trusted household slave/companion/adviser than like a farm worker or manual laborer. I cook, keep the house, care for the animals, and do some farm work, but for most of the heavy lifting he'll help me out. Last night we unloaded two cords of firewood into the woodshed and he did more of the work than I did. This is mostly related to him being bigger and stronger, and not so much what he feels my place is. My master's opinion on my place is better shown through my online name "ancilla", which my he gave to me, meaning "serving girl" or "maid" in Latin.

I don't work outside the home, except occasionally when he orders me to. Like a slave owner from Roman times, we've agreed that he has absolute authority over my life, to punish, change, sell, lend, rent, or even end me (the last of which he obviously wouldn't, but he sees those as within his rights).

As far as management, I oversee a lot of the house, always with his approval, but without a lot of micromanagement. So I shop, plan meals, cook and clean up often with very little input from him unless he has a special craving for something. I serve him most times, unless he sees I'm busy or just feels like getting up and getting his own. I am expected to be around and available in case he does need anything. He is in charge of the finances, but sometimes he'll give orders like "Pay these bills today" or "Take this to the bank". He makes all those decisions.

Our relationship might look like a 1950's male-dominant relationship from the outside, because we are married, with him working and me keeping the house and taking care of the kids. But internally we have different practices than most 1950s relationships, such as the extent of his authority and my submission. How it looks from the outside is pretty different than how it is, because he doesn't order me around willy-nilly in front of friends and family. Instead he makes "requests", which I know are orders even when nicely phrased.

As far as where sex fits into this, I don't know how ancient Roman owners felt about having sex with their slaves (although I can guess how the slaves felt about it), but that is a big part of our lives and relationship, alongside the BDSM activities we practice at home, at dungeons, or at parties. To me it is more of a pleasure and a treat than a duty.

My advisory duties include things like proofreading work-related emails for him, and suggesting new wording if his tone is coming across wrong. He often asks my opinion on other things too, not just for the household, but in dealing with all kinds of interpersonal situations. He thinks I have a pretty good sense on reading people and knowing how to treat them.

Currently, we are working on buying a new house, so he certainly wants my opinion on each one we look at. I'm in charge of all the animals, so determining whether a place is going to be suitable for a flock of sheep, some dogs, ducks, and other animals is up to me, as well as where the pastures and fences will go. Meanwhile, he's looking more at the foundation structures of the home—plumbing, electricity, layout of the rooms, as well as considering the distance from work. He always gets the final say, and sometimes does not follow my advice after he asked for it, but I figure that is up to him.

The other thing he mentioned to me at length was the basis for my slavery. Unlike some who (in historic times) found their justification in the complete inferiority of one race versus another, or the "males are naturally dominant" thinking going around even in some current M/s circles, he does not hold that his being the Master is based on his overall superiority. It is based only in our status relative to each other, not how either of us are intrinsically. I once disagreed with him and dared to say that I thought he was superior to me. He said, "In many things, yes, but not in everything, and not in overall worth, but just in certain traits and qualities." He felt this was similar to how the early Romans viewed slaves. Slaves or former slaves could be quite well respected in society; they didn't automatically become a lower version of humanity (as slaves in our country's history were thought to be back then).

Ancient Models, Modern Integrity
Sir Raven and slave jade

We are a Master/slave couple, with a heavy slant in the direction of Owner/property (O/p), and we operate within a consensual non-consent (CNC) dynamic. Sir Raven is fifty years old and a life-long New Yorker, identifying as a "center of butch" demisexual[1]. Jade is a thirty-five-year-old slave who identifies as a lesbian and a former Floridian. We have lived together in this relationship dynamic for about two years, 24/7. While we both thought that this collection of essays should perhaps be left to relationships that have more years behind them to tell their story, we also know that learning about the foundation of a relationship can get lost in translation when a couple is celebrating a fifteen-year anniversary.

Though we have only been together for two years, it feels like much longer, in a good way. We both partially ascribe this to our belief in the soul's ability to reincarnate; we have been together in former lifetimes. One might also take into consideration our initial six months of talking for three or four hours daily about what we each wanted from our relationship, finding ways that this could work best for both of us. With that knowledge in place, Jade moved from Florida, and we began our relationship that became M/s, CNC, and O/p.

We consider O/p and CNC to be a particular relationship style all its own. What this means for us is that as the slave, Jade agreed to retain no control over any part of her life for as long as the relationship exists. She further agreed that if the relationship had failed from her perspective, she could ask for release, but no matter how she might feel about her life, the final say could only come from Sir Raven. We both expect that the relationship will continue through our lifetimes, and a part of our core identities are tied directly to this relationship as Master and slave. As such, we would lose a vital part of who we are if we did not find a way to make our relationship work.

---

[1] "Demisexuality" is about desire and arousal, not just about a sexual attraction, but rather forming an emotional and intellectual connection. It's not merely that I'm only interested in having sex with people that I love; it's also that I feel a complete absence of desire or sexual feelings toward everyone else—ever—and that absence is what makes me a demisexual.

Influences

Sir Raven: We each read a lot about Roman and Greek slavery models at roughly the same tender age of twelve, and it heavily informed our dynamic. For me, there is no issue with Jade being my living muse, nor is there any with her educational level or other powerful attributes. As a master, these are only tools to be used by me, however I may feel I want to use them. We both know that both Roman and Greek societies had slaves who were highly prized for their skills and abilities and acted as tutors, writers, musicians, artists, chefs, and so on; many had their talents consciously cultivated for the pleasure of their master. This is certainly the case in our relationship. To me—and Jade knows this—it does nothing but add to the pleasure of my life that my slave can be used for many purposes beyond washing the dishes, although that's nice too.

In reading ancient Roman law on the topic of how they handled slaves, there is a wide array of information that can be useful to a master. The number and quality of slaves owned directly correlated to the overall wealth of the master. The master of the house is tasked with being certain that slaves are treated well and that their occupation in your household is suited to their intelligence and abilities. There are legal prohibitions against acts of extreme cruelty, or killing the slave without due cause. The Roman world of slavery explained that a master should consider a slave's health and education in order to make sure that the slave could best serve their needs. Roman law counsels masters to be comfortable joking with their slaves, and finding out their attributes by asking them about their interests.

Slaves were considered to be human beings who happened to be slaves, not lesser creatures, and several conditions existed for slaves to be manumitted (freed) at the behest of the master. One not uncommon reason to manumit a female slave was to marry her, giving her full status as a Roman citizen. It was not unheard of for a master to have a romantic, personal, and intimate relationship with a slave. There was also nothing unusual about tasking a competent slave to manage your property, including other slaves. In Roman society, unlike the slavery of the American South, the condition of slavery was often transitory. Children of manumitted slaves were automatically full

Roman citizens, and slaves could be highly educated and sought after for their abilities.[2]

Jade: In our relationship, as in Roman slavery, my accomplishments and money belong to my Master. When Sir Raven gave me my mail to open and I found a certificate from an Honors Society for my GPA, my response was to glance at it and just matter-of-factly say, "Oh, honey, this is yours." I was rather embarrassed when she wanted to frame it, but it is hers to do with as she will. I was surprised when she insisted on hanging my art on the wall, and decided where each piece would go, but those are hers as well. (When she decided to task me with painting wine bottles for a side business, I made so many that she had to tell me to stop!)

When she desires me by her side, that too is compatible with Roman slavery, because I am there as both companion and servant. We may have spent the night laughing and enjoying each other, but when she pointed out that her boot buckle had come undone, I knelt on the sidewalk to fix it without a second's hesitation. There is no conflict with whatever goals she has in mind for me for the future, because our slavery is not based on the American concept that the slave is inferior as a human being. Instead, Roman slavery informs our dynamic that it is just and right that I give all I have and all I will become. There is no conflict about her treating me well, because Roman law suggests rewarding slaves for good behavior, including asking them to dine with their masters during feasts. There is no conflict in desiring a slave to manage parts of your life, your home, or your other slaves, because there is no tone of racism present, no idea that the slave cannot be competent to manage your affairs, and no concept that a master cannot decide how to best educate their slaves for their tasks.

I have been assigned to write up notes for our monthly book discussion, keep journals to engage us in our relationship, research topics of interest for Sir Raven, and prepare work-related projects. Every act in my life is an act of service for Sir Raven, and I'm a living

---

[2] For excerpts of Roman law, see:
https://facultystaff.richmond.edu/~wstevens/history331texts/slavery.html

reflection of my Master's goals and values. We were also both inspired by concepts of Japanese concubines and geishas, so it is only a matter of service for me to be able to have a pleasant conversation with Sir Raven as another service. We also create art together and enjoy this as a sacred act, no different than a prayer.

While the idea of constant active dominance and passive submission may be hot, this is not what brings order and contentment to our lives. As her slave, I find the beginning of any new set of rules or procedures a challenge, but over time it just becomes "how we live". It is a struggle for any slave to learn that times of ease are a true source of pleasure for their Master, and not to internalize this as some deficit on their part because the active dominance has given way to a passive enjoyment of a life well-lived. For the slave, this can feel like the control has diminished, and it brings on fears of immense proportion. The reality seems to be that M/s relationships have a natural ebb and flow, with times that the leash feels pulled tight, and then a natural relaxation as the new ideas become internalized and the Master gets what they want.

I describe this as contentment, as an absence of friction that they (Master and slave) have each become accustomed to their relationship with one another as they learn how to acclimate to new expectations. I feel that it is the responsibility of the slave to ask for more active dominance as they need it ... but be careful what you ask for! It is also the responsibility as the Master to know when their slave is restless or may need a bit of a challenge. Being an introvert helps me since I'm always watching, observing, and paying attention to her—body language, tone of voice, right down to her breathing.

As a slave it can't be overstated how important it is to find out how to best provide this information to your Master, preferably before you are having a melt-down inside and are deeply worried about having failed in some way. One of the hardest things to do was just to simply and quietly find the right words to ask for what I need. Learning how to do that can take time, and it may feel deeply adversarial at first. Both people can feel defensiveness and surprise in response to being told that more is needed, especially if that "more" is elusive and hard to define. Knowing that the contentment phase is deeply valuable to many Masters (or at least to mine) may be key in adjusting expectations. It's important to internalize that you have succeeded as a slave if your Master feels comfortable enough to relax and enjoy the services you are now adept at providing. They don't necessarily think to tell us in those words, but ask them outright and you will be able to relax as well. Learning to feel comfortable with contentment can be a hard lesson for a slave, but a vital one.

How We Got Here

Jade: Our relationship progressed through stages that were more organic than structured, but we were always responding with our most authentic selves. We were introduced by a mutual close friend who was instrumental in providing basic backgrounds to each of us. At the time, we were both somewhat disinclined to put too much into our first meeting. While we liked each other, we were cautious. I had been instructed to be in service to Sir Raven and to see to her comfort during her stay in the family home. Having done this for other visiting masters, I didn't put much thought into it beyond wanting to be certain she was comfortable and that I was available to attend to her needs. What stood out for me was that first morning, when I woke up at six and prepared coffee. I had put it in a carafe on a silver tray, planning to leave it on the table right outside her door. I was startled when her door opened. I placed the tray on the table and poured her coffee. When our fingers touched as I offered her the cup, I had this premonition that I had known her before, in another lifetime. I have learned over time that sometimes a soul coming back into your life contains the lesson to learn how to work together or enjoy each other again, and other times the lesson is to learn to stay away from that person, despite the sensation of longing that accompanies your meeting. What stood out for me was her quiet presence, her calm sense of authority, and the way she carried herself with a great deal of intelligence and pride. Those are qualities I admire and that made me want to know her better.

Sir Raven: What stood out for me was Jade's subtle sense of service and attention to how I liked things. I noticed that she left a cold bottle of water for me, quietly made my bed, placed fresh towels in my room, and made a special trip to the grocery store to find the kind of coffee I like. When I commented that I really would like more coffee but was too unused to the Florida heat to drink it, she made some iced coffee for me to drink by the pool. I liked her, but it wasn't as if the Earth moved. However, after I returned to New York, weekly calls and emails gave way to daily calls that reached into the wee morning hours. Still, we both held off of expectations of any kind until I invited her to New York to help with the preparations of my spiritual birthday.

I invited Jade to come when I knew I would be at my worst. My spiritual birthday requires a lot of time and effort, and dealing with large groups of spiritual family members. This is hard for introverts, and we are both introverts. I knew I would be anxious because there was a lot to accomplish, and since my spiritual family is hierarchical in natural, I would not be in control of a large part of the proceedings. You might ask why a control freak like me would put myself in this kind of position when testing the potentials of a visiting slave, but I thought it would give us both a good opportunity to see how we work in times of stress, especially when I am not at my best. If she could handle that, then she could easily handle day-to-day life. I also believe that it is important for Masters to be vulnerable at times, and it is important to see how a slave handles that situation.

Although we were both expecting some stress surrounding the preparations for this large event, our arrival home from the airport definitely set the scene. On our return from the airport we found that the apartment above me had flooded, and water had filled the bathtub, overflowing onto the floors and seeping toward the electronics in the living room. Jade was dressed in a beautiful ankle-length black dress, but she immediately asked for towels, blankets, and the mop to contain the mess without a second thought. While waiting for the superintendent to pick up the phone. I burst into song, singing, "Bess, you is my woman now." Needless to say, we survived both the flooded apartment and the spiritual ceremonies intact.

Jade: I was originally planning to stay for about two weeks, but Sir Raven kept pushing back the date to leave until months had gone by.

Finally, after a hurricane and a nor'easter in November, she told me to collect my belongings in Florida and come home for good.

Sir Raven: So how do we do that, day in and day out? I'm not interested in micromanagement, and I prefer to leave Jade to handle the daily details of the running of our home. She is solely responsible for maintaining the home including all chores of shopping, errands, cooking, cleaning, laundry, and maintaining a straight-A average on her Master's program. In turn, I am responsible for protection, maintaining the household finances, and keeping a close eye on her maintaining her health. She is legally blind and suffers from fibromyalgia, although she's independent as all get out, which I love and admire about her. In short, I maintain total control of my slave's life and through her the household. If this sounds exhausting from both sides of the coin, let us assure you that there are days where it is. The payoff is that we each feel fulfilled, in a way that we do not when we are not in this particular style of relationship.

What we think is important is to condense down the layers of things that you need from a relationship and to closely examine what your core motivator is for getting into this relationship style. For both of us, we absolutely must have our control needs met. I feel most comfortable when I'm in total control and know exactly what to expect from my slave. For me, control is not only about my slave but my environment/home—I know what to expect when I walk through the door. And if I need a heads-up on any given situation, I know I will get all the information that I need to make a decision.

I have, and still do, hear African Americans balk at the term "Master/slave". I am an African American woman, born in America, a native New Yorker. I know all too well about America and its slavery past. I, like others of African descent who are far removed from the kidnapping of humans from their home to be placed into slavery (and for that matter, the people we refer to as white folks as well) are still feeling the effects of that time. And although that form of slavery is a thing of the past, I'm well aware of the effects of it still, although it may be dressed in different garb now. I felt the weight of my mastery when my girl, my slave, referred to me with that title. I came to know that I wanted to live in this form of power dynamic not based on the American slavery of kidnapping and brutality, but the slavery of antiquity where it was not uncommon for men and women to willingly become a slave for different reasons, such as paying off a debt.

This is not to glorify it, but I can respect a person who, of their own will, steps into slavery. They knew what it was they were getting into. They were treasured for their craftsmanship and other skills, and were molded to become an extension of their master and their master's will. Likewise, those masters had a responsibility to their slaves. I am one who takes on the deep responsibility of all that comes with owning another person. I am an African American woman who is the master of an Italian white woman. She willingly got on a plane and moved to New York to be with me, and like the masters and slaves of antiquity, we have both pledged to serve our dynamic (although it is true that the masters of that time have done what best served themselves). She gives herself to me as such, and I receive it. I continue to accept the responsibility of being her master while staying true to our household. I became her Master when she referred to me as such, and accepted her as my slave.

Jade: I feel most comfortable when Sir Raven has control because it makes me feel safe and protected. There are things that we each must give in order to get that core need met. Like many slaves, I'm a perfectionist and would be a control-freak myself were it not for someone else maintaining the control in the relationship. I've had to learn to view "perfect" through the lens of Sir Raven's expectations, and to be content in the moment. I had to learn to embrace mindfulness, and to live with the expectation of always having a "pleasant demeanor". Our house motto is that no one raises their voice in the house unless it's on fire.

We would both say that date that we became Owner and property was in January, when we filed Domestic Partnership papers. You tell this to a woman and her first thoughts are of weddings and such, but we didn't go that route at all. What we did was go down to the courthouse, which allowed us a sterile signing of a legal document. In a funny nod from the Universe, the woman never spoke to me, only telling Sir Raven to have me sign the document. Since I am legally blind, I could have literally been signing anything at all. I trust her, but that irony and humor wasn't lost on me. Afterwards, Sir Raven snapped a picture of me outside the courthouse near a beautiful statue, and we had breakfast at Burger King. When we went home, I signed documents giving Sir Raven full authority to make medical and psychiatric decisions for me, including trusting her decision to terminate life support if need be. So for me, at the signing of those documents I became her property and her responsibility.

Though Sir Raven never used actual collars before, she did decide to collar me the following May. Sir Raven calmly gave me a box containing an eternity collar as I knelt on the floor. Surprised and delighted, I held up the ring of steel and she locked it on my neck. There wasn't a need for words or ceremony. We had already made a vow to each other, and understood the foundation of our relationship responded to our most authentic selves—her vowing to take control and accept responsibility, and me vowing to obey and be an extension of her will.

Eternal Childhood

The Owned Daughter: Daddy/girl-Oriented M/s
Brett

People are drawn to age play for many reasons, but often the first they'll share is their desire to nurture or be nurtured. Just as commonly, age players explain that it offers a chance to recapture a good childhood or to revise a poor one—and, of course, nearly everyone in kink can relate to simple fetishism. Given how triggering age play can be for some, we present its most universal and wholesome aspects first, and then take an additional moment to distance it from its problematic associations, explaining how it's neither an incestuous yearning nor pedophilia (given that it is practiced by adults).

With that groundwork laid, we try to convey how the world of Bigs and Littles is an economy of vulnerability and innocence in which we share unaffected and naive excitement, silliness, and joy. It's when age play surpasses the moment, however, and becomes a way of life, that one discovers the real parenting in it: the long struggles and the hard-won successes. The pride is there, too, and the shattering disappointment. That disappointment, in fact, may have been my first indication of how deeply invested I was in the role of "parent".

In teaching about D/s and age play, I ordinarily define an "age play dom" as "any figure that can set expectations for an "age player", such as a teacher, classmate, or babysitter. As a master and "father", I carry that to its fullest conclusion in temporality and in authority. A parent-child dynamic is based not only on *lifetime* roles, but—unlike sibling identification or any other Big/Little pairing—roles in which one of us is explicitly the creator and the other the creation. Our roles are never suspended or set aside; if it wouldn't complicate marriage, I'd consider legal adoption.

Training a child-identified slave to be fit for service means building our M/s connection through a satisfying emotional connection and continuous fetish experience. Doing so only reinforces my awareness of its parallels in child-rearing: where a child is given latitude to explore within a strict boundary, so may be a slave. Where a child is raised in the customs of the family, to contribute gladly, belong, and confer belonging in the household, so might a slave. Where a child has no authority yet lives in an environment devoted to its thriving, so might a slave. The difference is that my slave will not undergo years of my care, conditioning, and training to enter the world and be scooped up by a younger man, or by one of those masculine women she adores! No, I keep her for myself, and raise her to be a fixture of my home. I may give some of her service and talents to the world, but we won't throw the baby out with the bathwater.

Because a child is small, unskilled, and captive to the self-centeredness of its age, it is a challenge for my "daughter" to prove herself through service: to be unfailingly reliable, thoughtful, cheerful and hard-working, and to put my desires above her own. She can learn housekeeping skills, secretarial skills, or any other role that can be preceded by the words "my little" (eg, my little chef, my little gardener, my little sex slave), to prove that she can fill the roles of both daughter and homemaker (wife). A Little determined to learn to cook in a kitchen full of mysterious spices, ovens with unfamiliar controls, and books with all-too-few pictures is a study of age play slavery.

The daughter/wife/slave role is a noticeable departure from those disclaimers I mentioned earlier—the ones we give near the start of most age play classes—as it is intentionally incestuous. It happens that incest is prominent in both of our sexual fantasies, and so it is at the foundation of our dynamic. While I refer to it as the "owned daughter" model for short, that title completely misses the romance of a girl's youthful, innocent aspiration to marry her father, and the labor that she diligently undertakes to deserve it.

Our own culture, thankfully, has no analog to this model. However, when I can go to some length to describe it, I suggest that someone imagine an ancient Northern European tribal culture, such as the mead-halls of Beowulf, or the barbarians of Kushiel's Dart, or the horse nations in Lord of the Rings. In these milieu, the daughters of the leader occupied a very low tier of nobility. While they might be marginally better-dressed and fed, and carry some advantage as brides, they were not idle; they worked. While this daughter's role is to oversee the servants, she is herself a working servant in keeping her father's home. If this is your fantasy and fetish, it isn't a great step to further imagine together that some daughters would remain as wives, marrying their father and owner and adopting the home of their birth as the home of their marriage. From her birth, training, labor, and the decision of her marriage, she is the property of her father, his asset. While the realities of child-brides are entirely reprehensible, I've found my little girl working to earn the role of wife to be a neat expression of growth in slavery in a committed age play relationship between adults.

Why I haven't called the relationship model simply the Electra Complex is this: it is her task to find her place among my household, not to displace others. Jealousy is endemic to age play relationships, which are often founded on abandonment or trust issues. This is true to the extent that young women in them frequently eroticize their being preferred to an imaginary mother or sister. While this makes for an exciting sex game—a supposedly submissive woman can delight like a demon in the debasement of challengers for her father's affection—it is no basis for a harmonious home life.

Not every parallel is so neat, of course. Training a Little to have emotional reserves can be tricky, since it's her surpassing vulnerability that creates her as a child in the first place. At those times, the language of parenting is useful; i.e.: "I'm going to need you to be a bigger girl right now." It's also the case in M/s age play as much as it is in conventional age play that partners can fall into an interdependency that is difficult to modulate; i.e., "I am trained to depend on you for emotional support, but sometimes you aren't there," or, more specifically, "..so I must be able to turn to other resources we've prepared if I'm having a PTSD incident while you're at work, without questioning your commitment or role." That's a very adult concept to swallow, and, since those crisis moments are widely-spaced, unpredictable, and strip her of some faculties, tough to train for.

Where it's less critical, however (and hot) I do instill dependence and remove capability. Because I enjoy invasive caretaking, I select areas where my daughter will remain childlike or even infantile and condition her accordingly. I then have the pleasure of fulfilling those needs myself, creating unusual intimacy and closeness. I'm careful of imposing more work on myself than I actually desire, just because it sounded hot at the time. For example, we don't strictly follow a bedtime routine of bath, bottle-feeding, and reading to sleep, nor could I commit to reversing her toilet training (a standard adult baby/diaper fetishist fantasy) without additional staff. And, while it would be ideal for us to have a lactating mutual partner, that would mean not only overcoming some considerable impracticalities, but accepting the ramifications of breastfeeding's oxytocin-driven pair-bonding.

Less dependence-oriented and more taste-driven, we have a larger gap in preferences than in many M/s dynamics. For example, her love of cartoons is a charming and attractive attribute, one that would be counterproductive to remove. I'm not a great fan of video as a medium in the first place, but when I bother, I prefer the slow-paced, the subtle, the old, and the British. Since I get some pleasure from indulging her, it's my responsibility to draw a line, and periodically set her to work to find for me something that I'd want to watch, and to then to be my patient, appreciative companion in watching it.

Other predictable gaps can engender some unusual protocols. My girl, raised on fast food, today has dietary preferences little-changed since actual age five. Since I follow an ancestral diet based on food quality, this presented not only an opportunity for parenting, but also to overcome my own frustration and grow as a parent. After reading on the formation of eating habits, I've required that she taste every food on the table before eating her own, at every meal. Her contribution to this protocol was a request that she be allowed to manage that process herself, and to follow it at the start of the meal rather than during. Provided that she does so, and chews with her mouth closed (and without the grimace of death), I'm satisfied.

I feel especially gratified when a protocol I create or decision I make falls particularly within ordinary parenting, such as medical decisions, permission for travel and social activities, or all aspects of her appearance. While any slave in my possession might get dental braces or be enrolled in a team sport, it's satisfying with a "daughter", knowing that we're like only so many other families in doing so. And what parent hasn't fielded, "So, I think I'd look great with a __ piercing..."?

In M/s, we cultivate the service we desire, and high among my needs is "service of personality". To have a spirit of fun, to bring delight, and to imbue our life with anticipation, hopes, and dreams, while growing into her own in discipline and duty, is what I desire in a companion. As intelligent, wise, and good-hearted as my girl is, I'm glad one of us craves ponies, pleads for a puppy, and is speechless at the beauty of a violently spangled tutu in a shop display.

Brett is a daddy and master active in the leather and kink community. He teaches on mainly age play topics and is a regular contributor to The Big Little Podcast. He lifts weights, eats Paleo, and lives with cats in Austin, Texas. He can be reached at creavero@gmail.com.

Daddies, Masters, Boys, and Slaves
Jimmy McA.

Daddies are wonderful people. For a gay man who was rejected by my own father at an early age, Daddies were the men who picked up where my angry, alcoholic father left off—and taught me that what I was is OK, even valued. They gave me my identity first as a gay man, then as a gay Leatherman, and then specifically—and most difficult of all—a submissive gay man. When I was first starting out, I thought that being gay and wanting someone else to be in charge meant that I was maybe supposed to be effeminate, or a doormat to be walked on. It was Daddies who taught me different, taught me to hold up my head and be proud.

All my life, it's been the Daddies among my lovers who have given me what I needed. They nurtured me, they comforted me, they mentored me, and they called me on my bullshit—and let me tell you, when I was younger I had plenty of that. I couldn't have been a real slaveboy then; as soon as things got sticky, I fled. My Daddies were disappointed, but let me go, because boys are like that.

But I could feel the magnet, even as I fought against it. At the house of one of my Daddies, there were two slaves. One of them was live-in, and the other came over several times a week. I watched these men half with discomfort, and half with fascination. They were completely devoted, self-effacing, and yet somehow proud. (*I was charming and would try to get out of trouble with a boyish grin, which didn't often work, but I kept trying.*) There was a quiet dignity in the way that they went about their tasks. (*Part of why I became a boy was so I wouldn't have to worry about being dignified.*) They didn't disobey. (*I couldn't help disobeying, or so I thought.*) They would put in great effort over little things, like garnishing a plate just right. (*What a narrow life! I thought.*) They mostly put up with me, although a few definitely didn't like me. (*I'd tease them, to see if I could get them to disobey. I couldn't. That always shook me.*) They were the bottom of the household, but somehow they made me feel … small. Not by any word or action of theirs, but just by being who and what they were. I could see that they were surrendering a lot deeper than I had the guts to go.

Before we go any further, we should stop for a moment and define the word "boy" in this context, because it has many meanings and can be confusing. In the eighteenth and nineteenth centuries, lower-ranking male servants were often referred to as "boy" by their employers. This happened even if they were elderly—a sixty-year-old might still be referred to as the "stable boy". This custom traveled to pre-Civil-War America and became the even more infantilizing custom of referring to any adult African-American, slave or free, as "boy"; as we know, this is still used as a subtle racial insult today. However, among people who practiced BDSM and had consensual slaves in the 20th and 21st centuries, "boy" was used to refer to at least three different things.

1. One definition was narrowly used as an adult male who does outright age play, usually in a heterosexual context. Today this is usually combined with "little" in order to avoid confusion, as in "I'm a little boy."

2. Another definition—probably the most common in a heterosexual and/or pansexual context—is "boy" as an affectionate term for any male submissive, with no suggestion of age play. (I have heard every heterosexual female dominant I know refer to her male submissive as her "boy" at one time or another, and none of them meant that he was playing a role that was less than adult and responsible.) In this context, "boy" and "slave" or "submissive" are interchangeable and can be used for the same person without confusion.

3. Gay leathermen, on the other hand—maybe because we needed more divergent role models for submissive men's roles, and the attendant specific labels—came up with a definition of "boy" that was separate from "slave". A boy was the counterpart of a Daddy; a slave was a counterpart of a Master. Boys were playful, exuberant, and in need of caring mentorship. They had fewer responsibilities, and more room to screw up. Their energy was youthful, but not (usually) "little". They could sass their dominants, even if they got punished for it. They might remain eternal boys, or they might "grow up" and become Daddies themselves. Slaves, on the other

hand, were entirely subservient, and full obedience was expected. They didn't usually grow out of being slaves and become Masters, although that has happened in the history of the gay Leather world! (As has Masters deciding that they wanted to submit to someone.) Slaves were a lot more committed, and the way that they acted and behaved was determined not by an internal "archetype", but by how their Masters wanted them to act and behave.

You can imagine that these definitions clashed when gay men came into community with straight BDSM people. A gay man would refer to his boy and his slave and mean two different people with different roles, and a straight woman would refer to her boy and her slave and mean the same man with the same role. There's still some scuffling around those definitional differences, and there probably always will be, because (as my Daddy says) human beings are perverse!

Somewhere along the line, though, I noticed that while it wasn't uncommon for a dominant gay man to be both a Master and a Daddy, it was pretty uncommon for a submissive gay man to be both a boy and a slave. (There were always exceptions, of course—one well-known Leather dominant that I've met has had men in his service who used the titles "boy", "slave", and "slaveboy".) When I was just a boy, by definition number three, I assumed that the two roles were mutually opposed—I was a boy *instead of* being a slave. I couldn't imagine being both at once.

The turning point came when I was between relationships and a former Daddy of mine came down with terminal cancer. I needed a place to stay, was looking into a job in his area, and his slave was overworked and traumatized with the situation. I offered to move in to help out during his last year, and the offer was gratefully accepted. It was a situation with more responsibility—and responsibility that you couldn't just blow off—than I'd ever held before in my life. It was also an incredibly sorrowful duty. His slave and I would sit on the couch and cry together after we'd finally managed to get him to some kind of peaceful sleep. At the same time, I wouldn't have traded that time with him for anything—I got to say goodbye, and I got to help two wonderful men in a time of terrible crisis for both of them.

I also got to watch their Master/slave relationship, close up under pressure. The more I saw, the more I admired my new slave friend, and the more I thought about their relationship. I would watch him kneel and kiss his bedridden Master's hand, and something in my belly stirred and tightened. *I couldn't be like that,* I told myself. *I can't surrender that deeply. It would kill me.*

Still, I "grew up" in a fashion during that dark time with Daddy J and slave hal. After the funeral, I moved to another state yet again, feeling a little lost and unmoored. I needed another Daddy to anchor me, and I found one at a gay men's soccer game. It was one of those moments when you see a man and think, "If I could be with him, I'd stay for the rest of my life." That was Master Hawk, and I approached him that day. We talked on the phone for about a week and then got together. I still insisted that I was a boy, not a slave, and that I wanted a Daddy, not a Master. He just smiled at me and said, "All right, boy," and the world was safe again.

We were in the Daddy/boy relationship for about a year, but I kept having thoughts about slavery. I'd think about it almost every night while I lay in bed, and every time I thought about it, it seemed even more appealing, although just as scary. I saw it as both an extra load of responsibility—being held much more accountable, and forcing myself to greater levels of obedience—and an extra load of selflessness, in the literal sense. My sense of self would be at least partially subsumed, and I wasn't sure if I wanted that.

I experimented with little gestures—putting my head on his boot, kissing his hand that lay on his knee, bowing when I said, "Sir, yes, Sir!" I made the gestures just a little more submissive than I was comfortable with, and I found that they gave me a strange thrill—and that feeling in the pit of my stomach. Eventually, I knew that I wanted more. I took these feelings to Master Hawk and haltingly stumbled through an awkward confession. He wasn't surprised at all. "I knew that you were heading in that direction," he said. He also listened to my fears that I just wasn't submissive enough to be a real slave, and he nodded. "You can be submissive," he said. "I've seen you be very submissive."

"But not all the time," I said.

122 | *RAVEN KALDERA*

"It doesn't have to happen all the time," he said, and then he took me in a very different way than he normally did. We did a whole scene with me as a slave—or rather, he put me in a deeper and more submissive headspace than I'd ever dared to be in before. That surrender that I feared, I did it. I completely surrendered to him and it was wonderful. Afterwards, I was even more confused, but Master Hawk explained things to me. He'd worked and played with me for a year, and he knew me pretty well. I was moving from being a boy to being a slaveboy, he said, and that was a difficult transition to make. I give you here his wisdom, as it was taught to him by the also wise man who trained him to be a Master.

As Master Hawk explained it, what a boy gets from a Daddy is caring, direction, and mentorship. What a Daddy gets from a boy is the breath of newness and freshness that we bring into their lives. Even a boy of fifty, he explained, if he's really a boy, can bring that youthful energy into his Daddy's life and be a source of joy. A Daddy also gets someone to teach, and to pass on the lineage that he got from his own Daddy or Master, or that he was taught by other leathermen.

A slave, on the other hand, gives service and surrender to his Master. Both the service and the surrender can come in many forms, but under it all is, as Master Hawk says, the work of the hands and the surrender of the ego. Both more and less responsible, in paradoxical ways.

Somewhere in the middle, Master Hawk told me, is being a slaveboy. To be a slaveboy isn't to be an abject doormat of a boy or a half-assed brat of a slave. It's the ability to go back and forth between those modes *as your Master desires it*, and be what he needs you to be in the moment. It's wearing two hats, and being able to switch back and forth between them at will—at your Master's will, but you're the one who has to do the switching.

Master Hawk explained it to me in a historical sense. In ancient Greece and Rome, a nobleman might have a caring, teaching and mentoring role with his adolescent son, although he might also be strict if he was training him to be a warrior, but the main role would be father/son. He would have a very different kind of relationship with his manservant, usually a slave who would be completely owned and do his bidding. They might eventually develop a friendship between them, but it would be hidden—no nobleman would admit that a slave was his best friend, even if that slave did the most intimate services for him. However, many noblemen had a third option. They would choose adolescent boys from lower-ranking families, maybe middle-class boys or even lower class if they were bright, and take them as "companions". Because of the class difference, it was automatically assumed that they would be a servant, and many noblemen took these companion-boys along as their assistants during battle campaigns when it might not be possible to bring a lot of slaves. But the nobleman would also educate them in such areas as philosophy, literature, and the sciences—partly as a way to help them out of their class, and partly to make them into a good conversational companion. They would also be the nobleman's submissive sexual partner, a point which upset a lot of scholars over the centuries.

Because they were a safe combination of "son" and "slave", they could also be the nobleman's friend and confidante. There was an assumption that they would eventually grow out of this boy-role, and the nobleman would find them a much higher career position than they would otherwise have been able to achieve. Many Greek and Roman generals, and even a couple of emperors, started out this way. The most famous of all these relationships was that of the emperor Hadrian and his companion Antinous. They loved each other so much that it was the talk of the empire, and when Antinous was murdered by jealous courtiers, the grieving Hadrian had him declared a god and set up temples to him throughout Rome and Egypt.

This, Master Hawk taught me, is the job of a slaveboy. Some grow out of the role, and some keep the role for a lifetime, because it's about what inside you, not what a culture says you should do. But if I was going to be a slaveboy, I had to be trained as a slave. For the next year, I was a slave five days a week, and it was hard. It was learning to live surrendered for much longer periods of time. It took more self-discipline than I ever thought I had, but somehow I found it when Master Hawk looked at me or gave me an order. It was also wonderful in a lot of ways, but if I hadn't had the weekends off I wouldn't have been able to maintain it, even with all my Master's help. Because he was my Master now, and not just my Daddy. On the weekends, we went back to being Daddy and boy, and while it was often a great relief, there were many times when by Sunday night I wanted paradoxically to be his slave again.

Over time it became less about days of the week and more about when he wanted it to happen. I think when I finally got the hang of becoming his slave or his boy at a moment's notice—maybe going back and forth a couple of times a day, even—something changed between us and we got a lot closer. He could trust me now, trust me to obey and not to bolt off if things became difficult. Like the Greek nobleman, I slowly became his best friend, and he became mine. I am his companion, his boy ... and his slave. And that's exactly what I want to be.

So that's how to have a Master/slave relationship with a Daddy and a boy. Not every boy will become a slaveboy. Most won't; it's too hard. Not every man with a slave heart has the personality to also be a boy, and many of those who do have both won't; it takes too much effort to juggle those two roles. But for me, it's the answer to a puzzle I tried to solve for ten years, and finally found the answer at my Master's knee.

Captains, Generals, and CEOs

Captain of Our Ship
Carolyn

I find "styles"—models or archetypes—to be very helpful to me, and I think to many other people, in maintaining a successful M/s dynamic. These styles are not scripts for role playing. They are not literal images. They are the running dialogue of how we of perceive ourselves. Styles are also a way to encapsulate and communicate parts of our life's story to ourselves and to others. In Master/slave and other authority-based relationships, being able to communicate about our relationships is important because the large number of traditional styles of relationships that are portrayed in literature, on TV, in the movies and all around us often do not ring true to what we feel is right for us.

Those of us in happy longer term relationships are often asked to describe what our relationships are like to give the newcomers a snapshot of one way of making authority transfer relationships work. In that context, I offer you two of our "styles".

We are a Female Dominant/male slave couple (although we don't use the term *slave* in our household). We've been friends for about eighteen years, a couple for almost seventeen years, and married fifteen and a half years. We're a middle-aged, upper-middle class, professional, white, suburban, fairly conservative couple.

The primary "style" or model we use is a naval one. I see myself as the ship's captain. Our relationship is the ship. This is really key to me because I consider my household to consist of myself, my husband *and* our relationship as a discrete third party, so the ship analogy works well for me. As captain, I am responsible for both the ship and the crew. Responsibility is a large component in our dynamic. I am not a "master gets what he wants" type of person. I am a "master is in charge and therefore responsible for stuff" type of person. I'm responsible for getting our little ship to our destination—to our life goals, whatever they may be. Being captain includes clearly identifying and defining the goals; ensuring they are viable; plotting the course to get us to the goals; and implementing the course by propelling and steering the ship in the right direction.

As captain, I don't decide things based on what I want, but on what I think is best for us and for our relationship. We, as individuals, plan on reaching our goals with this ship, so the ship's safety is important. But if the ship sinks—if the relationship ends—I'm still responsible for ensuring that all hands make it safely to land. However, that's not part of the ideal plan, so that's why I need to assess the needs all three of us—master, slave and the relationship—when making decisions.

My husband is the first mate. His job is to carry out my orders, but he's not a lowly person around here. He's second in command to me, and when I'm not around (which is very rarely) he's expected to run things as I would, not as he would. Whether I'm on the bridge or not, this is my ship, running on my rules, and he supports and carries them out. He's not here to anticipate me, or second-guess me. He's not here to pamper me or make my life easier—he's here to implement and assist.

As second in command he's a proud, competent, and highly respected member of the crew. He's not here as a worm or worthless entity. He's an important man. That there is no one below him in the hierarchy is irrelevant. He's still right up there next to me, but under my authority. The ship's captain is not served by his first mate, the captain is assisted by the first mate. There's a big difference in how those words feel in a relationship.

Other aspects of the "captain" style that ring true to me are that the captain gains and keeps his or her position through competence, not just by being loved, worshipped, or admired. Also, the ship is a little world unto itself—it's self contained, but not a fantasy. It has a role in the outside world, but also has a sense of unified autonomy. That's our household.

We also have another style that appears to be diametrically opposed to the ship's captain style—that of trophy spouse. OK, I know, you hear trophy spouse and think of a paunchy 50-something-year-old guy with gold-plated bling peeking out from a shirt that has too many buttons unbuttoned, and a 24-year-old blond with large breast implants and more bling than the guy, laughing at everything he says. That's close, but not quite it.

I married my husband when I was 50 and he was 33. He's attractive, very well-groomed, and can be taken out in all sorts of venues. He's intelligent and great company. When I brought him into my home I lived alone, owned my own home, had a professional career, and was pretty damned autonomous and happy. To a very large extent I wanted a companion to add to my life—a luxury. That's the trophy part.

I didn't need service. First, I'm competent, and second, I often prefer to hire a professional to do things. But I have a high-powered and sometimes stressful career, and I wanted a tranquil and charming person to bring companionship, intelligent conversation, humor, and grace to the dinner table, not someone who was going to play "who had the most stressful day at the office" with me over dinner, and not a house servant. I also wanted someone who would be able to travel with me when I want to travel, which pretty much limited what he could do for a career or job since I am Job #1 and anything else is secondary.

How we came to this idea as a recognized "style" tells a lot about the style itself. It also is how the ship's captain/trophy spouse styles can come together, because this all started when we met a couple on a cruise ship.

When we first spotted them, we laughed because they looked like the stereotypical short fat old guy with the tall young blond-and-dripping-in-diamonds trophy wife. We got to know them during the cruise, and boy, were we wrong. She had been a high level CPA at a big accounting firm, and been his accountant, but they had not met in person. When they finally did meet, he decided "I will have her as my wife!" There was more to it than that, but after two years he won her over and she quit her job as accountant and took the job as his wife.

Far from the ditzy bimbette, she was a charming woman who brought intelligent conversation, humor and grace to the dinner table. She was a *true* trophy for him, and made me realize how much my husband was my reward to myself for having reached a certain point in my life, and *my* trophy. Trophies are, after all, prizes.

One thing really stood out to show how similar they were to us. One night at dinner we were talking about movies, and she said some movie had been made in some particular year. My husband said no, it was made a year later. The man, being as proud as myself about his spouse, looked not at my husband but at me and said, "She is never wrong about these things." I looked at him and said "I'll bet on my husband on this one. Trust me, if he says he knows the year, he does."

That was an "aha" moment. He wasn't talking to them—he was talking to me and it was as "owner to owner", with not-so-subtle chest pounding. We had both put our trophies out there and were comparing them, both proud of what we owned. And yes, my husband was right, she was wrong. Win, Carolyn. Did I mention my competitiveness?

And that's when we adopted the trophy spouse model. It also is very appropriate to use because being the good provider and spoiling my subs is one of my kinks. I've seen the "spoiling" in parent/child styles, which don't work at all for me and my husband, but the trophy spouse seems to encompass spoiling quite nicely.

There's also a meeting of ship's captain and trophy spouse in our relationship. Our ship is a bit like a cruise ship. It's kind of plush, and heaven knows my husband's life is cushy as all get out. Ninety per cent of the time I'm easy-going. We have our routines, just as the cruise line serves dinner at set times, but it's not run like a sparse military operation. I view happiness as a moral imperative just as the cruise lines strive to ensure their guests have a relaxing wonderful vacation. There's lots of opportunity for happy fun times when the ship is well organized and well run.

My setting the course, watching the weather, checking all of the ship's systems, and keeping an eye out for rocks is understated and intended to go unnoticed most of the time. The goal is to have it feel as natural and unobtrusive as possible. I do it well without a lot of fuss and fanfare. My goal is to have a happy, cheerful, comfortable, and tranquil ship, and allow the trophy spouse dynamic to be more palpable.

But when the seas get rough or when there's a problem on the ship, the captain of even a cruise ship (other than the Costa Concordia) is still the captain of a ship—the only one in authority, the person who is ultimately responsible for the safety of the ship and the crew.

A common question on discussion boards is, "How do you keep the dynamic alive when things get crazy with health, work, family etc.?" But for us—when things get crazy—the captain comes onto the bridge, the second-in-command stands next to him (or her in our case) and obeys quickly without question. We function as a team, with calm efficiency. That's one reason that we always feel like our dynamic is turned up a notch when "life happens". What's really happening is that the ship's captain style is taking priority over the trophy spouse, and emergencies are dealt with efficiently, so that the joy can go on.

The CEO/COO Model of M/s Structure

Dr. Bob Rubel

It can be hard to explain your M/s structure to others. It can even be hard to settle into your own M/s structure due to the cultural load on words such as Master and slave or Owner and property. The world of authority-imbalanced relationships is filled with subtlety: subtlety of behavior and subtlety of meaning. In this subtle world, some seriously thoughtful people get bogged down as they try to explain the way their relationship works, leaving egalitarian folks—and even some other M/s couples—shaking their heads and saying, "Well, if it works for you, great".

While there are many reasons why it is hard to explain one's role in a relationship, perhaps the main reason is that unlike words such as "husband" or "wife", words that we use—"Master" or "Dominant" or "submissive" or "slave"—don't carry behavioral meaning within our American culture. While it's easy enough to explain that you have a dominant *personality*, it can be challenging to explain how you live and direct a relationship as a "Dom" with a "sub" or "slave". As we all know, most of this difficulty arises because these words don't have established definitions: you can't go to a marital guidebook and look up "Living as a Master" or "Living as a submissive".

Let me make this real for you. Imagine that you are at a casual party in Vanillaville. People are drinking and talking and introducing themselves around the room. In the spirit of friendship, you go up to a couple that you don't know. The man sticks out his hand and say's something like, "Hi, I'm Bill and this is my wife, Nancy." No problem. You got it. Husband/wife. Okay, you understand these roles. But… now it's your turn to introduce yourself and your partner. With a brave and smiling face, you extend your hand and say, "Hi, Bill, I'm John and I'd like to introduce you to my slave, tina."

Silence. Nothing. The handshake freezes in place.

Trying to explain, you add, "I'm her Master; we live in a Master/slave relationship".

Silence. Nothing. But Bill has released your hand, although neither he nor Nancy have moved a muscle.

"She's my property," you continue with a big smile on your face. You're hoping that once they understand your relationship you can be fiends and socialize, but you have a gut feeling that this isn't going to work out that way. You rush on, "I determine everything she does in her life and how she interacts in social settings such as these."

Still silence. Traffic stops, air is sucked out of the room, Bill's face takes on a contorted look that combines measures of confusion, astonishment, and repulsion. And you don't dare look at Nancy's face but it's her words you hear next as she suddenly realizes that she and Bill are being called from across the room and they excuse themselves.

What happened? A cultural clash, expectations clash. The goodwill you had hoped to establish goes to shit.

Why? A number of reasons. As we all know, the words "Master" and "slave" are emotionally loaded terms with lots of baggage and they mean different things to different people. You don't know what personal baggage triggered Bill and Nancy's reaction, but it was clear that their reaction was so strong that they don't want to know anything else about you. Who they *projected* you to be overwhelmed who you *really are* and they're not going to stick around long enough to learn about you. Unlike words such as "husband" and "wife", the words "Master" and "slave" don't communicate even a general understanding of socially-acceptable behavioral boundaries. For example, in an egalitarian marriage, if one person spends money after being asked by their spouse not to spend money until the next paycheck, there may be some heated words exchanged and some feelings bruised, but not much more than that. However, in an M/s structure, the Master's reaction is very likely to be far more immediate and severe if a slave willfully disobeyed a direct order not to spend money until the next paycheck.

In reality, the M/s dynamic differs from a husband/wife dynamic largely because of the relationship's reliance on personal accountability. But since each Master determines levels of accountability and related consequences, it can be challenging to communicate how we live even when we are speaking with other M/s couples.

Let's take the previous example and twist it a bit. Imagine that you are at a casual munch. People are drinking and talking and introducing themselves around the room. In the spirit of adventure, you go up to a couple that you don't know. The man sticks out his hand and says something like, "Hi, I'm Bill and this is my slave, nancy." No problem. You got it. Okay, you understand these roles—or think you do. But... now it's your turn to introduce yourself and your partner. With a smiling face, you extend your hand and say, "Hi, Bill, I'm John and I'd like to introduce you to my slave, tina."

You and Bill think that you are speaking the same language. You're both at a munch with your slaves. Ultimately, all you really know is that one partner identifies as Master and the other identifies as slave. You can assume that Bill is the dominant partner, as he extended his hand, but you don't know whether the slave is submissive or dominant, and you don't know anything about their relationship structure other than the knowledge that one is leading the relationship in the *Master* role.

Even within our own community, neither the words Master nor slave have definitions that will stand still. In part, this happens because various "camps" or subcultures have evolved within the larger Master/slave Culture. For example, one contingent says that slaves should let go of their own limits and entirely adopt the Master's; another says that slaves can have all the limits they want. One contingent wants slave to empty itself of ego in order that the slave's will be replaced (honorably and ethically) by the Master's will; another contingent feels that it's unhealthy for the slave to give up their will. One contingent requires the slave to sacrifice all their possessions and prior friends as a prerequisite to serving the Master; another feels that the M/s should not intrude into too much of the slave's daily life. One contingent is using M/s for spiritual practices while another sees it as mostly sexual.

Pushing this further, the Master's concept of his/her role within any particular "contingent of M/s" is a result of a lifetime of learning from other relationships, as well as from having been exposed to all kinds of popular media and myth about slavery, masters, and how one is supposed to behave when one is in authority. (Let's also remember that slave also has his/her own lifetime of experiences and expectations of what a Master is and should be.)

This all gets hard to follow, doesn't it? For me, too. So, one day—soon after Jen and I had decided to live in a 24/7 M/s structure—I explained to someone I'd known casually for many years that I had now fully embraced my slaveheart and accepted my role of being in service to Master.

The person blanched. "You!? How can *you* be a slave? You're one of the most dominant men I know. You've had a slave for eight years and, and, and..." And that sent me back to my thinking board. Clearly I was lacking the words to communicate the structure in which I had chosen to live. I started searching for a different way to explain authority-based relationships. Increasingly, I began to suspect that "disconnect" could be traced back to the way we apply English words to kinky relationship terms such as D/s and M/s. We hear someone explain that they "live D/s" or "live M/s" as if the terms explain how the relationship works. It doesn't. It doesn't communicate much meaning because—as I've already said—nobody agrees on what terms such as "Master" even mean.

"So," I said to myself, "What could account for this tangle of confusion over these words?" Eventually, I concluded that we in the BDSM world are confusing *behavior characteristics* with *role characteristics*. We're confusing assertiveness personality traits of dominance or submission with leader/follower terms such as "Master" and "slave".

Without going through an elaborate explanation about how I got there, here is a summary of how I now look at these words/concepts.

➢ **Assertiveness behavior scale:** Dominance and submission represent behavioral preferences that are part of one's personality. Not only do these characteristics exist on a sliding scale for each person on earth, but they are situational/contextual. A macho badge-heavy police lieutenant will behave very, very differently before an Internal Affairs inquiry board. That same police lieutenant will also behave very, very differently should he decide to pay for a session with a professional dominatrix.

> **Leader/follower role scale:** One's success as a leader is a function of at least two things—how well one can understand the world through the eyes of another, and how wise and accurate one is in guiding others with insight and compassion.

> Success as a follower depends—at least in part—on choosing a leader whom you believe is better able to make key life decisions than you can, and upon whether or not one has the skill and wisdom to get out of one's own way and accept the leader's guidance. Again, this is situational/contextual: You may be a great leader when directing person "A" and also a marvelous follower when reporting to person "B".

"So," you ask, "What is this all supposed to mean? What does all this mean in practical terms?"

Try this: We have a person who fits somewhere on the assertiveness scale of dominance/submissiveness, who has some combination of wisdom and leadership skills, and who is interested in having a thoughtful relationship with another person within defined authority roles. Hmmm. I'm not sure we've made it to "kinky", but at least we're teasing apart the outlines of the components that comprise someone's personality and behavior. But wait, there's more!

Because I think of these characteristics on a sliding scale, I'm now able to envision relationship combinations that are not commonly discussed in the D/s or M/s worlds. I would argue that once situational assertiveness personality characteristics (dominance/submission) are separated from leader/follower roles, one can envision a follower who is generally dominant or a follower who is generally submissive or switchy.

It is my further contention—actually, my conclusion—that where someone falls on the dominant-submissive scale is unrelated to whether or not they can successfully serve and obey another person.

This leads to my thesis: While D/s relationships are defined as a "dominant-acting D-type" paired with a "submissive-acting s-type", an M/s relationship is much more defined by the Boss/Master's qualities of *leadership* plus *integrity*—as those attributes relate to the Master's ability to empathetically lead a subordinate. Where the subordinate's personality falls on the dominance/submission sliding scale only concerns the Master to the extent that it affects the quality of the subordinate's service and obedience. That's how it happens that when you speak with experienced slaves—those who have been doing this for more than five years—that some of them will tell you that they're dominant in all aspects of their lives except in their personal M/s relationship.

While no one else may really care how someone else identifies, my own curiosity was triggered by the seemingly endless nuances that comprise relationships within our larger kinky culture. This became very personal for me, as I have changed sides of the slash and petitioned a strong female dominant to be my Master ... after having owned a slave of my own for eight years. The petitioning was easy; the self-identity part was much harder, for I see myself (and those who have an opinion about it affirm that they, too see me) as a dominant man. This conflict about my own self-image drove me back to my computer and blank pages to work through the discord of being a dominant man self-identifying as the slave to a dominant woman.

That's when it dawned on me that the corporate world demonstrates this schism every day (as does the military or a monastery). In the corporate world, the CEO (Chief Executive Officer) leads the corporation and the COO (Chief Operations Officer) handles internal operations. Typically, the distinction between a CEO and a COO has to do with vision, as opposed to dominance or submission. The CEO is looking outward and interfaces with other CEOs and the world in general; the COO is looking inward to ensure that the company is running smoothly and that "problems" are solved before they reach the CEO level. As anyone in the corporate world knows instinctually, the last thing you want as a COO is that a problem gets by you and lands on the CEO's desk.

Translating this corporate model into our M/s language: the COO (slave) is responsible for taking care of the CEO (Master), and the CEO is responsible for taking care of the company that also includes the COO.

Sound familiar?

As it happens, I have a corporate background. As it also happens, I work for a female CEO. Once this idea crossed my mind I realized how well this model also described the structure my partner (Jen) was using to direct me personally. Now, when asked how our relationship works, I explain that Jen is the Family CEO and I'm the COO. This sidesteps discussions of dominance and submission and related entanglements. And everybody "gets it" immediately.

So here's the punch line: It is my observation that M/s is concerned with the integration of a slave's service and obedience with their Master's responsibility to provide wise guidance. It is my further contention that where one falls on the assertiveness scale is only an issue if the Master sees it as an issue.

Yes, I call her "Master". Yes, I like it when she calls me "boy". Yes, I have been known to become overly submissive when serving … and yes, I've also been known to become overly dominant when serving. But I'm no less responsible for ensuring that my Master's wants and needs are met, wherever I happen to fall on the D/s personality spectrum on any particular day.

Gays in the Master/Slave Military
Justin B.

I was in the Army for eight years, as a gay man. It was the era of "don't ask, don't tell", and I didn't. I indulged my leather-bar habits when I was home on leave. Luckily my parents live in San Francisco and are fine with me being gay; they were just worried for me while I was in the Army, because they knew that I was playing a somewhat dangerous game. (In fact, when I first told them that I was signing up, they both looked disappointed and said, "We thought that you'd be spared that, since you were gay.") They didn't know that I was into leathersex, though, and I still haven't told them.

I met Jake in the Army. He was a private when I first met him, and he was only a PFC when I met him later, a few months after I got out with a sergeant's rank. I'd had enough, after eight years, of not being allowed to have a meaningful personal life like my heterosexual counterparts. I wanted a real, actual, relationship, and I didn't want to have to hide it. After all, my parents had told me that they'd pay for my commitment ceremony if I found the right guy, so there was no need to hide from them. Of course, I went straight into a leather bar, because I'd also decided privately that I wanted a partner who would be my slave. I've always been a dominant sadist, and I wanted a partner who craved the other side of that package, but for more than just play. I wanted someone who understood service. Being in the military is, in the end, about service for everyone of any rank.

It wasn't hard to pick up men for SM hookups; I was in shape, crew-cut, and fresh from the front lines. I was also somewhat shell-shocked, but the guys I played with didn't see that. I kicked them out when the scene was over and didn't let them stay the night, so I wouldn't have to explain any screaming nightmares. On some level, I think I was waiting for the right guy whom I could trust with that. There were some really great guys that I played with, and some of them were even serious slave material, but they just didn't click with me. Some part of me wished that I could have stayed in the military, but in no way was I willing to give up my new out-of-the-closet full-on gay-leatherman identity.

Jake had been fairly newly enlisted at the time when I was a year from getting out. I was working in boot camp and he was a new recruit, but he didn't really register against all the other new recruits. When I walked into the bar and saw him there, it took me a few minutes to figure out who he was. If he hadn't still been in fatigues, I wouldn't have remembered him. I figured he was out on leave, but after I bought him a drink and talked to him, I discovered that he'd been discharged, and had barely avoided a dishonorable. He and a few others had gotten drunk and stupid, some fag-bashing words had flown, some violent brawling had happened with some property damage as a side effect. I remembered how he looked at me, saying, "If there was any way I could redo that night, I'd do it. I really feel like I failed. Except that I'd probably do it again." He felt that the incident was a combination of military homophobia (which was unfair to him) and his own lack of discipline (which was completely his fault, and he owned it).

I asked how he'd ended up here, and got out of him that he was secretly a SM bottom. He'd been living his own double life, without understanding family. So I asked him, "Well, I can't do anything about what's already happened, and neither can you. But if you've got some guilt to expiate, maybe I can help a little with that."

So he came back to my place, and I put him through some boot camp paces, except that it got a lot more sadistic and ended with some really hot sex. Then off he went, feeling at least a little better—everyone does after they get laid—and I figured, that's that.

But then he called me up the next day and said, "Sir, I really think that I need some discipline in my life. For real. Can you teach me, Sir, not just about play but how to obey properly?" So we met up the next night and negotiated things. I would be his CO for all practical purposes. He would be my grunt, assistant, bottom, and anything else I needed and wanted. He would come over three times a week and spend the day with me, on his days off. The first assignment I gave him was to find a job that would work with my schedule.

It was supposed to last six months this way, but three months in I was taking Jake to meet my parents, and they loved him. Four months in, he discarded his room and moved in with me. Actually, the most important landmark was much earlier, probably at the two-month mark, when I got the courage to talk to him about PTSD, and he understood. He was the first man I let sleep in my bed since I'd gotten out. I instructed him on what to do if I had nightmares, and he did it. I could feel certain that he wouldn't think less of me for it. At the six-month mark, I officially collared him and made him my slave. We've been that way ever since.

I'm still his CO, I'm just also his Master. Our protocols are easy—they're what we already learned, maybe tweaked a little for informal situations or public ones where our more formal protocol would be strange-looking. We do incorporate a few protocols that the leather community would recognize, but that's mostly because those protocols were copied from the military to begin with. I've also studied protocols from armies and navies throughout history and around the world, and integrated some into our way of doing things. You'd be surprised how much interesting information is out there, and how much we who have served would still recognize, even with hundreds of years in between us and them.

While our military-style M/s has a strongly gay, or at least men-only, flavor to it, that doesn't have to be anyone else's answer. Women are just as capable of military discipline and being good soldiers (and leaders) as anyone else. There are quite a few women in the armed forces now, and the numbers keep growing. Any couple of any gender combination can take this on, if it works for them.

I wasn't ever an officer in the Army, but I'm the officer in charge now, in our relationship. We have our own uniforms now, because we don't belong to the U.S. government any more, we belong to our relationship. He serves me and I serve the relationship; that's how we see it. Service is an important value in our way of doing M/s, and we do a lot of service in the local leather community, as well as the gay community at large. We are active in local politics, because having served our country does not mean that we don't still have an obligation to it. We were married in our dress uniforms from the Army, but after that we created our own. We joke a little about "paramilitary organizations", but really there's only two of us, so we aren't much of an organization. (Although we are organized.)

We take care of our bodies, keeping ourselves and each other in shape. Respect is a big part of our relationship, and it is a little more formal in a lot of ways during the day, but we are intimate with each other at night. Do we love each other? Of course. We're just not sappy about it. Neither of us are the sentimental sort. We both believe that love, and respect, are both shown with actions, not words. Respect comes first. Love is a side dish.

Discipline is very important to us as well. My home is run with military precision, and that's the way I like it. Jake knows the correct way to do everything, and that's the way he does it. You could eat off my floor, and in fact he's done just that. Even when I'm making him do difficult and perhaps somewhat degrading things (which he is in fact hot for), it's all part of teaching him self-discipline and inner strength. When he came to me, my slave was a boy who couldn't hold himself back. Now he's a man who knows when it's right to defend the line and when he should shut up and keep his head down.

That's one of the important points of military-style Master/slave relationships, I think—the slave is expected to be a responsible adult at all times. Obedience is not something that you fight with the slave to get out of them. They can either do the job, or they can't. If you as the Master don't give them the right tools to do the job, or give them shitty instructions or an order that is going to turn out badly, it's on you, and you take responsibility for it. The other side of "only following orders" is that those orders had better work. However, "only following orders" doesn't mean that the slave is not supposed to give information if he or she sees something going wrong.

Another strong point is honor. In some relationships, while the Master has a code of honor (or is supposed to), the slave doesn't have to hold a code of honor for themselves. The Master is supposed to keep the slave in line morally with his or her orders, and the slave can be basically amoral so long as they are obedient. In this relationship, we are both expected to hold to this code of honor, and both believe in it fiercely. It's not my job to keep him from being an asshole. It's his job. I would only step in to discipline him if it was clear that he wasn't able to do it himself.

I do punish, when I have to. I don't usually have to. I save my sadism for SM scenes, not punishment. More likely, punishment is going to involve doing some rare chore that is necessary but nasty. If I don't have any, my friends certainly might. There's always something to find for a slave who needs reminding that this is serious. However, I don't think I've punished him for more than a year. He is too invested in getting it right to screw it up.

If I were to advise people who were interested in this style, my advice would be different depending on whether either of you was a veteran. If you were both veterans, then it's not hard. If only one of you is a veteran, you will need to be patient with the other person, and make sure that they understand why it is an honor to serve in this fashion. You might want to make them read some military history, to get an idea of what sort of tradition they are living in the shadows of. If neither of you are veterans, then definitely read military history together. Understand where this all came from, and why every protocol was put in place. Military protocols are about function and practicality, not show. That's important to understand. If you mostly want show, look for something else.

I figure that we'll end up growing old together, like an elderly general and his military valet, except with a lot better sex. (Well, I shouldn't assume—who knew what happened between elderly generals and their old war-buddy valets?) We'd like to get a couple of new recruits in, soon, and we're thinking about doing that. After all, we can't be the only veterans who want their own little barracks where being gay is not only OK but part of the deal, right?

Spiritual Discipline

Spiritual Practice
Master Fire, slavelliot, and the House of Fire

Who we are

Our name is Master Fire and We are a single person who identifies as a Master, Dominant, Top and occasional bottom. We are a het-flexible, cisgendered woman on an eclectic Neo-Pagan, animistic, and metaphysical spiritual path.

Part of the speech protocol of Our Household includes Us using the "royal We", but it is not done for reasons of aloofness or perceived egoic importance. In addition, the slaves adopt the impersonal "it" pronoun, but this is not done as a means of humiliation. Some argument could be made about its use as objectification, but this is not intended to be done in a negative way. The plural "We" is used, not as an indication of aloof royalty, but as admission that We cannot exist without All Our Relations.

Our slavelliot identifies as a slave, bottom, cisgendered gay man; it has been collared to Us about five years at the time We are writing this and its spiritual path is also an eclectic mix, primarily with aspects of Neo-Pagan, metaphysical, Hindu, and Buddhist practices. Both of us find that being in a Master/slave relationship is part of a larger spiritual practice and see the relationship as a natural manifestation of our shared life philosophies.

Definitions of "Spiritual M/s"

So, what is "spiritual M/s"? Of course, there are many definitions of M/s, so We won't explore them here. However, We have run across only a few definitions of spiritual M/s, so We will share the two that have influenced Us the most. The first definition We discovered and practiced involved SM. Not every M/s relationship contains SM, but in the spiritual relationships that do, SM is used as a ritual tool in order to evoke and/or invoke spiritual experiences. The chemicals the brain and body release during SM are conducive to producing an altered state of mind. Many know this as "sub space", but We can assure you that the phenomena doesn't just affect submissives who bottom; it affects anyone who bottoms, no matter what their role in a dynamic happens to be. It can also affect the Top; administering SM has created altered states just as frequently as receiving it, though they are often different in nature. So the first definition of "spiritual M/s" is actually more of a definition of "spiritual SM".

The second definition We have experienced involves the actual dynamic of the M/s relationship. How and why the Master and slave interact has a spiritual purpose in these kinds of relationships. A gut sense of "rightness", or perhaps even destiny, dictates both the beginning and ending of such relationships. It is common that the Master is the spiritual head of the relationship, though they are not usually worshiped as a deity.

It is also common that the slave has their own spiritual practice and, many times, this practice is of a different wisdom tradition than the Master. For example, We have known a Buddhist Master who owned three slaves, each of a different path: a Druid, a Christian and a modern primitive. We know a Christian Master who owns a Muslim and We know a Muslim Master who has owned a Wiccan. In these relationships, We have observed that the Master takes a role ranging from simply having the requirement that the slave have a spiritual path to actually ordering them to participate in certain acts and rituals within the slave's personal religion.

Most often, however, these two definitions manifest at the same time within the spiritual M/s relationship. For some, they cannot be separated; for others, they can. Regardless of whether they can or cannot, the fundamental foundation of the relationship is spiritual. This can trump any differences in religions/spiritualities, sexual orientation, gender conformity, or a wide host of other experiences that define how a person views themselves. In addition, practices of being transparent (open about emotions), authenticity (being true to who you really are), and spiritual development through service and shadow work (discovering who you are) are common to both definitions.

Personal Evolution

When We first began in this lifestyle, We were much more focused on the physical aspects of SM. It wasn't until We began to explore M/s that We found the subculture of spiritual "woo" in the M/s/SM communities. In particular, We explored this idea and practice with the Butchmanns Experience, a small weekend intensive focused on the life- and heart-transforming power of these things. Southwest Leather Conference also played a large part in this development, being informally known as the "woo" conference in the M/s circuit. Our slavelliot already had the knowledge that SM could be a spiritual experience when it came into the lifestyle, and was looking for those who also believed that neither SM nor M/s had to be about sex or sexual gratification. So slavelliot was much further along its spiritual path when it began in comparison to Us when We began.

The experience of being in this lifestyle was the impetus of Our "dark night of the soul" in which We began questioning if We believed what We believed because it was Our Truth, or did We believe what We believed because We had been taught to believe it. More often than not, We discovered it was the latter. The religion into which We were born became antithetical for Us as We progressed along Our path. To this end, We are now an ordained Reverend of Metaphysics, a past and present leader of several eclectic pagan groups and teacher of a wide variety of relevant topics.

Our slavelliot has always felt a connection to nature and spiritual beings, even as a young child; it learned to listen to these at an early age and began the practice of meditation well before its teens. All along, its path has never been one of a single religion, but an eclectic collection of practices from any source that felt right to it. Being in the spiritual M/s and SM communities has felt like a natural extension of its beliefs and practices and it, too, serves through teaching.

Integration and Manifestation

For both of us, the actual practice of spiritual M/s has manifested in both expected and unexpected ways. The aspect that has been perhaps most surprising is the separation of M/s from SM. This is an area of deep puzzlement for both Ourself and slavelliot and, sometimes, an area of emotional struggle. There are other aspects of both our lives that have changed, or apparently dropped away, in our service to Spirit (what we tend to call our Higher Power, for ease of discussion). There is emotional, and sometimes physical, struggle with those aspects, too. As a spiritual being, We personally have a gut feeling that these things are temporary, though it is quite unclear how long "temporary" might be. Regardless, the two of us currently feel that what we are doing together is spiritually right and important, even if neither of us really understand why or how.

All of the ways that We and slavelliot have integrated this into our lives are based on having the kind of relationship between Master and slave that we each have with Spirit. As the Master, We work hard to emulate Spirit's guidance of Us as Our guidance for the slave. For example, because directions about Our life come to Us from Spirit in the form of orders and directives, it is right for Us to do the same with the slave. Spirit, in Our belief, has only Our best interests at heart and, fundamentally, operates only from a place of good stewardship for Our life. We attempt to emulate that for the slave as much as possible and issue orders from a similar place. If that goes awry—because We are, after all, human—We understand that there are, and should be, consequences.

Emulation of Spirit is fundamental, and because of this, working to develop each of our ranges of compassion, acceptance and emotional boundaries is a spiritual practice. This, too, is reflected in the M/s relationship. When a mistake happens, the introspective work behind the emotional reactions and actions of all involved is a fundamental philosophy. Creating a sacred space in which this can happen requires a certain level of spiritual, emotional, and philosophical development, a process which is ongoing throughout the M/s relationship. As the Master, We attempt to create this space for slavelliot and any other slave that might be in the Household, as much as they, in particular slavelliot, attempt to create it for Us.

Conclusion

Our greatest example of how an M/s relationship can not only be spiritually based, but can develop into an actual spiritual practice all by itself, is about taking the dynamic We have with Spirit and translating that, as best We can, to the M/s dynamic. It doesn't have to be about the worship of a person or deity, but can be instead about the practice of life philosophies that are spiritually-based and expressed. It is a synergistic dynamic where we support and uplift each other, based on this spirituality. For the two of us, and for any who have been in the Household since these principles came into being, this expression is an integral focus and has lead to a meaningful and rich relationship.

Shiva Gurudev: Finding Spiritual Relationship
Master Thomas and slaveboy jimmy

Master Thomas: In late summer 2012 I retired from a job in Western New York and moved to Portland. Six months earlier, slaveboy jimmy and I had started to correspond on Recon, an internet site used by gay men interested in BDSM, and had begun a potential Master/slave relationship. It was clear to both of us that this would always remain part-time, because jimmy has been partnered to another man for over twenty-five years, and they were finally married in California shortly before Prop. 8 passed in 2008.

I was excited to find someone who wanted to explore a Master/slave relationship where "spirituality" was central. We both knew that what we meant by "spirituality" would not be conventional. As I identified myself as Master over the last fifteen years, I experienced a great wholeness and well-being when I developed serious Master/slave relationships, and I have searched for ways to understand this experience. I dislike religious fundamentalism and any literalistic understanding of spirituality, but my experiences did seem similar to those described in religious traditions.

slaveboy jimmy: I was on a long and meandering path, from being just a sub-boy to becoming a slave. Six years ago, when I was in my mid-forties, I would occasionally play with a Bear Top in Chicago who would spank me and pound my ass. The last time I was with him, he told me firmly, "You need a Daddy or a Master." This stunned me into silence, but lit a small but tenacious flame in my slave heart. With my partner's permission to explore my sub/kink side, I posted on Recon, opening myself to my destiny. Despite the controlling fears of my ego, some deep part of me sought a Master.

Then Master Thomas reached out across the country to contact me, touching my slave heart deeply with the spiritual possibilities in his Recon profile. In his second message, he told me that everything would be different when I was with someone I considered my Master, and that I would get even greater pleasure from being a total slave. I had no idea what this meant, and still am discovering its power, but I immediately knew that I wanted and needed to become his total slave.

I was created to be a slave, and I joyfully accepted my destiny to submit totally to my Master, to serve, to please, and to obey. Now I understand how a slave can become an extension of his Master, bringing submission, obedience, and service to yet a higher plane. I am incredibly grateful that he reached out across the country to touch me, a boy wandering lost in aimless search for his destiny, to teach me to serve him.

Master Thomas: Five months after slaveboy jimmy and I began to explore a Master/slave relationship in Portland, it had deepened considerably. Since I had begun to feel like his Master and Owner, I gave him a provisional collar, telling him that I expected it to become permanent in time. I explained to him it was "provisional", in order to give us time to let its meaning develop in the dance between Master and slave. The one thing I reiterated to him very clearly and strongly was that this shouldn't mean any change in his relationship with his partner.

I will let slaveboy jimmy describe a particularly important session, seven months later when the collar became permanent.

slaveboy jimmy: I knelt before my Master in submission and obedience, head bowed and hands clasped behind my back. He told me that in this session we would return to the beginning. He stressed that he owned me as his slave and that I was his property to use however he desired.

Then Master removed the provisional slave collar from my neck, and my heart sank. Seeing directly into my slave heart, Master said that he knew that taking off the collar would hurt more than any whip. He told me that before the day was over, I would beg him to put the slave collar back on my neck. He buckled the thick leather training collar around my neck instead, the same collar he had used when I first came for training and service as his slave. He pulled my T-shirt over my head, stopping to leave it covering my eyes, to teach me that Master owns even my sight. He probed my mouth with his fingers, testing his property and checking that I had obeyed his command to floss each day. Master slapped my face and chest, crushing down my ego and allowing my real slave self to come forth.

I was stripped naked. Master buckled the leather restraints around my wrists and ankles, placed the leather slave hood on my head, closed blinders over my eyes. He hooked the wrist shackles to the metal loops on the training collar, just like he did the first day I came as a potential slave. The feeling of bondage, of Master's total control of his slave, welled up inside me. I obeyed his order to lie across the edge of the bed, and he firmly and repeatedly beat my slave ass, the pain of each blow sending his energy coursing through me. When he unhooked the shackles and ordered me to encircle his body with my arms, legs interwoven with his, my head buried in his chest, a flood of emotion welled up in me. I felt my full submission and complete trust in my Master, totally owned and safe.

Now with the hood off my head, Master Thomas pulled me up beside him, allowing me the privilege of looking into his piercing blue eyes, his energy coursing into me. He asked me what I wanted, and I froze, as I usually do whenever he asks me more than the simplest yes or no question. I knew, however, exactly what I wanted. I wanted him to place his slave collar back around my neck. He unlocked my tongue by yanking on the thick leather training collar, and I begged him for the slave collar.

Master unbuckled the training collar, and stunned me by asking if I wanted the slave collar not provisionally but permanently. My slave heart leapt at this. Every fiber of my being shouted out the answer: *Yes, Master! Thank you, Master!*

He instructed me that I should change my Recon profile to declare that I am the owned slave of Master Thomas, and could be used by other Doms only with his approval. I was to spend as much time in his service as possible, within the bounds of my relationship with my partner and my work. Then I followed him to the bathroom, and at his command laid down in the tub. He temporarily removed the slave collar to protect it and then gave his owned slave the honor of baptism with his piss, the warm fluid streaming over my body. He ordered me to keep my eyes closed and to open my mouth, and I swallowed two small mouthfuls of his piss.

After rinsing my body, he commanded me to lie back down in the tub, and he shaved my crotch and ass clean and smooth. I had long dreamed of getting shaved by a Master. My submission as his slave and his ownership of me as his property were crystal clear as he placed the permanent slave collar back around my neck. Permanently collared, cleansed by my Master's piss, shaved clean and smooth, I felt born anew as Master's owned slave.

Master Thomas: Masters don't often talk about their own experiences in the dance of the Master and his slave. When I feel the power and strength of my Master heart, I am at the center of the Universe. When I take control and use my slave, paradoxically I am both greedy and have lost my ego, as I find myself serving something greater than myself. Over the last fifteen years, I have learned to be spontaneous and not to over-prepare scenes. I feel like I'm submitting to an interior force within me that is far greater than my everyday self.

Over time, we have developed a series of protocols for his arrival which serve to put both Master and slave into their respective roles. I open my garage door five minutes before he gets here. He parks in my driveway, enters the garage, and takes off his clothes after having closed the garage door. He waits until I open the door to receive him, enters, kneels down, and kisses my feet until I touch his back, when he rises to his knees. He repeats his mantra:

> *I am your slave.*
> *I have no rights.*
> *You possess me.*
> *You own me.*
> *As your property,*
> *You use my body, mind, and soul*
> *However it pleases you.*
> *I exist to please you.*
> *I exist to serve you, Master.*

I do think in advance about a theme that I will emphasize in my play with him. Such themes have included "ownership", "gracefulness", "the slave as extension of his Master", etc. A large part of our formal play explores these themes, their meanings, and the feelings they engender.

On the occasion when I decided to make slaveboy jimmy's collar permanent, I had meditated long and hard about whether we were ready for this step. I also thought about what this particular slave collar would mean in our relationship together, knowing that it had varied for me in past relationships. I knew I would have to give slaveboy jimmy a free choice about whether he wanted to accept me as his permanent Master, but beyond this, I had not thought through any of the specifics of the day's play. I let the play develop from one thing to another, as my intuition led us from one activity to the next. As jimmy knelt before me, wearing my collar, I felt the wonderful power of ownership, the incredible responsibility of interacting in healthy ways with my slave, and the overwhelming feeling of joy. Our play and his service the rest of the day took on a new vibrancy for me. It was now my obligation to make him stronger and more confident as a beautiful slave.

Typically our time together is divided between BDSM activities, sexual service, and service tasks to be fulfilled. The BDSM activities are ritual ways to symbolize our growth together, and they help transform him as the perfect slave for me. The sexual service gives him a chance to give me pleasure and show me how special I have become in his life. His household duties and other service tasks allow him to be the submissive slave he was destined to be. After making his collar permanent, the BDSM activities and his service to me that day took on new spiritual significance and transformative power. They seemed to free us to become our true selves—Master and slave.

slaveboy jimmy: I worshiped Master's cock in total devotion as his slave. On my back, my eyes locked into his eyes, he fucked me—my submission complete, the pleasure building as Master's energy coursed into me through his eyes, his touch, his mouth, his cock. He applied clips to my dick and balls, my newly shaved crotch magnifying the sensation; he finished by putting clamps on my nipples.

My slave task that day was washing the kitchen and dining area floor. It was just where I needed to be; a fully owned slave serving my Master on hands and knees. The growing pain from each clip on my body made me know that I belonged to him, that I was his complete property. He has very particular ways of doing household tasks, and that gives me a wonderful certainty that I am serving as he wants me to serve him. I have learned that he is a man of very definite habits, allowing me to be secure; yet he can also be spontaneous and somewhat unpredictable, giving our time together an excitement.

With Master probing my pain level from time to time, I finished washing the floor and followed him back to the dungeon. Grasping the handholds hanging from the ceiling chains, he buckled the restraints back around my wrists. I stood with legs spread, arms bound upward to the ceiling, naked and collared, with clips on my tits and dick and balls, an owned slave in great joy and some pain, open and exposed in obedience to my Master-Owner, my Guru-Teacher.

He methodically removed the clips, instructing me to dive deep as the pain built fast. I rose up on my toes, pulling down on the hand restraints as I worked to absorb and transmute the pain. Removing the tit clamps from my body, he rubbed his hands across my chest and balls and dick, at first amplifying the pain and then quickly transforming it into heat and light and pleasure, as I sank back down onto the soles of my feet and breathed deeply. He unhooked my arms from the ceiling chains, resting them on his shoulders. I hugged my Master tightly in total devotion and gratitude for all that he had given me this amazing day. Wearing the now permanent slave collar, I knew to the very depths of my slave heart that I exist to obey, to submit, to serve, to please, to worship my Master.

Master Thomas: I began to realize that the religious formulations that helped me understand what was happening in a Master/slave relationship were poetic or metaphoric truths, not scientific or literal truths. Our culture has relegated poetry and art to insignificance—so to use "artistic truth" or "poetic truth" seems strange. Yet poetry and art are ways that most other cultures have tried to understand their religious experience. Perhaps in the West we have lost the understanding of our spiritual experiences as poetic, because we have been encouraged to think of religious truths as literal propositions.

With that in mind, I sought out religious myths and images to make the spiritual experiences of Master/slave relationships understandable. Christianity seemed to have a kind of truth that speaks to some slaves. One beautiful submissive (who had disavowed Christianity when he accepted himself as gay) told me that this passage in Philippians really spoke to him: Jesus "emptied himself to assume the condition of a slave, and became as men are; and being as all men are, he was humbler yet, even accepting death, death on a cross" (Philippians 2:6-8 in the New Testament). That might be a poetic image for a slave, but it didn't help me understand my growing spiritual experience as a Master.

I finally realized that the figure who spoke to me was Shiva, the ancient Hindu God who is still worshiped today. He is the destroyer and the creator—the destroyer of our petty egos and creator of our fullest human potentiality. Shiva destroys the social norms that we so often use to define our self-worth (money, job status, social conformities, etc.), but in destroying this artificial ego, we gain a new understanding of our deeper human nature.

The image of the Dancing Shiva (the *Nataraja*), who is the destroyer dancing on the demon of ignorance/ego, has become my own poetic image for my experiences in Master/slave relationships. However, the Master also needs to destroy his petty ego—and that is why I submit to Shiva. For me Shiva isn't some supernatural being apart from the world—he is more "true" than a literal figure. He is poetic truth, a way that many humans have tried to understand our deepest spiritual experiences. This image is extraordinarily profound, and it has become a part of my life.

I introduced this image to slaveboy jimmy early on, explaining that I wasn't attempting some new kind of fundamentalism. The image of the *Nataraja* expresses what I am doing as Master—trampling on a slaveboy's superficial ego. But the image also expresses my extreme humility before the "Universe" (to use Raven Kaldera's term), presenting me with a rare gift and an incredible responsibility—and in this sense I bow before Shiva. And through me, Shiva has empowered slaveboy jimmy.

slaveboy jimmy: I grew up as a weak and unathletic boy in a deeply Catholic family (true to the pattern) and was very observant religiously right up until I finally came out as gay in my mid-twenties. At that time, I dropped the whole religion thing like rock. A few years ago, I was struck by a radio discussion that religion could be better understood not as something one believed, but rather as something one did. At about that time, Master reached out to me on Recon. His discussion of the spirituality of BDSM, and the image of Dancing Shiva as the destroyer of my ego and creator of my slave self, began to make my inchoate feelings and desires clearer to me. My service and submission as a slave is recapturing the lost spirituality that I had felt in my youth, but through a path that is fully true to my nature as a slave. This empowers me to give my Master strength and service.

Master had me read the essay by Raven Kaldera and his slaveboy Joshua Tenpenny, "The Path of Devotion: *Gurubhakti* in a Master/Slave Context" (*Sacred Power, Holy Surrender*, Alfred Press, 2011). Deeply meaningful to me, it provided a framework for many aspects of my service to him and my journey to becoming his slave. He told me that the part of me which had asked for a Master was not my ego, but my deep slave self. This strengthened the powerful feeling of destiny I have in becoming his slave.

Master Thomas: One of my East-coast slaveboys had introduced me to the concept of *Gurubhakti*, or love of one's spiritual teacher, about six years earlier. I named that slave Apasmara, the name of the demon boy that Shiva subdues in his wild dance in the famous image of Shiva Nataraja, the dancing Shiva. (The demon boy represents "ignorance" and "superficial ego".) My slave called me his "*Gurudev*", the teacher who opens up divine consciousness for his *chela*, which means "disciple," "slave" or "servant" in the Hindu tradition. So I had already begun to practice "*Gurubhakti*" long before I read Raven and Joshua's essay. When I read it a year ago, I was amazed that another

Master and slave had developed the same symbolic play—and I now cherish their essay.

BDSM play opens up both the slave's and the Master's hearts. The absolute submission of the slave frees him from his petty ego and from artificial social restrictions. Even though the slave's submission demands that the Master is totally dominant, I also feel a sense of humility before the beauty of the slave who offers himself to me. Slaves are "gift-givers," who desire to please their Master above all else.

When I feel jimmy completely submitting to me, something happens inside me. My feeling of power is absolute, but I simultaneously feel an incredible tenderness and responsibility. Paradoxically, that arises when I am fully demanding, feeling a slave sacrifice all of his own desires. Then a mysterious exchange of power occurs, and I feel that the slave and I are so attuned to one another that we are in a spontaneous dance, with energy flowing back and forth between us. The theme of one of our sessions was, in fact, the dance between a Master and his slave.

slaveboy jimmy: I knelt before Master Thomas, listening intently as he began to teach me to dance as a slave with my Master—the slave never leading, always following, yet moving together. He explained that this dance is more than a slave moving smoothly and gracefully, and more than a slave obeying his Master's commands. It is the slave becoming an extension of his Master. This thrilled me even as it remained a mystery.

Master was playing the *Guru Gita*, an ancient chant that countless *chela*-slaves have learned as praise to their Masters. Although I didn't understand the Sanskrit words, the hypnotic sounds and feeling of devotion and submission in the voice of the *chela* were deeply moving to me. I followed Master in the dance, kneeling before him, head resting on his body, swaying together to the music. Master touched me with just a finger to direct his slave's body this way and that. I stretched my body naked across the floor, beneath Master's feet. Leading me now with just a touch of his finger, he positioned me under the hand-holds hanging from the ceiling, buckling the leather restraints around my wrists, and lacing the leather hood over my head.

He granted me the privilege of gazing directly into his eyes, and I felt his energy flow through me.

Master flogged me long and hard, building intensity in my body, mind and soul. After whipping me with "Cobra", his quirt, he grabbed me, his arms pressed directly into the tit clamps. This sent a sharp jolt through me, and he commanded me to go deep and follow the pain down. This was breath-taking, and sent me deeper, reaching into my slave heart more than I had yet experienced. Master returned to the leather flogger, merging the sharp pain from my tits into the broad red glow of the blows on my back and ass.

The flogging ended, he stood before me as I breathed deeply and grasped the hand-holds tight. Master removed the clamps from my tits, sending astonishing energy through my body. I rose up on my toes in reaction to the pain. He ordered me to dive deeper into the pain and transform it, as he grabbed my chest and worked my tits. Very quickly the pain was gone from my mind, and a flood of heat and light and pleasure filled me. I followed this rushing flood downward deeper yet, my body lowering off my toes and relaxing into Master's grasp.

Later, Master Thomas asked me where I go and what I experience when he flogs me. The best I can describe it is like diving downward into a deep pool of water, which I love to do when swimming. Unlike diving deep into water, this diving gets easier and faster the deeper I go, and I am traveling toward the light, not away from it. It is much like the feeling of rising upward through the water of a deep pool, as the dive is finished, rising faster and faster toward the light playing on the surface.

Master is there diving after me, following my body a bit behind as I plunge deeper, his arm outstretched to gently touch my leg and guide me. Diving ever swifter downward toward the light, with my Master right behind me, guiding his slave's path with just the touch of his outstretched hand, is my unique spiritual experience. It is the most awesome sensation of my life.

Master Thomas: When he is flogged, jimmy goes deep into the "zone," a spiritual place where he experiences a deep connection with me as his Master and a feeling that he is intimately connected to all of creation. Since we have developed a deep trust, I also feel myself slipping into another dimension, where I feel an incredible connection with him and with nature. This connectedness flows back and forth between us. The intensity and rhythm of a flogging puts me into a spiritual space as well. More than any other activity, I feel like I am dancing with my slave when I am flogging him as he reacts to the various tempos, rhythms, and intensities.

Perhaps the word "freedom" comes the closest to what I'm feeling. I feel at peace and I feel a total freedom as I let my true Master-self emerge. Metaphorically, I feel that I have merged with Shiva and am at the center of power—the power to destroy and the power to create. I feel "free" from all social restrictions, but would never harm my slave who has given himself so completely for my use and enjoyment. I feel a sense of gratitude in that freedom. I am humbled before his trust that I will re-create him as a wonderfully strong gay man who becomes even stronger in his enslavement.

The freedom that a slave feels in being used completely is emphasized in bondage play. Masters often use bondage so that a slave experiences his enslavement and ownership. "Ownership", however, was something that jimmy understood intuitively from the very first day of our play. He seems happiest when he is serving me by doing tasks in my house and yard; then he knows he is truly owned. Bondage punctuates and reinforces this feeling of being owned. Being physically controlled with ropes, restraints and chains frees him psychologically and spiritually.

slaveboy jimmy: Master grasped my slave dick and balls firmly in his hand. I truly love this, because I then feel my total submission to my Master, and his total ownership of me … and I am sexually wired to be totally turned on by having my dick and balls grabbed tight and pulled. I listened intently to his teaching on the two principle goals of bondage: to teach a slave to submit completely to his Master's control, and to provide the freedom of total helplessness and surrender.

He ordered me to lie on my back in the middle of the dungeon bed, buckling the leather restraints around my wrists and ankles, snapping the leather parachute around my slave balls, and lacing the hood tight around my head. I focused on clearing my mind to open myself completely. Master hooked the ankle restraints to the wooden spreader bar, stretching my legs wide, and he pulled my balls tight downward to the bar. Slowly, methodically, he threaded the ropes through the eyelets and around my body, pulling my arms downward and tight at an angle, until I was completely immobilized and yet free. I could not move, and because I had no option but to submit on a physical level, I was freed to completely submit and obey him as he directed my spiritual flight.

He started to tickle me. I am very ticklish, and each touch on the bottom of my feet or finger tips dancing on the sides of my chest threw me into convulsions of laughter and uncontrolled body jerks. This gave my Master pleasure commensurate with my embarrassment as I struggled without success to absorb the sensation. With some relief the tickling ended, and he clamped my slave tits and clipped my body, running the Wartenberg wheel across my chest, legs, dick and balls. In the total helplessness and surrender of the tight bondage, the clamps felt great and the Wheel was not nearly as painful as I had remembered it. I had the same sensation of diving deep underwater that I experience in flogging, only slower and longer, with him diving as always close behind me.

Master edged my dick, and I felt his energy course into me from his hands and mouth, and felt his control; even control of my slaveboy hard-on. The total experience of the bondage was astounding across three dimensions: the sounds, smells and physical sensations, the sense of physical helplessness and exposure, and the mental and spiritual freedom that arose from opening myself to my Master. In thinking about this later, I remembered attending Catholic mass as a boy. The power of both experiences came from the total integration of physical sensations with an interior poetic state that integrated my body, mind and spirit.

He ended the session by slowly releasing the ropes, and I could hear him methodically wrapping them back into the intricate pattern used to store them. The slow, measured pace of my Master's work brought me back to the dungeon gradually and softly. I was filled with gratitude for the experience.

Master reminded me that a slave has no rights, which creates a great freedom that I felt very strongly. He opened a window for me on the reciprocal nature of the power exchange between Master and slave. He told me that he will hurt me but never harm me, because a Master is responsible to the "Universe", and if he harms a slave he would be destroying his own Master-nature. Trust flooded into me at his words.

As I think about the bondage experience, an image or diagram forms in my mind. When I first read Master Thomas's Recon profile two years ago, I was especially struck by the four virtues of a Master/slave relationship—trust, respect, honesty, and courage—and keep them written on a sheet of paper by my desk at work. In his profile on Recon, Master Thomas wrote:

> A Master/slave relationship depends on four virtues—trust, respect, honesty, and courage—but the greatest of these is courage. Only if we have the courage to look deeply into ourselves and take action can we begin to respect ourselves and each other. And it takes courage to trust. Joseph Campbell wrote: "It is only by going down into the abyss that we recover the treasures of life. Where you stumble, there lies your treasure. The very cave you are afraid to enter turns out to be the source of what you were looking for."

The four virtues are deeply meaningful, and help articulate for me the intellectual and spiritual dimensions of being Master's property. I picture them arranged around the edge of an ellipse, with respect and honesty placed at the ends of the minor axis, and trust and courage placed at the ends of the major axis.

In each BDSM experience at his hands, the whole ellipse lights up, but with different levels of intensity in different parts. Getting flogged lights up the "courage" end of the ellipse most strongly, with the "trust" end in a supporting role, while in bondage it is the reverse: "trust" is brightest with "courage" in support. Honesty and respect are always present in each activity. With his teaching, I find courage the first of the virtues, and perhaps this is why I may love bondage but I love getting flogged the most.

Master entered the dungeon next day and gave me a firm morning spanking. Then he granted me the privilege of worshipping his body with full devotion. I focused my whole being—body, mind and soul—

on giving him pleasure, which is the reason for my existence. More than ever, I plunged into a sense of worship and connection, the very boundary between my slave body and Master's body somehow dissolving until I was merely an extension of him. It magnified manyfold my physical pleasure at touching him with my hands and mouth and legs. The experience of total physical and sexual service to my Master merged into and emerged out of spiritual devotion. It was the complete spiritual experience of *Gurubhakti* as described by Raven Kaldera and his slaveboy Joshua.

Reading "The Path of Devotion", I understand that I worship my Master, not as a human being but as Shiva—the direct connection he provides to all that exists. Raven Kaldera writes of the meaning or folk etymology of Gurubhakti: "to raise up from darkness into light", "to make a great effort", "to belong to", and "to worship". This has powerful meaning for me: I am my Master's *chela*-disciple-slave, I belong to him, he possesses and owns me completely as his slave, and I serve, obey and worship him as my Guru-Teacher-Master. This is so right, so natural to me, filling the spiritual hole within me with a wondrous connection to what I can only describe as the Universe itself, as a slave to a wise Master-Teacher who deserves my complete service and devotion.

When I was in New York for work, I visited the South Asian collection of the Metropolitan Museum. The sculptures of Lord Shiva were very moving to me, as they reminded me of my Master whom I long to serve, to obey, and to worship as *Gurudev*, my Master-Teacher and my Connection with the Universe. These sculptures helped me see Lord Shiva as the great generative force: Creator, Preserver, and Destroyer of the Universe. I am grateful beyond words for Master leading me to embrace the process of destruction and creation—to be alive. I am a leaf carried along in a stream, slow-moving and meandering at first, but then pulled forward in an ever swifter and stronger current toward my destiny.

Master Thomas: The Master/slave dynamic of the power exchange depends on two things. The slave must feel that he is giving his Master a great gift and must desire to make that gift special in everything he does. The Master must be totally demanding and have no hesitation in acting on his desires, which can only happen when Master and slave trust each other completely.

When both slave and Master have these attitudes, the M/s relationship can become magical, opening a spiritual dimension that both experience and an ecstasy that connects everything. When that begins to happen (and it always can get deeper), the slave becomes even more grateful and wants to give even more to his Master, and his Master will want to demand even more of his slave. Slaveboy jimmy and I have now entered that realm.

Jimmy's reports of his training showed that he understood with both his mind and body what was happening. A slave is an extension of his Master in two ways; both feeling himself as his Master's instrument (the dance and scrubbing the kitchen floor) and feeling a Master's energy flowing into him (the tit clamps, my hands on his chest, and the fucking). The reason that flogging has always been really important to both of us is that we experience a total connection there. The slave feels the flow from his Master's whip, and the Master feels his slave's response. As I flog jimmy, the world narrows and I am intently focused on his reactions to the intensity and rhythm of the whip, almost as though I was experiencing them myself.

As our BDSM play has developed over time, jimmy began to develop an interior grace that he didn't even know he had. He also mastered the art of turning pain into erotic/spiritual energy. At one point, I asked jimmy whether he was a masochist. He told me he had come to understand that he did not desire or seek the experience of pain itself, but rather the experience of being fully and completely used by a Master for his pleasure. This deep-seated, burning desire to be used as a slave often comes in the form of suffering for his Master, intersecting pain with liberation in a most mysterious way.

So the question from my side is why I like to give pain in BDSM play. Why do I like to see a slaveboy suffer? The shortest answer is that I like the connection that occurs when a boy willingly suffers when I flog him or bind him and put clips on his body. I am poised on the knife-edge of power and caring. When my boy suffers I feel the power, but I also feel an amazing caring and love for him; the paradox of the desire to give pain and relieve pain at the same time. I think my happiest moment is when I comfort a boy after I have relieved his pain, a pain that I enjoyed giving him.

When I think of slaveboy jimmy prostrating himself at my feet, I feel his humility and nobility. I feel ennobled and humbled at the same time by his total submission. I gratefully look forward, as does he, to the times we can spend together, and I will continue to enjoy using him completely as he needs to be used.

In describing our spiritual journey together, we have perhaps overemphasized the BDSM activities a bit in this essay. He also spends significant time serving me with physical labor when he is here, and instinctually he knows that his deepest aspirations are fulfilled in serving a Master in any way he can. I am graced by his acceptance of my slave collar. I love watching him work for me, naked in the house, and minimally clothed in the yard. He has done very little physical work in his life. As a professional, he uses more brains than brawn—and I like watching this man, who never felt competent doing physical work, discovering the joy of serving his Master by scrubbing floors, pulling weeds, washing dishes, and cleaning stoves. He has removed hideous wallpaper borders in the house and with my help repainted the rooms. His comment to me on doing this painstaking task: "It's a good job for a slave."

As we have now written this essay together, I foresee using him more in his intellectual capacity to help me work on my future academic writings. He has become my complete slave—service slave, sexual slave, and BDSM slave, limited only by the part-time nature of his servitude. The spiritual freedom and connection we have experienced together have been remarkable. He is bound to me with mental chains, stronger than chains of steel. He serves me in gratitude, because I've allowed him to fulfill his destiny—and, of course, he has allowed me to fulfill mine.

slaveboy jimmy: Once. as I knelt before him, Master Thomas asked for a single word to describe my enslavement. I answered "Gift". All I have to give my Master is the submission and surrender of my body, mind and soul to be used fully for his pleasure. The mystery of a slave as both gift and gift-giver fills me with wonder and joy.

Master said he liked my word "gift," then told me his word: "Transformation". In a flash, I understood. On his Recon profile, after quoting Joseph Campbell that the cave one fears to enter is the source of what one is looking for, he says that this is where a good Master will take his slave, an arduous journey that both Masters and slaves with courage take together. When I first read this, I knew in my slave heart it was important even though I did not really understand it, but his word "transformation" linked us together in our descent into the cave. He has transformed me from a sub-boy seeking an experience of submission to an owned slave realizing my destiny, allowing me to fulfill my reason for existence: to obey, serve and please my Master. I still have long to travel in the journey as his slave, much to learn and deeper to go. Yet in my transformation Master has granted this slave a spiritual gift beyond measure.

THE REALM OF GOR

Gorean Consensual Enslavement: A Short Study
Malkinius of Chicago

Prologue

What you are about to read is somewhat unusual. It is a Gorean writing about Gor and consensual slavery in the Gorean style for a publication and for people who are not Gorean. This is something most Goreans will not do, and something I would not normally do. I am only doing so for two reasons. The first is my respect for Raven Kaldera and the work he has done in understanding and teaching about consensual enslavement and especially due to his work integrating how to do it when working with people with physical and mental disabilities.

The second reason is that I am one of the few Goreans who can, or even possibly should, properly speak about consensual slavery as Goreans view and practice it. This is because I not only own slaves, but I also study and train consensual enslavement. I might have been a member of the Gorean Caste of Slavers if such a caste existed on Earth.

I obtained Raven's agreement that I could spend the first part explaining what we who call ourselves Gorean (and who are not part of a game or fantasy, online or off) mean when we say that we are Gorean. If you don't have an understanding of what we believe and how we live, you cannot understand why we say and do what we do, and you will never be able to tell the fakes and players from the real thing. Regretfully, there are many times more fake Goreans than real ones.

Many things are said about Gor and Goreans, but few actually know the truth. Many people talk about us based on what others say without any work or study to learn the truth. We make an excellent boogeyman for many to target so as to advance their agenda and beliefs.

Some ideas and practices have gone both ways between Goreans and those who practice Leather and BDSM. Even some of our onlineisms have been…borrowed. There are those who try to live as Goreans and there are the types who like to add a little bit of Gor to their BDSM play or slavery just to spice things up. I will mention those, but mostly I will be talking about those who follow the philosophical tenets written into the books by the author, John Norman.

One of the qualities that set Goreans apart from most groups is that we have a specific large body of written material on which we based our shared culture. However, what we are *not* is any form of cult or religion. We lack a written guide that everyone is expected to follow, and we have no one leader. We all draw from the same source—the *Gor* books—and from a few influential writers about what is and is not Gorean. After that, it has been fighting tooth and nail, sword and spear, shield and axe to decide what we can agree on and call Gorean. That is still an ongoing process. This is why when you ask what is Gor and what are Goreans, you may get more answers than people you ask. Most will be similar, but not all.

What is Gor?

Gor is three things. First, it is a series of science fiction novels all ending in "of Gor." Those books started with "Tarnsman of Gor" by John Norman, which was first published in 1966 and currently ends with book 33, "Rebels of Gor" which was published in the fall of 2013. John Norman is the pen name of Dr. John Frederick Lange, who holds a PhD in Philosophy. He is still, as of the beginning of 2014, a professor of Philosophy at Queens College, which is part of the City University of New York on Long Island.

Second, Gor, in the books, is a planet hidden on the opposite side of the sun from Earth. Some of the ancient Greeks and especially the Pythagoreans believed such a place existed. (We believe there is a connection between Pythagoras and the name of the book series. The fact that Pythagoras was born on the island of Samos and there is a main character in the books named Samos is just such one connection out of many.) In the books, a race of highly intelligent aliens known as the Priest Kings (who resemble praying mantises) used their very advanced science to bring their planet from another solar system to ours and conceal it from us on the opposite side of our sun. They also imported tribal and ethnic groups of humans from Earth to Gor over the years, so there are cultures based on the ones of the Greeks, Romans, Norse, Zulu, Inuit, Mongols, Sioux, Huns, Japanese and others. The permitted human technology ranges between classical Roman and medieval but without firearms or explosives. This is one of a few technological limitations placed on humans by the Priest Kings. Medicine, on the other hand, is much more advanced in some areas, including serums that extend life and can even reverse aging.

Third, Gor is also the Gorean word for Home Stone. A Home Stone is a rock that symbolizes a Gorean's place and allegiance. It is similar in some ways to a national flag, or other items that are the focus of allegiance and community. It is the object on which Goreans pledge their citizenship. It is something that matters only to the free men and women of Gor and to them it matters very much. Understanding the concept of the Home Stone is a requirement to be Gorean. A person may have a Home Stone in their home, and may also pledge to the Home Stone of a city. (Goreans who have pledged to a location Home Stone will often add "of somewhere" to their names. I am Malkinius of Chicago because the Goreans of Chicago, Illinois in the United States of America have created a community with such a stone.) A Home Stone is always an object; never a place, an online chat channel or some abstract concept. It is always two capitalized words and never only one word. This is important to Goreans, and a great filter to identify the people who use it otherwise as being players who have not read the books.

On the fictional planet Gor, slavery exists as a legal institution, as it did in almost all of the societies brought from Earth to Gor. This is not the slavery of eighteen-hundreds America, but more like the slavery of classical Rome and Greece. That was an economically-based slavery, not ethnicity, gender or sexually-based. A person of any race, gender or group can be enslaved.

Not all slaves on Gor were female. According to Norman, only about one woman in forty was enslaved; the rest were free. He also stated that there were more male slaves than female ones, but almost all were work slaves, and official numbers of them were kept low so that the male slaves would not know how numerous they were. Most slaves as described in the books worked on farms, in factories, or took care of people and households. They were not slaves kept just for looks, sex, or because someone loved them or they loved their owner. Consensual slavery is mostly a type of relationship slavery rather than economically-based slavery.

There are many myths and misunderstandings about slaves in the books, even among Goreans, and especially among the "players at Gor". There is much more written about Goreans and what is in the books by people other than the author than I can reference here, but I have added a few references at the end for further reading about Gor and Goreans. However, nothing beats reading the books themselves for the correct information. This is why almost the first thing we tell anyone who is interesting in Gor and possibly being Gorean is "RTFB!" or "Read The F'n Books!" This scares most people away, and honestly, we like it that way. After years of doing this, those who are unwilling to read will never make it to becoming Gorean. At best, they might, especially if female, become the slave of a Gorean. Even then, many owners require their slaves to read the books. I do.

What is a Gorean?

In the books, a Gorean is someone born on the planet Gor or who is taken there from Earth and adopts the culture. On Earth, a Gorean is the follower of the philosophical tenets or ideas that Dr. Lange put into the books to show how he believed men and women should live their lives. Norman also put ideas into the books as a counter-argument to situations and groups that were common at the time he wrote the books. We do not take everything he wrote as gospel, and we certainly don't try to emulate all or even one of the cultures of the books, even if some Goreans do tend to identify with some of them. We know that the books and planet Gor are fiction; we don't need to be told that. We know that slavery, as it existed in the books, hasn't been legal here on Earth for a long time. This is why we say that we practice a form of consensual slavery that is similar to the consensual slavery of other groups who practice it on Earth.

Goreans try not to be, or act, stupid. We also, like the Goreans of the books, tend to be practical and do things for reasonable and practical reasons, not someone else's ideology. It is only those who play at Gor who want to emulate merely the culture of the books. We strive for the *why* of the books, not just *what* they do or sometimes say.

Goreans tend to be opinionated, and we are usually not shy in stating our opinions. We also tend to be very politically incorrect. We believe in equality under the law, but not that everyone is equal, let alone the same. We know men and women are both built and wired differently. We had that as part of our philosophy since the 1960s, even if science didn't catch up in the proof of it until the 1990s. The minds of men and women—not just their bodies—are noticeably different in many areas. Men and women do think differently from each other, which, of course, lead to many misunderstandings. We believe that our nature makes us different but complementary. "One is not whole without the other" is a point of Gorean philosophy. While in the books slaves could be male or female, among Goreans here on Earth, most slaves are female and most owners are male. Therefore our default assumption is a male owner and a female slave. This was true in the books as well.

The Chronicles of Gor are our connection to each other. They have become the source of a shared cultural background that gives us a cohesion that does not exist among many other groups. As I said before, RTFB! Read them first for the story, and then read them again for the philosophy. Thirty-three books shouldn't take you more than a year or two. There are no "Cliff Notes" or "Gor for Dummies" books. Goreans believe that if you want to be like us, then do the work we did to get here. There really are no short cuts to reading the books so that you can understand, first of all, what we are talking and arguing about, and second why we do and say what we do. Third, if you have read the books you will know when someone claims something to be Gorean and it really isn't Gorean in the slightest.

You will hear that the books are badly written. While not the best writing you can find, they do read better when the books are read in order. Norman writes in a more archaic style, and the books are full of allusions and references to things of Earth and Earth history as well as multi-linguistic puns. Norman even mentions the Gor books themselves in the story as literature that some captives who are taken to Gor have read themselves. He also frequently writes in sequences of three, and in very long sentences. He does not write in the sparse Hemingway style.

Most people see only two types of individuals as being Gorean: free and slave. Goreans see two types of Goreans: men and women. Slaves are property and technically not "Gorean", as being a Gorean means that you can choose how you act and react, and an obedient slave will act and react as her (or his) owner wishes. To us, this definition prohibits slaves from being Gorean as long as they are enslaved. Actual Goreans are not Doms or subs; we are just free people living our lives in a certain way.

Men and women who wish to live their lives according to the Gorean philosophies are just that: men and women. They are free to speak and act as they choose within the constraints of the society where they reside and in accordance to their own specific beliefs on a matter. Goreans take responsibility for their speech and actions. It is not the fault of someone else or some other group that made them do it, unless there really was force applied to do so. Goreans choose, and then accept what comes of that choice. Personal responsibility is one of the hallmarks and easier-to-spot identifiers of Goreans. Not everyone who acts that way is Gorean, of course, and in fact most are not, but you should expect it from the philosophically-based Goreans on Earth. Do not expect if from those who just play at Gor or use Gorean as a title to pick up slaves.

Goreans believe in strength, whether it is of body, mind or will. The academic will have more strength of mind than of body. The warrior will be the opposite. Strength of one type does not mean that there is no strength of the other types. It is also a type of strength to impose our will and our control on our environment and our lives. A friend of mine says the he realized he was finally Gorean when he put his will to changing the way people used a certain computer program, and succeeded in getting tens of thousands to change their use of it as well. He wanted the change badly enough to push it through, and his strength of mind and will changed something he cared enough about to work at.

Goreans believe in the Theory of Natural Order, which states that some of any group or species are dominant over others, and some are submissive to others. It is a spectrum between dominant and submissive with most people in the middle. In humans, as in most mammals, the distribution along the spectrum for males is shifted to the dominant side and for females it is shifted to the submissive side.

This does not mean that all males are dominant and all females are submissive; they are not. Males and females both have individuals who go to the extremes of each end of the spectrum. See the chart below for a representation of this spectrum.

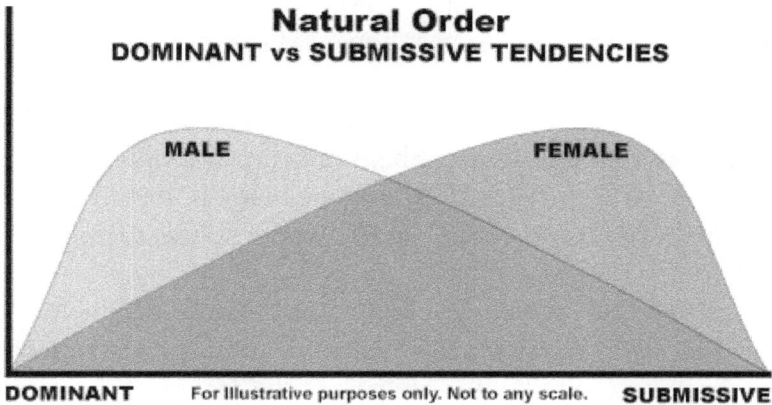

Natural Order
DOMINANT vs SUBMISSIVE TENDENCIES

MALE   FEMALE

DOMINANT   For Illustrative purposes only. Not to any scale.   SUBMISSIVE

© Copyright 2010 Malkinius

Chart of the Dominant vs. Submissive nature of humans illustrating the concept of Natural Order. It does not represent any specific or aggregate studies, is not to any specific scale, and no real numbers were harmed in its creation.

Goreans believe that the most complete expression of the Natural Order is the Master and slave relationship. The dominant seeks out someone as submissive as they are dominant, and vice versa, to complete themselves. Like many other ideas from the books, this theory was rejected when it was first written, as it did not meet the political correctness of the time. We believe that it is scientifically true, and based not just on what a few want to believe, but how humans actually are. It is part of the basis of consensual enslavement as done by Goreans.

Slaves of Goreans on Earth are primarily, but not universally, female. They are women who have decided that their nature and purpose in life is to submit to and to serve others they believe are worthy of their service. These slaves, or *kajirae,* are not doormats or women incapable of making any decisions on their own. They may choose to let others decide as part of surrendering themselves to their owner, but no woman who is not strong will succeed as a slave.

Gorean slavery is a form of what is generally called TPE (Total Power Exchange) or TPT (Total Power Transfer) consensual slavery. The other term for this type of consensual slavery is Owner and property. The key understanding to all of these is that the Owner or Master has all the authority, power, and responsibility in the relationship, and the slave has none. There are no time-outs or safewords for a Gorean's slave.

Another concept that is not unique to Goreans, but is Gorean custom, is that a slave is a slave. She is not the slave only to her owner. Her status is that of a slave to anyone who is free. How that is expressed varies by however the slave's owner chooses to do so.

Goreans are human beings, and we do what others in their societies do. We work, we play, we love, we hate, we have friends and we have people whom we don't like. We are part of the society of the country in which we live, and like most people we pretty much live according to its laws and rules. Some will claim that being Gorean means you do not have to obey anyone else's rules or laws. However, Goreans also understand that we are responsible for what we do, the good and the bad. If we violate those laws, we accept the consequences. Goreans do not make themselves victims. Those who wish to be victims are not, by definition, Gorean.

Gorean couples are often, but not always, married. This version of Gorean marriage is called Free Companionship. It is based loosely on classical Roman-style marriages and often is done first for a year and then renewed. Gorean owners and slaves can be married to each other as well. Some people were married before they became involved with Goreans or consensual slavery; some marry afterwards. Many of them also have children, either together or from previous marriages with blended families. This is the same as in any other form of consensual slavery or general relationship. For most Goreans, a family begins with a couple; male and female, whether free or slave. In a few cases, it is a free couple and a slave, or an owner with multiple slaves. A family may also include children, although all consensual slavery relationships are much more complex when they involve children.

Gorean couples raise their children pretty much as any other couple does. The problems with enslavement and children are the same for Goreans as with any other Master/slave group: What Gorean things do you do around family and children? With most, this means the outward forms and rituals of enslavement, as well as how much to tell children and relatives. Goreans add one other major decision: How much of our Gorean philosophy and ethics do you pass on to your children and others in your life? These are questions Goreans have debated for years, and we have yet to decide on one answer to almost all of those questions. Some of us do one thing and some do another. I do not know if there really is one majority answer or not, but I will cover the answers chosen by those whom I know or whose writings I have read, and who have stated what they do.

When it comes to Gorean philosophy and behavior, Goreans seldom outright teach others; we mostly show it by example. *This is what I do and how I live* is our usual answer, and only when asked do we expand on that answer. Otherwise, think of your classic 50's—60's TV household with the competent father who kindly rules and cares for his family and gets respect back from them. The mother cares for her family and husband and sees to his comfort as a primary consideration in her life. The children tend to be polite both to their parents and to others outside of the family. If all this sounds a bit idyllic, consider it the goal that we try to come as close to as we can. Just like everyone else, not everything goes according to plan and not all children behave as they should—nor do all adults for that matter, including Goreans. However, we strive to come closer than most realize.

How much do our children know when their mother is a slave to her husband or the man with whom she lives? The simple answer is: It varies. We know the reality is that as children grow up they learn things their parents don't necessarily want them to know, and they don't always tell us until later, if at all. For most, what they learn if they ask is somewhere from nothing to something age-appropriate. We don't tell a five-year-old as much as someone who is fifteen or twenty-five. Some are told the full truth from the beginning, but most are not. I have found that full disclosure is more common when children are in late high school, or college-age or older, than for the very young ones.

Greater disclosure seems to happen more often when it is a blended family.

Not unlike in the books, both Gorean free women and slaves usually work outside of the home. Their types of employment are as varied as anyone else's. Some slaves are in a leadership position or even own their own businesses, others only work a few hours a week. How much a slave works is entirely her owner's decision. With Gorean women or Free Companions, it is more of an equal decision.

Gorean Slavery

In the books, slavery is a legal institution in all parts of Gor. It is, in one form or another, universal among all the cultures and locations. Both males and females may be enslaved. While the books mostly speak of female slavery, male slaves are fairly frequent and main characters are often enslaved, especially in the early books. Tarl Cabot, the main character of the series was enslaved about once a book through most the first twenty-five books where he was the main character. In each case, one way or another, he freed himself. On the other hand, most females who were enslaved stayed slaves. Only a few were freed and some of those were re-enslaved. There are many long paragraphs describing and declaring that the nature of woman is to be submissive to men and that slavery is the natural extreme of the understanding of Natural Order as it applies to humans.

Female slaves were said to number about one to every forty free women. Male slaves were never given as a percentage of the population, but since the slavery in most of the books was based on classical Greek and Roman slavery, the percentage of male slaves working in mines, mills, farms and on public work projects and such could have been higher than the one in forty given for females, since that was a fate of many men captured in wars or sentenced for crimes.

Most of the female slaves, or *kajira*, specifically mentioned in the books were used for personal, domestic and sexual service. There were some who, like males, worked in factories, businesses, and farms, but not usually in mines or other heavy labor. Slaves kept only for pure sexual service were a small percentage of slaves in the books.

In the books there is a Caste of Slavers whose job is to buy, sell and train slaves. They may also be involved in the initial capture of slaves. Despite the large number of comments and examples of Slavers being the main trainers of slaves, most Goreans, like many in BDSM, feel that only the slave's owner can do such training.

What is a kajira? A kajira is a slave girl.

What is a slave girl? It is a girl that is owned.

The first Gor books were primarily located in areas based on classical Greece and Rome, thus the language of the books is primarily based on Latin roots. In the books, the language is universal so that all Goreans can communicate with each other, even though there are local dialects that include words from the many cultures brought from Earth. *Kajira* is the common term for a female slave. *Kajirus* is the similar term for a male slave. The terms use standard Latin endings. The plurals are *kajirae* and *kajiri* for female and male slaves respectively.

In the books, the first words taught to a female brought to Gor are *"La kajira,"* or "I am a slave girl." The male equivalent is *"Lo kajirus,"* or "I am a slave boy." Those statements are enough for someone to legally declare himself or herself a slave on Gor, and once the declaration is made, it cannot be undone. It does not work that way on Earth, however, despite what it says in the books. (Remember, we do not emulate everything in the books.) On Earth, in almost all cases, a potential slave must beg someone to be their owner. We always warn them that whomever they choose for an owner is one of the most important choices they will make, and it is the last *free* choice they will ever make.

In the books, the most common types of slaves are work slaves, domestic slaves, tavern slaves, and pleasure slaves, plus a few kept as trophy slaves based on their former status. In our reality on Earth, they are domestic and general-purpose slaves. Sometimes a slave may also work outside the home to provide income to their owner. Many, but not all slaves are married to their owners. They may or may not start out that way, but it certainly happens. They may also be the mothers of their owner's children or children they brought into the relationship. Caring for children can also be a part of their service to their owner.

Goreans may have one slave, or they may have several. The difficulty of having multiple slaves goes up by the number of slaves one person owns. Over the years, we have noticed that the number of females wanting to be a *kajira* is much higher than the number of Goreans who wish to own slaves. Someone who is known as a Gorean usually does not have great difficulty finding a slave if they wish one. Potential *kajirae* who have read the books can usually easily tell the difference between those merely claim to be Gorean and those who really are.

The publishers have stated over the years that more women buy the books than men. In many ways, this is because the books are romances, and that is what brings many women to Goreans to become their slaves. There is a term in the books called "love slave". This is considered to be the perfect match between a Master and a slave, where the love between the two of them causes mastery and submission to be total. It is one of the more common things new slaves are looking for in a Gorean owner. Unfortunately, it does not happen on Earth as often as it does in the books. Whether or not a slave finds it, or how they end up if they stay, is unknown until it happens. Reality is not always a perfect match to the theory.

There is one other consideration that is not limited to Gorean slavery that I wish to add. In my experience and study, most slaves have two to three owners before they settle down, or give up when they do not start out in a committed relationship with their first owner. This observation is true not just for Goreans but for all groups that I have studied involved in consensual slavery. This reality can break the romance of slavery for some or add to it for others.

What is the difference between what we do and what is done in Leather/BDSM? The answer to that question could be nothing and everything. The problem is that there is no one true way of doing consensual slavery. Most people just make it up on their own. For most BDSM consensual slavery relationships, there are no more than a few conventions and general practices that carry over between what each group of slaveholders do. People make up their own styles and protocols as they go along. For them, there cannot be only one way of doing things. Everyone is supreme and correct in how they do consensual slavery.

I am not part of the Leather traditions, but I have read a small amount about them. They are more of what people think of as the classic BDSM slavery style, and by my reading are based on enslavement going back to the gay Leather bars and clubs with biker and military aspects to their protocols. My impression is that the way to do things is passed down the various family or group lines, from one teacher to the next. This is closer to how Goreans see and practice consensual enslavement, but without the formal lineage.

How do we do what we do? Very well or very poorly depending on the people involved. Goreans seem to take some of the best and worst of the other groups—or perhaps the other groups take the best and worst from Goreans? The first books were written in the mid to late 1960s, and this means they predate much of current BDSM, but not all of the Leather traditions. The Gor series is older than the term BDSM but not the practice. Norman did not take most of what he wrote from BDSM, but from historical slavery. BDSM, however, has taken many things from us. The slave positions are some of the most obvious things taken from Gor to BDSM, but there are other more subtle things, which have been copied. Some are Internet based, and some are not. I do not claim to know in which direction everything has gone, but in some cases, what Goreans did came first.

Among the problems Goreans have is that while we have sources from the books, some also have assumptions as well, which can be troublesome. For instance, one of these is the assumption that being male, dominant, and Gorean somehow makes you knowledgeable and capable of successfully owning and training a slave. Most overlook the fact that in the books, children were trained from a young age in the handing and mastery of slaves, either first hand or by observation. That just doesn't happen for almost everyone here on Earth.

For Goreans, there is both the theory and the practice of what we do. In theory, *kajirae* have the same legal status as any other mobile property, or that of domestic animals. It is a form of chattel slavery, but not the form practiced in North America up to the 1860s. All slaves are in a lower position socially and in status to any free person. Any Gorean free person may command a slave, and they are expected to obey or to be punished. Any Gorean may punish a displeasing slave whether or not they are the slave's owner. (In practice, both of those last two ideals have limitations.) There is a hierarchy of slaves. Male slaves rank below female slaves, and when an owner has multiple slaves, he may assign a First Girl over the other slaves. In other styles, all slaves are usually equal in status. For Goreans, free are free and slaves are slaves; there are no subs or switches.

A *kajira* is expected to be deferential and respectful to any free person at all times. There are no "You are not my Master so you can't tell me what to do!" attitudes among *kajirae*. Does that mean that anyone can command a *kajira* to do anything, including sexual activities? No, it does not. All of this is a reminder that a slave is a slave, and is not a slave to only one person. Since a *kajira* is always a slave, she must respond as a slave all the time. It is part of the Gorean mindset that is not always present in all other forms of consensual slavery.

Most Goreans who own slaves do have only one slave, although some have more than one. When Goreans add a new slave, existing slaves get no say in the final decision, even if they are allowed some input. (Although while it is technically true that slaves have no say in how their owners do things, anyone who thinks slaves cannot have an *influence* should rethink this immediately, and that includes Goreans.)

There is a Gorean saying in the books that all women are slaves, but some have not yet been collared. While there are many such "sayings" in the books, they are almost always presented as just that—a saying, not a practice. It is the same as all the "sayings" that a slave may be killed for any reason if they are displeasing. In the books, this is true, but it never happens "on camera". It is only referred to as something that has happened. Slaves are usually considered too valuable to be killed out of hand. It is better to sell them and acquire a new slave. In real-life practice, however, the slave is also often the wife, lover, domestic servant, plaything, or any and all of those combined. She is the complement of her owner. This is especially true when the owner and slave are married to each other.

Most Goreans are not cold and callous towards their slaves; they do care for and about them. The feeling of responsibility for your property is only a part of it. Also, as in most other types of consensual slavery, the owner cares for their slave somewhere in a range between fondness to romantic love. That does not mean the slave can do whatever she wants; he is still Master and she is still slave. You can love, but not be in romantic love with, your slave.

Goreans believe that a woman becomes more beautiful the deeper she submits. It is not just a physical beauty, but also something that emanates from them. I have seen this happen. It is a beauty that Goreans look for and *kajirae* work towards.

Training the Gorean Slave

In the books, the Caste of Slavers were responsible for the initial and general training of slaves. They also did specialized training for skills an owner wanted their slave to know, but that they could not teach. On Earth we have no such caste or professional trainers, because Goreans generally believe that being Gorean and reading the books is enough to enable them to train and properly master a slave. In this, they match most of the create-your-own-style BDSM Master/slave relationships. This is one part of the books that we seem to reject. The Goreans of the books were trained from a young age to master and control a slave. People of Earth are not.

Among the most common things a new *kajira* may be trained in are the basic cultural concepts from the books, the Gorean slave positions, and the basic Gorean form of serving. She might also learn the general expectations and customs we have taken from the books, or sometimes what has been created online.

Perhaps the best known item about Gorean slavery is the aforementioned "slave positions". They are also the most-copied-by-non-Goreans cultural item. In some cases, a few of the positions are so obvious that others have created them on their own. In other cases, they have just become standard items that many slaves of all types learn and do. There are many web sites that give lists and occasionally pictures of the positions. Many are, at best, partially correct; most have been copied from older lists that have been circulating for over a decade. Some include positions not from the books that were created long ago, mostly on IRC. Most Goreans use some of the positions, but not all, even if they have their slaves learn them at some point. They are part of the cultural glue that holds Goreans together as a group. They are also practical—not just for show, training or humiliation. However, not all Goreans know this. Some just consider them an activity to learn, or something that makes them Gorean if they know and use them.

The most common Gorean slave position is *Nadu*. *Nadu* is kneeling on both knees with thighs spread at a 90-degree angle, the back straight and head held upright with eyes down. The hands are placed palms down on the thighs, and were only turned palm up when begging for something. (I have my own list of positions on my web site. I also have a practice sequence for those who wish to learn and practice them. Everyone is welcome to use it, but please do not repost it anywhere without asking me first. Links to it are fine and the URL is among the links at the end.)

The culture and expectations of what we consider Gorean and Gorean slavery comes to most people via the Internet. People have tried to live according to the books, including practicing Gorean-based slavery before the Internet as we know it was created. However, most of what is considered Gorean today was created or finalized on the net starting in the late 90s, much of this by the men of the IRC channel Silk&Steel. This is true of both the good and bad things that are called Gorean. Some things that we have adopted come from online usage, which have references in the books, but not all of it. Most of these things have to do with slaves and their behavior or activities.

These things include third person speech, which was used at times by slaves in the books and was commanded with the phrase, "Speak as a slave." However, it was not something that was used all the time by slaves. It also includes the online idea of collar tags attached to nicknames or slave names used in writing. The forms vary, but the most common is the form slavename{Initials} or for example, dina{HM}. Another is deciding not to capitalize slave names. Whether they came from Gor to BDSM or go the other way I am not certain, but I have seen references to both being originally Gorean but now used online by others. The lower-cased name was used to easily distinguish slave from Free in a text-based medium. Capitalizing words like Free are connected in the same way. At this point, they are common Gorean usages.

There are also ideas created online that we wish hadn't been, such as the strictly "onlineism" of ranking slaves by silk colors. There are references in the books to slaves being called white or red silk slaves. Those terms mean "virgin" and "not virgin", nothing more. Virginity in slaves was not as culturally highly prized as it is on Earth; it was considered a problem to be remedied so that the slave could serve her owner completely. A sexually experienced slave was much more valuable in the books than an inexperienced virgin. There have also been one or two "Gorean" or "Kassar" languages created that are supposed to be Gorean; they are not. There are occasional Gorean words in the books, but there is no whole language available akin to what J.R.R. Tolkien created in "The Lord of the Rings" with Elvish and Dwarvish and so on. Silk color ranks and fake Gorean words are common among the online players but not among those living as Goreans on Earth.

We also have unowned slaves who serve Gorean masters. There are precedents for this in the books; sometimes it is a former slave, or someone looking for their first owner. They present themselves as a "slave" to learn and to attract a future owner. The online term we have adopted (mostly due to being unable to agree on a better one) is that of unowned slave. They are also subject to all Goreans as a slave, and often to one specific person or the host at one of our gatherings.

One sometimes sees the acronym CINBIAK, which stands for *Curiosity Is Not Becoming In A Kajira*. The full phrase is mentioned several times in the books. It does not mean that slaves cannot or will not be curious about many things, because they will be. *Kajirae* are very curious creatures. It does mean in practice that slaves do not need to know the things their Master does not want them to know. It is also used in training a *kajira* to simply accept what is happing to her without questioning, or it might be used when the owner just doesn't want to be bothered by lots of questions.

The main outward symbols of Gorean enslavement are the collar and the brand. The brand denotes that the person is a slave, and the collar shows who owns the slave. The collar may be metal, leather, or occasionally something else, but it is almost always something worn around the neck. For public wear, Gorean slaves sometimes wear something less obvious such as a necklace, anklet or a simple chain. Turian collars (named after a type of collar common to the city of Turia on Gor) are the most common metal collars I have seen Gorean slaves wear. The Turian is a round steel bar formed into two half-circles with a hinge and a lock holding the two parts together. It is also very common now among others involved in BDSM. This is probably because it is less obviously a slave collar and can pass as a type of necklace. I have heard that a version can even be purchased at Macy's department store. There are a number of online manufacturers as well. The first person to make them for sale that I know of was a Gorean from the Chicago area.

Flat collars, which are the most common ones in the books, are sometimes worn, but I have seen less of them. They are usually more expensive than the Turian and a bit harder to find. They are also much more obviously a type of slave collar. Some Gorean slaves wear leather collars, often with D or O-rings attached to them, but not usually full-time. They are the same sorts of collars that are often found on BDSM subs and slaves, except that Goreans almost never add spikes and studs. Gorean collars also usually lock, not just buckle. Non-locking collars are often considered fashion accessories rather than symbols of actual enslavement, as the slave can easily remove them. When a collar is locked on a slave and she does not hold a key, it has a very large psychological effect on her.

The most common Gorean brand is a *Kef*. The word *kajira* starts with the letter *kef* (Gorean for the letter K). The female *Kef* resembles a script lower case *K* with a tall stem and the male *Kef* is a block capital K according to the books. There are also other common brands such as the *Dina*, which is a flower shape that is the second most common Gorean brand; the books also describe a few others. However, most Goreans do not actually brand their slaves; if they mark them, it is most commonly done with a tattoo instead, although some do have their slave branded. The most common place for a Gorean brand is on the outside of the top of the left thigh where the palm of the slave's hand would cover it with their arm hanging at their side. The second most common place is the front of the thigh. Slaves in the books were almost always permanently marked in some way.

One of the things done online which *was* taken from the books is a stylized form of serving. "Serve" is not a word that was used in the books in that form, but it is an online term we have adopted for a way of serving a drink described in several books. It became the most common way to describe serving a drink online, and we brought it offline as well. I call it Serve 101 because it is a basic way of serving something. The simple description is that the slave kneels in Nadu before the person she is serving, holding (for example) a cup in both hands. The cup is first touched to her lower belly (or "slave belly" as it is called by Goreans), then brought up to touch between her breasts, and finally up to her lips where she kisses the side—not the rim—and extends the cup to the person she is serving with her head lowered between her outstretched arms. She waits in that position until the cup is taken from her and she is released to return to Nadu. When done smoothly and gracefully, it is very pleasant to be served in such a fashion.

What do *kajirae* wear? It varies from nothing at all to full formal clothing, depending on where the slave is, what she is doing, and whom she is with. In the books, the slaves commonly wore nothing or very little at home; this works because most of the books take place in a Mediterranean climate. Not everything was located in that area, so people wore what was appropriate to where they were located. Both free and slaves wore furs in the far north, loose robes in the desert, and almost nothing in the jungles. On Earth, we wear what is appropriate to our climate, culture and work. In general, most kajirae wear clothing considered more "feminine", such as dresses, skirts, and blouses. It is the same in the home, but in cases where there are no children present, a slave might wear nothing at all except a collar.

In the books, slaves often wore what were called "slave silks", which were diaphanous or translucent flowing fabric made out of silk or similar natural material. At other times they wore clothing of a more coarse, cheap material for working in. Slave clothing from the books ranged from a simple over-the-head poncho (the *camisk*) to tunics that are classical Greek and Roman in design. Some slaves have garments based on the costume of the books, but it is not universal among the slaves that I know. A nude slave at home is more common. However, slaves in the books almost never wear pants, and that can influence how they dress on Earth. It is part of bringing the customs and items from the books into our lives.

Few Goreans wear fetish clothing, except for those also involved in BDSM. There are no fishnets, corsets, knee-high stiletto boots, or leather/latex outfits with lots of shiny spikes and studs on men or women. We also don't usually wear clothing from the books when we get together; most of the time our clothing will not attract much attention. The exception is when Goreans gather in private; then the *kajirae* sometimes get to wear clothing from the books. It is not role-play in the normal sense, just bringing a bit more of the cultural aesthetic into what we do.

Non-Goreans Interacting With Goreans

There are only a few places where we interact and it actually matters who is Gorean. Those can be in person, online, at some group's event, or at Gorean gatherings. In some cases, if you know someone is Gorean, you might just as likely have met him or her at other places (such as work) that have nothing to do with either Goreans or BDSM.

The old adage, "When in Rome, do as the Romans do," does apply to Goreans to some extent. We may not agree with something to the point of doing it, but if you do, it is your responsibility to abide by the consequences of your choice. If a Gorean goes to a BDSM event or other types of events, expect them to abide by the rules of the hosting group or the event. If you come to a Gorean gathering, we expect the same behavior from you. Always ask before you do or bring something or someone. This politeness solves many potential problems.

If you meet with Goreans at the times we gather offline, it helps to know something of our expectations and the terms we use. We do tend to distance ourselves from BDSM in our nomenclature. We have gatherings, not munches. We do eat and talk, but we don't follow that with play parties. Like BDSM munches, many gatherings are held in public restaurants; some are in private homes. The restaurant gatherings are almost always open to the public, but not all of the gatherings in people's homes are open. There are places online which list some of the public meetings and unless you are coming to cause problems, you will be welcome to attend them.

Slaves are expected to act as we believe a slave should act at all times. Every free man is referred to as Master followed by their name; every free woman is Mistress followed by their name; but just Master and Mistress respectively are appropriate. Slaves are expected to act polite and respectful towards all free people at all times. How they actually feel may be at odds to that, but we are speaking of public behavior. What their owner does about exceptions to this standard mostly happens later in private. For Goreans, a slave is a slave all the time, and how they address people is based on their status in relation to others rather than a declaration just of personal relationship.

A slave may be commanded to do some things by anyone. The limits of what others may do with them is based on what their owner allows, but simple commands like bringing food or drink and answering questions are expected to be obeyed without discussion. Do not expect any *kajira*, owned or not, to obey commands for sex or sexual activity. If you attend a Gorean gathering with a slave you own, and you have placed restrictions on your slave, expect many of those same restrictions to be placed on you in return with other slaves, and possibly some amusement at your expense as well. Do not expect Goreans to follow BDSM or Leather customs, rules, or expectations. This is not kinky play. This is how we live. We don't need safe words for a slave serving her owner.

Epilogue

There are a few points I wish to summarize about Goreans and our *kajirae*.

+ The primary point is that many to most Goreans here on Earth do not own slaves and do not post on BDSM web sites such as FetLife or CollarMe even though there are Gorean boards in both places. We do not play at being Gorean online; we live it offline. Yes, we know the books are science fiction and not real. Telling us that only makes the speaker look stupid, which I am certain the discerning readers of this book would not wish to do. When you remove the slaves, Goreans have nothing to do with and are not a part of BDSM. We are not part of most of the groups described in this book. We do our best to be honorable and ethical people according to our own concepts of moral and ethical behavior, not yours.

+ Second is that the books are the glue and the cultural basics that hold Goreans together as a recognizable group. It is also what sets us apart from other groups that try to include us.

+ Third, Goreans consider women to be complementary to men, not less than men. Despite the claims of many, Goreans are not misogynists. Goreans are male-led and follow the Natural Order. The Natural Order is a Gorean tenet and expectation, but not a requirement to be Gorean on an individual basis. Being free *is* a requirement to be Gorean.

+ Fourth, most Goreans don't care that we are not what you expect or want us to be. We tend to be very politically incorrect and we don't care for those who are PC. We don't have to like what you do, or say that we like it. We are not you, and you are not us. If you want to be like us, do as we have done and become like us. If you want to become Gorean, we will point you in the proper directions, but you will have to do your own work. There are no instant Goreans. When we say Read The Books, we mean it.

+ Fifth is that the slaves of Goreans, where they do exist, are predominately female, but not all females are slaves or even potential slaves, despite some of the frequently quoted passages from the books.

+ Sixth is that Gorean slaves are best described as Total Power Exchange slaves or better yet, slaves in the Owner and Property style of consensual enslavement. The power only goes from the slave to the owner, and the control only goes from the owner to the slave. The only power that slaves have is to be pleasing; such ones are treasured. The only choice a *kajira* has is to be or not to be a slave. Like all consensual slaves in places where slavery is not legal, that choice is still theirs and Goreans recognize this. To Goreans, a slave is a slave at all times. There are no time-outs or non-slave times for *kajirae*.

✦ Seventh, we take from the books, but they are neither a bible nor their author a guru that lays out for us how to live.

✦ Finally, Goreans are people of Earth who were raised according to the society in which we were born. We found something in a philosophy that called to us. We choose to be Gorean. (There are very few who were born to and raised by Goreans. I know of a few second-generation Goreans, but no third generation, although they may exist.) We are human, and our philosophy is created by and based on philosophies created by humans.

I am including a few online resources to follow up on what I have said here. The links will give you the opinions of others whom I consider as or more knowledgeable than myself, or at least worth reading, and places I send people who wish to become Gorean or a Gorean's slave.

All of this is but one Gorean's take on the topic; something that will give you some understanding of Goreans and Gorean-based consensual enslavement. Not all Goreans will agree with all that I have said here. Some will be in agreement, but feel that I said too much or too little; I leave that judgment to others. If you wish to know more about Goreans or enslavement in the Gorean manner, or just to speak about what is here, you can find me online or through my web site. Send me an email or a message and we can talk.

Links:

◇ **House Malkinius.** This is my personal web site that was started in 1999. It contains some things from my time online and some more recent. The older the content the more likely it was online based. *http://www.housemalkinius.com*

- **House Malkinius Slave Positions and Practice Sequence page.** *http://housemalkinius.com/Positions.html*

- *Silk and Steel.* This is where much of what we do now started. *http://www.silkandsteel.com*

- *The Gorean Public Boards.* This is one of the first of the online forums by and for Goreans. *http://www.pantheus.com/forum/*

- John Norman's *Chronicles of Gor.* The official book web site and forum. *http://gorchronicles.com/*

- **Gor on *Wikipedia.*** You can also search for *Gorean*, *Kajira* and *John Norman* for other useful pages. Like many wiki pages, they are not totally correct, and there is some argument. *http://en.wikipedia.org/wiki/Gor*

- *Bear's Gorean Musings.* These are collected old and new essays by Bear of Ar, one of the earliest writers about things Gorean. *http://bearofar-bearsgoreanmusings.blogspot.com/?zx=5ca7fe287c8481f7*

- **Marcus of Ar on *What is Gorean Philosophy.*** *http://www.silkandsteel.com/3k/marcphil.htm*

- *Life on Gor.* This is one of the better descriptions of how the books and Goreans developed, by a non-Gorean. It does contain numerous errors of fact but is worth reading. *http://www.literaryescorts.com/?act=non-fiction&item=519*

Being a Thing

Human Pets

Silje Wyn

My name is Silje Wyn and I am a human pet. A human pet is a person who identifies as a pet in the same way that other people may identify as a dominant, a bottom, a rope bunny, a slave or a vampire. It is a label that signifies how we relate to people, especially those people we are in intimate relationships with. It explains our behaviors and motivations. It guides many of the decisions we make in life. It is one part of the parcel that is our lifestyle.

If I can impart nothing else, then I hope to convince people to assume nothing when it comes to human pets. I will relate what I know to the best of my ability but nothing is set in stone. No single rule applies to every single human pet or human pet relationship. Human pets are self-defining. Each and every single human pet has their own definition of what makes them a human pet and how they relate to their partners as a human pet. If someone identifies themselves as a submissive or a slave, there are general rules of behavior that a person might feel safe assuming that person would be guided by. When a person identifies themselves as a human pet there are no general rules of behavior that can safely be assumed will guide their actions. It is best to ask each person what it means to them to be a human pet.

What is a human pet?

Defining the human pet is tricky at best. A basic dictionary will define a pet as a domesticated animal kept for companionship or pleasure and treated with affection or cherished. Since there is no basic definition for human that encompasses all that a human being is—suffice it to say that humans are complex and complicated beings—a human pet is a person kept for companionship or pleasure, usually treated in an affectionate and cherished manner.

There is no right or wrong way to be a human pet, nor is there a right or wrong way to have a relationship with a human pet; however, there are some similarities in the ways that many human pets define themselves and relate to their partners. For example, one attribute that I have noticed in every human pet that I have met to date is a desire for attention. Not every human pet wants to be fussed over, but each pet wants attention in their own way. For some it is a desire for constant human touch and interaction, or to be degraded and humiliated; for others it is a need to be objectified sexually or in some other way. Many pets want to be the apple of their partners' eyes, to have their constant attention, or to be their partners' loyal best friend. Some human pets are sexual with their partners and others are not sexual at all.

There are two main types of human pets: those that identify in some way with a non-human nature and those that do not. I cannot speak in great detail about the former—what I call Human-animal pets—as I have no personal experience with that identity. Basically, though, the Human-animal pet is a person that identifies with, mimics the behavior of, or attempts to transform mentally and/or physically into some type of animal or non-human creature. If a person identifies as a puppy, they may wear accessories like mittens that confine their hands and feet in such a way that will both reduce their mobility and at the same time give them the look of a canine. They may engage in behaviors like playing fetch or barking that outwardly express their identity as a dog. They may interact with people and their partners while in a mental headspace that is simple and free of human worries, where they seek out the attention and love of their humans and seek to engage in ways that are more natural to their canine mind than their human mind. I have read definitions on human pets that state that Human-animals are less likely to be sexual with their partners than their pet Human counterpart, but in practice I have not found this to be true. Each relationship is different and dependent on all the people involved in that relationship.

A person that retains their human identity while also identifying as a pet—the latter type of human pets—are what I refer to as pet Humans. While this type of human pet will not mimic the behaviors of an animal or transition into an animal state of mind, they may model some animal pet behaviors, since domesticated animals are the only working models for pets that we have. Our behaviors help us define ourselves, but what you assume is not always what you see. For example, I might eat out of a bowl on the floor, but I would not be doing it in order to be humiliated or so that I can act like an animal; I would be doing it in order to please my partner and in order to clearly establish my status as a pet.

The important part of being a human pet is having the necessary mental and emotional state, and it is often easiest to reach said mental and emotional states through certain obvious behaviors. When everyone else in a room is clothed and sitting on the furniture talking about their day, the weaker power position of the naked person sitting on the floor tethered to their partner with a leather leash is obvious. The power dynamic and the status of that person is clear in the minds of everyone in the room. If everyone in the room is eating dinner at the table, but one person is eating dinner out of a bowl on the kitchen floor, the status of that person is clear physically, mentally, and even emotionally. If everyone at the party is mingling, but my movement is restricted through collar and leash and my ability to communicate is limited through voice restrictions, then my place and my status are confirmed in my own mind if not in the minds of the other people at the party. Many times it is what makes us different that clearly defines us.

Pets are Property

Most people do not like to think of their animal pets as property, and yet we call them "pet owners". Putting aside philosophical questions that ask if any living being can ever truly be owned by another living being, it is important to know that pets are property, and human pets are no exception to this rule. When one owns a pet, one is responsible for keeping them in good physical, mental, emotional, and even spiritual health. The extent of personal responsibility toward a human pet, much like toward an animal pet, is entirely dependent on the type of pet one has. Some pets need their partners to have absolute control—yes, even micromanagement—over them, while other pets are far more autonomous and require attention only in certain situations or at certain intervals.

Most human pets will refer to their partners as owners, handlers, or masters. This is the point at which many people question the difference between a pet and slave. For some, there is no difference except how the person defines themselves. For others, the distinctions are more obvious. As an example, slaves and pets both usually consider themselves to be cherished property, but my experience has been that slaves will often emphasize the "property" aspect while human pets will often emphasize the "cherished" aspect of the definition. As another contrast, human pets are more often given some level of autonomy. Many (though not all) human pets retain the right to say no to any given situation at any time, while many (though not all) slaves feel that giving up all of their rights is what makes them a slave, and is a basic part of their service towards their partners.

Slaves and human pets alike wish nothing more than to please their partners. Slaves will often attempt to be everything that their partners need, while human pets are more often likely to do whatever is in their power in order to support their partners. While a slave wants to be everything to their partner pets would rather be their partner's best friend. I don't say this to mean that a slave does not wish to be a best friend to their partner also, but rather to show the difference in the ways that slaves and human pets are usually motivated. Slaves give their partners pleasure by serving them, by whatever means necessary or requested. A pet's service is to be pleasing and to give their partners pleasure in whatever way they have negotiated.

Human pets do not all fall on the dominant-to-submissive spectrum, either. Some people that identify as pets and seek to please their partners are neither dominant nor submissive, but are just pets. Some pets are somewhere on the dominant spectrum while other pets are somewhere in the submissive spectrum.

How does the Owner/pet dynamic work?

A master may have many slaves, but it is uncommon for a slave to have more than one master. Many pets will not only have multiple owners, but their owners may be anywhere in the spectrum of kink. This gets confusing, as the possibilities are endless. However, many pets do thrive on hierarchy. If a specific hierarchy has not been negotiated ahead of time, pets will often create one in their own mind. Whoever is at the top of the totem pole gets the pet's primary love and loyalty. More than one person can hold that top position, but once that top position is taken it is hard to break. A pet may be submissive to (or may *submit* to) anyone above them in the hierarchy of their relationships. However, if a pet is at the bottom of the hierarchy, they will still retain certain rights and privileges that other submissives and slaves in the relationship do not have, as defined by the nature of their pet identity. Although a pet may have many owners, or be in a relationship with multiple people, they may not identify as polyamorous. They may not have sexual relationships with all or even any of the people that they are in a relationship with.

The owner/pet dynamic works in whatever way the people involved want it to work. It is possible to define an owner/pet relationship so that it includes protocols, rules, and hierarchies, and many pets will welcome such definitions, but for owners and their pets, all relationship dynamics are completely dependent on the people involved and how they define themselves.

People often ask what the owner/pet dynamic looks like on a regular or daily basis. There is no easy description; it takes some work and imagination. You know what your daily life looks like. Figure out why you would want to own a pet or, in contrast, why you would want to be a pet. Feel free to use animal models as examples. When a person considers owning an animal pet, they usually do so for specific reasons like wanting companionship, more exercise, something pretty to look at, or wanting to get rid of vermin. Imagine how your life would be different if you had a specific animal pet in your life. Would you get up earlier to feed and groom it? Would you come home earlier so that it wouldn't be lonely? Would it be inside all the time or would you let it out to roam or get exercise? Make a list of questions that you would need to consider. Also, make a list of things you might need to take into consideration that you didn't think of when picking out the animal.

Then do the same thing with a generic human in mind. Ask yourself why you would want to own, or be, a human pet. How would your life be different from what it is now if you had a human that you could treat as a pet? Would you want to micromanage the care and feeding of your human? Would you want that person to do many things for themselves? What behaviors do you think would be different or similar to those of slaves? Change the situation until it meets your needs and desires, and then all that is left is finding someone who shares your ideal.

This may be a frustratingly vague way for many people to understand or explain the owner and pet relationship, but it can also be very freeing to know that you can set the terms in any way you please. The owner/pet dynamic inherently contains the same kind of freedom to naturally be what you are that a master/slave dynamic does.

Objectification

slave will

> *Today I am a small blue thing*
> *Like a marble or an eye…*
> *…You are perfectly reflected,*
> *I am lost inside your pocket,*
> *I am lost against your fingers…*
> *…I am turning in your hand.*
> —Suzanne Vega, "Small Blue Thing"

Instrumentality: *The objectifier treats the object as a tool of his or her purposes.*

That's the first of seven rules of objectification created by Martha Nussbaum,[3] delineating how to treat a person like a thing. I ran across them when I was in college, and I couldn't finish reading them. At first I told myself that was because the idea of being treated like a thing was so awful I couldn't even think about it. Many years later, I admitted to myself that my reluctance to think about it was because I wanted that, somewhere deep in my soul, and wanting that was so awful that I must be a terrible and sick person. How could anyone healthily want what thousands struggle to avoid every day? I'd closed the book and walked away, but when I became a slave, I went in search of it again. I found that my beloved Mistress was doing every one of these things to me, and I was loving it.

I am, most definitively, a tool for her purposes. One purpose might be getting the meal she wants to eat tonight, without having to hunt for a restaurant. Another might be getting her taxes done with a wave of her hand, or getting that fence rail finished, or having another bed appear in her garden, ready to plant. It might be having exactly the sex she wants without having to worry about whether the other person is sexually satisfied, or not having sex when she doesn't feel like it and not having to worry that her partner is taking it personally. It might be getting luggage to magically appear in a hotel room, or having a floor

---

[3] Nussbaum, Martha. "Objectification." Philosophy and Public Affairs, Fall 1995, pg. 249.

that magically cleans itself. If there is a job to be done that she doesn't want to do, and I am capable of doing it, by definition it is my job.

Before I go any further with this, I should make it clear I am aware that most people—and even, perhaps, most people who use the labels "submissive" or "slave"—do not enjoy or feel comfortable with the level of objectification in our M/s relationship. Just because I happen to love it doesn't mean that it's necessarily anyone else's glass of vodka. Many people would feel negated in a bad way by such treatment, and I do not mean to suggest that they should seek it out or endure it if it makes them miserable. However, I think that serious objectification is often treated like it's "only something that happens in porn", and I want to address that here. While pornographic objectification is usually of the silly type (like making someone into a useless pet or locking them in a cage all the time), real objectification can also be a very practical day-to-day lifestyle, and still give a thrill. I get that thrill every time my Mistress does any of the things on this list. It may not seem thrilling that she assumes I will, of course, pick up that paper she just dropped, but it is for me. We may be a minority even among M/s people, but some of us really do like being treated this way.

I'm one of those people. I don't know why, and I have certainly thought about it a lot, but being a thing brings me great peace. It relieves most of the stress that was present in my life before M/s. The closer I get to being a thing, the better I feel. There is an egoless-ness about it that is almost spiritual for me. Well, perhaps it is spiritual, but I don't have the words to describe how.

It isn't just about some sort of Freudian regression to childhood, either. The way that I am treated—while not unkindly, certainly—is not the way one would treat a child. I've got kids, and I know that. Kids don't do well when they are treated like things, even though some of that has to happen when they are very small, and one could see making decisions for them—especially when they don't agree with the decisions—as treating them as having no agency. But for me, it's different. I am an adult who understands exactly what is happening to me, and I actively enjoy it. That makes it hotter for both of us, and makes it entirely different from a parent/child relationship.

Denial of autonomy: *The objectifier treats the object as lacking in autonomy and self-determination.*

My Mistress knows that I am an intelligent human being who can make my own decisions, but she also knows that I enjoy it when I don't have to do that. She controls everything about my life—when and what I eat, when and how I perform hygiene, what I wear, which doctor I see and when, when I go to work and how I handle my lunch hour, who I may have in my social life, when I can see my kids or my friends, even how I am to treat my ex-wife when I see her. She makes all these decisions with a good mixture of both consideration for the feelings of others and strict boundaries around their access to me. Because of this, I can relax and go along with her orders automatically.

My money is hers. My body is hers. That's literal, not symbolic. I do not determine anything for myself any more, except for how to apply the rules she has given me to a specific situation. I gain more skill in doing so as we go along. I love this. It's great. Honestly, when it comes to my personal life she makes better decisions for me than I ever made for myself. I am much better at being considerate to others now, as my children attest.

It took a while to get used to reporting everything I did and having it tweaked, critiqued, and polished, right down to interactions with co-workers. After a while, though, it became automatic. Here's what I did. *Changes? Please walk me through that, ma'am? Thank you, ma'am, I'll do my best.* And I try.

Inertness: *The objectifier treats the object as lacking in agency, and perhaps also in activity.*

She wants the end of a string held for some craft project. I stand there and hold it, for as long as she needs it held. She wants my leg in a different position as we sit on the couch, so she moves it as if it was a pillow or newspaper, and expects it to stay where it was put, or at least away from her pile of books. I bring her a drink while she is working on her laptop on the porch; she is not ready to take the drink until she has finished typing this paragraph, so I stand there with the drink until the work is done. My convenience is put aside; I'm here to be convenient to her, always.

She wants to know that not only do I love being treated with so little agency—and, sometimes, as a stationary object—but that I am sturdy enough to bear the little difficulties of doing so. In a sense, being a good object and enduring some discomfort for that—and not feeling resentment afterwards—makes me strong. Practicing it makes me stronger. I can endure more at work without getting upset, now that I've learned this discipline.

Fungibility: *The objectifier treats the object as interchangeable, A) with objects of the same type, and B) with objects of different types.*

Sometimes my Mistress has other submissive men over for casual sex. She might want me to stand there holding a drink while she torments them, or rides their cocks. She might want me to perform with them for her amusement, if they will go along with it. I am not shown special treatment during this. I am not called anything but "boytoy". The other submissive man is just called "boy", but that's largely just to reduce confusion when giving orders to us. He is an object of the same type, and we are interchangeable in this situation.

Sometimes my Mistress has non-submissive men over for casual sex. She prefers them to be bisexual, and sometimes they do not understand our M/s. My job is to pretend to be her pleasant, easygoing boyfriend who is happy to engage them in sex for her amusement, but I have to do it in a way that looks like we are equals and I just think it would be a good time. (I am straight, but I've learned that when it comes to making her happy, sex is just another service to perform.) Here I am interchangeable with objects of different types, who probably don't know how much they are being objectified. (Actually, considering the guys she picks out, they're probably pretty clear that they're being objectified, but many guys tend not to mind that for a couple of hours as long as they are getting off.)

Violability: *The objectifier treats the object as lacking in boundary-integrity; as something it is permissible to break up, smash, break into.*

While my Mistress is not interested in smashing me, any more than she'd crash her own car for a lark—she doesn't want me rendered useless—my physical boundaries are not my own to guard against her.

If she wants to fondle or hurt me in passing, she does so, even if it's inconvenient to me. I cannot touch her without permission, so it is more than just a quick exchange of affection, as it would be for many people. I might be on my knees scrubbing the floor, and she might walk by and stick a finger in my exposed, up-tilted asshole, and my job is to hold still in spite of surprise and arousal. Then I'm to suck her finger clean, and clean it further with the rag attached to my toolbelt (worn even when I am naked) because the best messy object is one with automatic cleaning attached. I do keep my anus washed out for her, just in case something like this happens. But every time it happens, it reminds me of what I am—a thing to be idly toyed with as she chooses, and not as I choose.

Sometimes what's even more hard to bear is when she doesn't touch me for days because she's busy. Having her walk by me and ignore me is worse than being violated, but it's important as well. I need to remember that I bend to her pleasure, and not the other way around. Every time she walks by and ignores me, this lesson is driven home.

Ownership: *The objectifier treats the object as something that is owned by another, can be bought or sold, etc.*

This is actually how we got together. I was owned by another Mistress for about three months. It was wonderful and I still have a great deal of respect and affection for her, but she had to move to the other coast and couldn't bring me along. I have a decently-paying job (and the paycheck is one of the perks of owning me) which is pretty much bound to one area, and uprooting me would reduce my value. I also have regular visitation with kids from the marriage of my youth, and uprooting me would upset them. Sadly, she decided to rehome me. That's how she put it—not "sell me" exactly, but "rehome" me as if I was a dog who couldn't live in the new apartment, but was going to be placed somewhere else regardless of how I felt about it.

Yes, I suppose that unlike an actual dog, I could have walked out at that point (although I should point out that actual dogs run away too), but I took a lot of deep breaths and trusted her to do the right thing. We were not romantically involved, which helped. She interviewed her friends and chose my current Mistress, but there was a trial period during which my new Mistress definitely treated me as if I was something owned by someone else, which I was. When it was clear that we got on very well together, they officially transferred my ownership, and I was "rehomed".

Denial of subjectivity: *The objectifier treats the object whose experience and feelings (if any) need not be taken into account.*

Obviously this isn't always true—we have check-ins where she asks me how I am doing, if there are problems, if I have ideas on what might make things easier. I am required to be honest with her and tell her about any negative feelings I have about her orders or my life as her slave. At first I had trouble with that, because I felt that a thing oughtn't to have any problems, or at least things didn't complain about them. I loved the subjective experience of objectification so much that I felt doing relationship processing would ruin it. However, my Mistress set me straight in a big way. First she pointed out that she wouldn't keep a thing that couldn't follow basic orders like, "Be completely honest with me." Things were to do what they were told. Complex things, like a car or piece of intricate machinery, had readouts that would tell an owner how the thing was performing, and when it needed maintenance. It was stupid, she told me to deny that I was a complex and valuable tool, or that I needed maintenance. Checking in with me was checking my readouts so that she could maintain me properly.

She also informed me that she wanted my reports to be simple, honest, and clear of my baggage around what I thought my slavery experience should be like. If I didn't know how to do that, she would train me in it—she referred to that as "installing the dashboard"—but by damn there was going to be a dashboard, and I was not to make her job harder by sabotaging it. She also pointed out that it wasn't very "inert" of me to decide that I shouldn't have a dashboard, and to shut off all my dials when she had expressly commanded otherwise.

Well, that shut me up good.

I'm an object, but a complicated one that needs maintenance, and that's all right. I'm property, but I'm living property like a dog—and with as little say in the decisions over my life, and that's all right. I am a thing that she values and keeps around, and that is truly wonderful. Sometimes, being reduced to the basics can show you who you really are, and that the thing you are is a beautiful thing.

Eclectic Examples

Building a Household Style
Master James

Sitting on the terrace of an outdoor restaurant in DC about ten years ago, with the first hint of autumn in the air, I contemplated how my first serious long term D/s relationship came to an end. There had been no throwing of crockery and few harsh words, but as I stared down into a drink and looked at the leaves in the park starting to lose their color, the realist in my guts reared its ugly head. I hadn't handled the relationship as well as I might have and, while I had a hard time admitting it to myself, I'd been looking for a new relationship to "start again". When I faced myself I was aware I'd quit. There was too much beyond my control and too much I didn't understand.

For twenty years I'd been producing some kind of interactive theater. After every production I tore what had been done to pieces. This wasn't self-punishment, but the opposite: as long as I could be honest about what I'd done wrong, I could easily forgive myself for it, providing I remembered it and did not repeat the error.

Being a quitter was not my style. I wanted to "do it right" the next time. The problem was that I did not have any sort of clear road map as to how next time was going to be better. I had gathered some suspicious dogma about what I should "always" do as a Dominant, but much of it seemed perilously close to "always behave like an asshole" and I doubted I *would* do things that way next time.

I was also at a confused place in my life in regards to BDSM. The things I wanted out of it were emotional depth and darkness, but the prevailing norm was a scene in which a girl was flogged into an endorphin-induced high, which looked like service topping to me. I wanted to reach inside people and change them.

All my life I'd been taught that the answers to questions could be found in books. I was very familiar with *fiction* on the subject of slavery. A good friend suggested that the term "Master" fit what it was that I wanted to do—to control and change people, not just top them in a scene. Since then I've come to put very little stock in terms like "Dominant" or "Master" per se, but at the time it seemed that the whole of power exchange was defined by categories. If I wanted to train people, that made me a "Master", and if I was a Master then I should find books on Mastery and do what they said.

Armed with this new knowledge of the "correct" slot for my vocation, I began to study. I wasn't naïve enough to think that the terminology meant that much, but it did give me a starting point. I found very little written nonfiction on how to be a Master in a modern context, less on how to be a heterosexual Master. I found two or three lists of "slave rules" on the internet, and short essays that tended to focus on the subordination of the will of the slave to the Master. I found some depth in Guy Baldwin's *Slavecraft*, but by intent it was more the start to an understanding than a textbook for building M/s relationships. I found an outline of structure in work published by Bob Rubel, who had attempted to put together a set of basic household protocols, and discovered other guides and suggestions such as a marvelous outline presented by the late and very distinguished Jack McGeorge.

Unfortunately, as I studied these documents and attempted to make use of my learning, I began to see several issues that were not widely addressed. First, what worked for one person did not always work for another. A lot of traditional M/s presumed a militaristic mindset that one assumes evolved from actual military services. There was a top-down mindset, elegant to those who craved a certain type of structure and discipline, but strangely distant and irrelevant to girls raised in the 1990s or 2000s in the US East Coast suburbs. Nothing about growing up watching *Full House* and *Boy Meets World* had prepared them for life in Boot Camp. Authorities in M/s assured me that life in Boot Camp would make them into models of stark maturity and personal power, but this didn't seem to be the case. What it accomplished was to annoy the *fuck* out of them.

Second, I did not want to recreate slavery, or someone's idealization of slavery mired between Barbary Coast Sex Slavery and John Norman's *Chronicles of Gor*. I did not even want to recreate the depictions I *admired*, such as those by Pauline Reage and Laura Antoniou. I wanted a functional form of power exchange that worked for *real people*, not characters in a novel.

Finally, most writing about power exchange seemed to be aimed at the healthy and well—people who at least appeared to be shining exemplars of normalcy. These idealized slaves were not Bipolar or Borderline, did not suffer from PTSD or crippling depression, and did not have OCD or ADHD. In the real world I found these things very common, particularly because these conditions and others often created a profound lack of control. People who suffered from them often instinctively or knowingly sought power exchange as a way to help bring order to their lives.

I'd set out with the idea that a Master was a specific thing to be, and that if I could find the "real" guide I could be a good Master. What I came to realize was that the idea of a "blueprint" for power exchange was as absurd as a blueprint for a painting or symphony. Not only was there not "one true way", there could not *be* one true way. There were skills and techniques that *could* be taught, but how they came together were a matter of individual style. Some authors had approached power exchange with the idea of presenting a *method* rather than a *skillset*, but the most useful had focused on understandings and skills.

Some styles did not seem right for me or the people with whom I was involved in power exchange. For example, I was often assured that the correct spiritual orientation would make the household thrive, and was even a necessity. The point of M/s was to progress to a sort of enlightenment. The people who put this forward weren't stupid, and they weren't suggesting some narrow fifteenth-century religious doctrine. I could understand ritual as an assembly language of the psyche, and I accepted the general concept of self-actualization, though I was dubious as to Maslow's idealistic interpretation of it. I appreciated this might have a place for many people, but after several "spirituality" events, I was pretty well convinced that it was not a primary focus for most of us.

In 2008, I walked into the lobby of the Crown Plaza Hotel in Silver Spring, Maryland, briefly convinced I'd found the nadir of M/s. I was in a sea of patch vests, jeans, boots, and even black Master's caps, enough that I wasn't sure a gray wool business suit was quite up to the occasion. Every year this suburban enclave of Washington D.C. plays host to the Master/slave Conference (MsC) organized by MTTA and its President,

Master Taíno. MsC and MTTA produce a program called "Our Traditions Live", highlighting the history of the Leather M/s community. Watching the lighting of candles for deceased members of the community, the display of leather awards and patches, and browsing the Carter-Johnson Library's vast room of old books and magazines, I felt strong kinship and great reverence for people who had struggled and given their lives to make it possible for me to post that I was a Master of slaves in a public forum without inviting police investigation.

I learned a great deal from thoughtful and well-spoken presenters who seemed just a little more mortal, if no less intelligent, once I'd met them in the flesh. Yet I was not quite *of* them. Close kin perhaps, or the mortal child of a generation of heroes; reverential but facing a different world, less threatening, more mundane. I could watch with genuine emotion the award of a Master's Cap, yet not only not wish such an honor for myself, but feel that should such an honor by some strange path come to me, it would at once turn faintly ridiculous, like the visitation of knighthood on Sir Mick Jagger. I sought to discover a style which suited us.

Style is a combination of both ideals and presentation. The power-suited boss and the Hawaiian-shirted party guy might have similar ideals but net very different reactions. There were a bewildering range of ways in which Masters could "dress" a household, and clothes do make the man, woman, or idea.

Style is also a joint undertaking. A Master may prefer a style and, if he's willing to draw lines that may lose adherents, dictate style—but in most cases there is give and take. I found that it was more the job of the Master to set *tone* and let a confluence of ideas establish the details of style. My girl Miranda had a preference for informality which likely helped save me from some exercises in overblown pomposity. My other girl JayLynn's forceful and no-nonsense personality certainly created a hesitancy to hound after some of the more extreme elements of M/s tradition. We got along well because we shared a certain pragmatism, and if we did not always agree on what was fulfilling, we did have some shared sense of what was wasted time and effort.

Flexibility was also core. As we began to enlarge our circle of acquaintances, the household grew until it was no longer a hierarchy, but a collection of associated individuals who chose on occasion to serve each other, but not all or most of whom are in service to myself or anyone. Each of these autonomous people brought their own idea of style and shared purpose, and while I may provide some guidance and direction, they can and do make their own decisions about time, commitment, and beliefs. However, here I am focusing on the specific dynamics between myself and my partners in power exchange, with the understanding that these convey our style by example to other associates of the household, but not as any sort of manual of practice or set of expectations. The best way to teach and set standards is to exemplify and maintain them.

Part I: Presentation

Edwardian Manners

Through Sir Stephen, now Director of the Master/slave Development Center of MTTA, I was first exposed to the concept that one might actually operate an M/s household along Victorian lines. In the early nineties, well before the dawn of "steampunk," I'd run a "Victorio-Edwardian Society" and since the mid-nineties my wife and our "household" of the moment had produced an annual Victorian and Edwardian Holiday Tea.

I was uncomfortable, early on, with the idea of snapping orders at a "slave". Growing up in the 1970s, I'd watched *Upstairs Downstairs*, and *The Duchess of Duke Street*, both of which shaped my idea on how people of quality speak to people serving them. I also had a distinct opinion that people who were rude or impolite to service people— including their own—were uncouth. This probably came from decent parenting and a southern grandfather who was the retired owner of a Department Store, a gentleman farmer and Quaker, and a man who seemed at times to have strode with quiet ferocity out of the 19th century. I recall many things about my grandfather, but one is that he had little patience for bad service or tasks poorly done either from his own employees, or from others. One sunny vacation summer morning around 1972, in a hotel restaurant in Myrtle Beach South Carolina, I watched the whole family try to crawl under the table while he called a waitress over, ascertained she did in fact make the coffee, then proceeded to instruct her, gently but firmly, how to properly make that beverage.

It had not quite occurred to me to organize a household along those lines and, while this was no more of an exact fit than any other style, it spoke to deep-seated beliefs. My manners in this regard caused some friction within the household. It was not always satisfying to receive orders in the form of "Could you..." or "Would you be so kind as to...", whereas in my world having to bark "That's an order!" was a pathetic last resort, something that only happened at a moment of near mutiny and which called for an implicit direct threat. To me, "That's an order!" was subtext for "I am about to refer you for discipline and/or Court Martial," and had no place in a well-run household.

Our household formed during the occasion of a sad gap in most references for polite service. The BBC series of my youth were long gone from the screen (and not yet readily available online) and *Downton Abbey* was not yet popular. I required the household to see *Gosford Park*, but it failed to convey well-intentioned service and had unnecessary *drama*. Over time, however, through events, cultural reference, and my influence, an Edwardian manner has become a part of our household ethic. Orders and demurrals should be polite, allowing for an interchange and correction or new information, so that the process of orders is never a source of embarrassment on either end.

The concept of barking orders, in addition to being bad manners, always seemed comical to me, reminding me of Yul Brynner in *The Ten Commandments* intoning gravely "So it shall be written. So it shall be done!" To me, "I'll endeavor to do my best, Sir," "Was that a priority, Sir?" and "I'm afraid that may be impossible with the resources at hand, Sir," were all perfectly reasonable responses.

Military Discipline

As military families go, mine fell pretty far from the tree. While my father *was* in the Air Force, he spent the Korean War as a typist in Riverside California, where he contributed to the war effort by typing the morning report for the 320th Bombardment Wing, developing an interest in motor racing and, as revealed by photographic evidence to the chagrin of my grandmother, picking up hot Hawaiian girls. My own first three years of schooling were through a private school full of the children of officers and diplomats, and which led me to see military discipline as something both exotic and desirable.

Likely because military discipline and tradition was a scarce and exotic thing in my childhood, I became rather fascinated with it. I acted out the normal games of war common to most children, but I had an unusual fascination with the human and social elements of military life. I actually played at being in barracks, on base, at sentry duty, and other uninteresting tasks. Before one children's war game, in which our side was to issue forth to skirmish in a particularly significant battle with the enemy, I gave a short and solemn address and suggested that the company take time to write and deposit last letters home before the upcoming fray, a bit of realism that only a few of them appreciated. I wanted my father to "play army", and I think he rather thought he'd gotten the best of me when he explained that this would consist of cleaning my room and preparing it for inspection, though it may be the only time I voluntarily cleaned my room. As an adult I'm more a bohemian than a militarist, yet I have no doubt it is one reason that "Leather M/s" initially appealed to me. When giving examples, I tend to default more towards Air Force or Navy, because they emphasize pulling together to make something run smoothly rather than sacrifice or winning the fight.

Initially I was shocked to find that military discipline and even ideas such as "chain of command" had very limited utility when teaching people who had no cultural exposure to the idea of actual military discipline. For all that America went "back to war" in the late nineties with accompanying patriotism and flag waving, there was no widespread increase in the understanding of military life as there had been in previous wars. The number of troops was more limited and the media seemingly had little interest in factual stories about deployments that were mostly dangerous occupations, rather than fights in which suicide was a constant threat and the army worked to suppress any sort of hijinks that might cause local friction, no matter the cost to morale.

I realized that military discipline, whether it came from the Leather Tradition or any other source, needed explanation and points of reference. Even then the understanding can only go so far; but still, there is some utility. In the run-up to a recent event, one of our newer associates noted that everyone seemed more tense. Realizing that he was still getting used to the changes when we are in "down to the wire" mode, I explained it to him by saying, "When the ship is actively engaged in operations, responses are expected to be short, crisp, and to the point."

Possibly the most useful thing which we've taken from military culture is not discipline but a far more recent concept: Commander's Intent.

Commander's Intent

In April 1980, eight US Combat helicopters set out to rescue Americans held by the Iranian revolutionary Government at the U.S. Embassy, the focus of the historic "Iran hostage crisis". Real-time control of this operation went all the way to the President, with the commanders on the ground given very little discretion. At the "Desert One" staging point, one of the helicopters collided with a C-130 transport, setting off a catastrophic explosion that wrecked both aircraft and killed eight men. With shots being called from halfway around the world, catastrophic confusion ensued, classified documents were abandoned, and without ever even *encountering* the enemy, the U.S. surrendered at least four operational helicopters and many classified papers to the Iranian Revolutionary Government. The debacle would contribute heavily to the subsequent electoral loss of then U.S. President Jimmy Carter. Following this humiliation, the U.S. Army conducted a review of its centralized decision making doctrine, realizing the need to empower subordinate commanders on the scene.

In finding a solution, the Army looked back nearly two centuries to a time when Napoleon's Armies were rolling across Europe. With their principalities crumbling before Bonaparte's advance, German strategists realized that iron discipline and blind obedience were no longer effective in a fast-changing world, and that they needed to *empower* their subordinates rather than *control* them. This led them to develop the concept of mission-oriented command. It's cornerstone trust between superior and subordinate, based on intimate knowledge of each other. This concept, called *Auftragstaktik*, became the center of a culture of trust within the Army which allowed "The Desert Fox" Erwin Rommel to smash military forces vastly larger than his own. While we may not think much of Rommel's boss, his ability to do more with less is legendary.

Leather Tradition came from an adaptation of military discipline to Master/slave relationships in the late forties and fifties, which may suggest we still have a page or two to take from the military—not so much iron discipline as two modern concepts that emanate from *Auftragstaktik*: *Imparting Presence* and *Commander's Intent*, which were classically summarized by Lt. Col. Lawrence G. Shattuck, U. A. in a 2000 article in *Military Review*.

Imparting Presence means bringing subordinates a sense of yourself. Shattuck writes, "Imparting presence is the process of developing subordinates decision making framework so that they respond the same way the senior commanders would if they were able to view the situation through their eyes." In our world, imparting presence is key to the concept of "internal identity" which female Dominants sometimes refer to as the "WWMD—What would Ma'am do?" principle. The process works on the following principles:

- ✓ **Start early.** Begin imparting presence from the day you find yourself in charge.

- ✓ **Establish boundaries.** Make sure your subordinates have a good intrinsic feel of what *is* and *isn't* okay in your playbook.

- ✓ **Explain rationale.** A military commander might say "Don't take risks that get our people killed for a crap objective nobody cares about." In our world, it may include favoring substance over appearance, or speed over detail for priority projects.

- ✓ **Get feedback.** Some Dominants are allergic to the idea of taking their submissive's opinions into account. There are "old school" Dominants who would say this is "touchy-feely", which is why it's good this isn't advice from Dr. Phil. This is advice from the Army, those nice people who level your town with howitzers. Get feedback.

✓ **Allow for individuality.** Let people be themselves and they'll give you the best of themselves.

Commander's Intent focuses on instruction by *priority,* not by *method.* Long lists of techniques and may be part of instructions, but they can become confusing or irrelevant as events change or point of view changes. Commander's Intent focuses on making sure that the people doing the job know what it is you *actually want done.* It focuses on *end-state.*

✓ **Formulation.** Give concise statements of intent that focus on the results desired.

✓ **Communication.** Think about how to effectively relay information. It's not enough to have a clear idea in *your* head. You need to get it across clearly, and different people don't all remember things the same way. One submissive might need things written down. Another might tend to obsess on a specific detail and forget the overall message.

✓ **Interpretation.** The quality of interpretation depends on how well you have imparted presence.

✓ **Implementation.** In order to implement, your submissive has to actually have skills. Whether the job is buying advertising, handling public-relations, ironing a man's shirt, or polishing boots, you may have to teach the skills you want to see.

The Theater

For years our household operated a live-action theatrical concern, and theater still plays a big part in the values I tend to live by. "The show must go on!" is a powerful and imminent value to me, and at times the devil lurking on my shoulder. Occasionally putting the individual misery of an associate or intimate ahead of that has been very difficult for me, requiring me to recall that people are a priority. Usually it works well, allowing us to establish difference between "a production" and "day-to-day-life". Often we hear stories about power exchanges rent by disagreements over the dry cleaning or a cup of coffee. For us it's simple: Sloppy service or omissions on downtime may not be *favored*, but will generally be *forgiven*. When the house lights go up, excuses are much less acceptable. This is helpful on a daily basis, but can create a level of anxiety to our events which I've tried to allay in recent years using Commander's Intent to focus on the important details.

Theater also underscores a certain air of pragmatism, which tells associates of our household where to put effort. For example in some households, the master is always served on the best china. In our household, the stained, bent spoons and cracked plates go to me first, then are passed down through the household. The reason is obvious if you understand show business. To create a lovely storybook experience, *point the good side towards the audience.* We already know the stuff has flaws, but our guests need to see our best silver and china because it's their perceptions we care about. Hopefully we already think we're awesome and, if we don't, an unbent fork isn't going to make a difference.

Part II: Ideals

Flexibility

> *If a system is to be stable the number of states of its control mechanism must be greater than or equal to the number of states in the system being controlled.*

> *–The Law of Requisite Variety, W. Ross Ashby (1956)*

Imagine you have a fan that has a switch that says off/on. Now try to set the fan to low speed or high speed. You'll have a hard time. You need more than two settings ("control states" in engineer's parlance): on and two speeds. You need *three* control states: off/on low/on high. There's no getting around this. If you turn the dial halfway between on and off and it runs slower, you've created or discovered a third control state, even if there is no printed label on the dial. This principle has turned out to hold true in a lot of other areas in nature and life, and a simpler way to put it is "The most flexible element will control the system."

The law describes a truth about how humans must act to control each other, and forms a core concept of our household. In the long run, the most flexible person will "win". This seems a little counter-intuitive, since many traditional approaches to power exchange and household organization stress inflexibility as an expression of strength. Being flexible doesn't mean being wishy-washy or giving in all the time. It means never having your option to choose what is wise or right constrained by the expectations of others about what is "domly" or "traditional". The *capability* to flex doesn't mean you always *will*. On the submissive side, flexibility is about not needing to play "Simon says", a model where absolute and blind obedience is demanded. Since the Master can't anticipate every possibility and the submissive must obey "absolutely", this often turns into a grim game where the Master must work to give an order that cannot be subverted.

Commander's Intent means that we expect results, even if that means a substantial deviation from planned orders. Imparting presence means that partners know what flex is "reasonable" in getting the job done. Flexibility means being able to act as a free human agent, not as a robot following a set of logical instructions even if it means obvious doom.

Respect, Tribe, and Fellowship

"Clean my boots, slut, before I kick you to the curb," may make a hot scene, but it's a tough long term dynamic even for just *two* people. Add a few more to the mix and it's likely to be disastrous.

When Dave Logan, John King, and Halee Fischer-Wright talk about tribes, they don't mean uncontacted Peruvians or the legal jurisdiction of Native American run casinos in upstate New York. A tribe is a collection of people who come together, which includes people who come together to support each other in alternative lifestyles. In *Tribal Leadership: Leveraging Natural Groups to Build a Thriving Organization*, Logan and company suggest that tribes exist at five levels. (If you don't have time for the book, search for David Logan's TED talk on Tribal Leadership.)

✓ **Stage One**: "Life sucks." This is the culture of street gangs and other groups that "live for today for you'll die tomorrow."

✓ **Stage Two**: "My life sucks." This is the culture of Dilbert, the culture of call centers, failing discount stores, and the DMV. The people in these tribes know that there are better things ... but not for them.

✓ **Stage Three**: "I'm great, you suck." This is the stage of most of corporate America, and even many lifestyle BDSM or power exchange communities. It's a compete and win stage, every man for himself. A lot of successful people live at Stage Three.

✓ **Stage Four**: "We're *all* great." This is the stage of cooperation consideration, and respect inside and outside the tribe.

✓ **Stage Five**: "Life is great." This is the state of global change and profound impact, of living by values and ethics. This is where Nobel prizewinners live and create profound positive change.

We'd all like to be at Stage Five, but that's tough. Some of our household were raised in families that acted as Stage Two and Stage One tribes. We work hard to maintain a solid Stage Four basis and part of my job is trying to keep us out of Stage Three.

Several of our associates keep a distance from their families. One has rejected her family altogether due to a history of sexual abuse. Within the household, we don't promote using fictive terms of kinship to refer to each other. Partially this is because the very concept of *sibling* has negative connotations for some of our associates while others feel that a "sister" is a very different sort of person than a partner within the household, however intimate.

In Western culture, at least, fictive kin relationships may be made no stronger when they require willing suspension of disbelief. We have built-in associations for members of our tribe, and trying to label our associates as "brothers" or "sisters" with middle class Americans who have limited cultural basis for a ritualized acceptance of fictive kin may create cognitive dissonance that makes the relationship seem awkward and forced. Some of our associates occasionally *use* family labels, but we don't force them or make their use official. The household is expected to be gregarious, with different associates having different levels of stake; an alliance rather than a social "end all and be all". We've seen groups collapse when the inevitable "drift in" and "drift out" of individuals who form new relationships or move brings a crisis in how they are to be considered. We're friends first and everything else second.

Likewise, in many groups, falling out of love with a principal of the group is grounds not just for an invitation not to let the door hit you in the ass on the way out, but for demonization. You are not just someone for whom there is no use, you are "that bastard who hurt our little girl," and there is no pit of Hell too deep for you. In theory, this serves the same function as societies where divorce is difficult, exerting an external pressure on bonded pairs to find a way to "work things out." In practice, anyone who feels their emotional bond with a member of the group slipping has three choices: maneuver out of it politically through deception and manipulation; pretend the attachment remains while betraying it at every turn; or run away fearful and volatile, often denouncing the group as a preemptive measure. This does not seem constructive.

All that said, our model is one of a "family of association", focusing on a right to invest our energy in others based on their value to, and acceptance of, each other.

The Primacy of Learning

A rationalist and humanist point of view is fairly essential to us. Obviously, as the household grows, it becomes harder to characterize any value that is shared by all its associates. We include a fair split of those who are theists of some kind and those who are agnostic or atheistic. We value both science and learning, and both will trump nonsense and wish-fulfillment.

My wife is a Priestess in the *Ordo Templi Orientis*, an esoteric lodge which practices ritual magic; others among us attend Pagan events or Christian religious observances. None of us have much use for granola-driven pabulum, demonic possession as an excuse for mental illness or day to day character failings, literal creation, or any other belief that places the supernatural in the realm of an excuse for ignorance, bad behavior, or makes it a barrier to self-awareness rather than a tool for achieving it. My personal motto regarding things spiritual has been "Pray to God ... but row for shore."

Since most people we know are not evangelical adherents to a faith, and most of the spiritual people we know are prone to a fairly pragmatic take when it comes to real-life issues, it is a different sort of mythology that has been a more serious concern: Otherwise enlightened people have dogmatic beliefs about the human mind that "just ain't so". One of the most common is the idea that *anyone* can do *anything* if they just apply *raw willpower*. Usually this is paired with a blind inability to fathom *willpower* as a thing of finite reserve, or the concept that a task that may take *little* willpower for one person can be incredibly *costly* for another.

Bad ideas about this are commonplace in the world of power exchange relationships, chief among them being the idea that if someone is just "slavey enough", they can simply be ordered to stop having mental health issues or find new energy. Certainly both Dominance and submission can be revitalizing and can alleviate stressors, opening new reservoirs of emotional energy in a variety of ways. Submission can allow an individual to feel that some worries, particularly ephemeral concerns, are in the hands of another, and do not require further attention. Catharsis can help free emotional energy. Discipline and sadomasochism can provide structure and outlets. Still, it's important to avoid the belief that having the right "slave heart" means neurochemistry doesn't get a vote.

The realities of neurochemistry are a particular focus of our learning, especially understanding the biological basis of romantic love, particularly in its first stage which is referred to by various terms including *crush*, *new relationship energy* or *the honeymoon phase*. This energy is wonderful, heady, feels great, and tends to rip apart relationships, communities, and even nations. From the moment of "Hey, why don't you ditch Menelaus and run away to Troy with me?" love has been a troublemaker.

By understanding that this sort of love is the reward mechanism for a basic behavioral drive, and distinguishing it from emotions such as attachment which our society also calls "love", we establish a framework for accepting some common inevitabilities, such as the fact that the "honeymoon phase" does not last forever. Many family-like structures are built on the fiction that we can control who we are in love with ... and sometimes, some individuals can. It's difficult, doesn't always work, and may be harder for polyamorous people who expose themselves to the potential for intimate attraction, rather than carefully keeping others at arms' length where they aren't in a position to activate behavioral and physical triggers for attachment.

In less flowery terms, we believe that people are going to act like people, and that declaring a power exchange does not magically change that. If I need someone's behavior to change, the more I understand about *why* the behavior exists, the more likely I will be able to have a realistic idea of how it can be moderated or changed, and how to make that happen. Also, because not all behaviors are amenable to modification, that may mean explaining to others that the behavior is not going to change (or is not going to change overnight), and working with them on adjusting and coping.

Responsibility

Individual responsibility for our actions starts ... unsurprisingly ... with each person taking responsibility. Including me. I have not always been wise, foresightful, or helpful. I have at times played the role of a stage-one-through-three tribesman. If I cannot accept that and take responsibility, how can I expect anyone else to do so? This is an area where people, whether they are in service to me or not, are not going to *do what I say,* but may *follow my example.*

Especially in regards to my personal power exchange relationships and, in a more general way as a nominal leader, if things go wrong it is *always* my fault. This isn't some rubric to ignore, like a politician pinning the blame on an underling: "Of course it is my fault that this bad thing occurred, and I take full responsibility for firing the bastard who did it on my watch." It means reviewing, pragmatically, what I did wrong. The times someone in a social group willfully fails are pretty low. If people fail, there are reasons, and those reasons start with management. If someone failed, then either I gave them a job they couldn't handle, or I failed to support them adequately (which is poor management), or to explain the job, or train them to do it (which is poor communication). That doesn't mean they don't need to learn new skills or do things better next time, but if a leader doesn't take real responsibility, nobody is going to let them lead, and we need to remember that all consensual power exchange is a voluntary commitment.

Pragmatism

We mean this in the sense of practicality and ethical flexibility avoiding social dogma, without losing site of humanity and positive goals—a social *realpolitik*. Ideals are good only if they allow us to do good things, not if the pursuit of the perfect is the enemy of the good. In particular, we should never uphold ideals so impractical that we must come up with systems for subverting them in order to be socially functional.

We see some individuals and households put forward high-minded (and sometimes excessively simplistic) ideals. As an example, there are ideals which runs contrary to basic human nature and social health, such as "Don't gossip." Gossip is a derogatory term for "learning rumors and details about the behaviors and intimate conduct of others", which is the core of human social interaction. Forbidding gossip is a means that despots or oligarchs use to ensure that they are the only ones who have good and accurate information about the social landscape. I've always laughed when I see Masters who forbid "gossip" but are happy to "exchange important ideas about problem people in the community with other leaders." There's a term for that. It's called *gossip*.

Of course, some people probably define "gossip" exclusively to mean "lying and spreading false rumors", which is a different matter entirely. That's just unwise. A lie is a way to get a major advantage now, but lose trust in the future. For anyone who is not a fly-by-night con man, that's penny-wise and pound-foolish. With pragmatism, the value of avoiding lying and cheating comes naturally and obviously because it's a bad idea, not because of some dogmatic sense of honor.

On the other hand, social lying is permissible. I'd rather have someone falsely say, "Your singing was great, we loved it!" than some passive-aggressive slight like "Your singing was ... interesting," or a stinging silence. The focus is the objective (prevent pain rather than cause pain), not a dogmatic reference to the truth. Of course, there *are* times to tell a friend they might want give up singing in public, or to relate some other hard truth, but those occasions are infrequent enough to be handled as special cases.

An additional example of pragmatism is the decision to let duties fall to those people who do them best. Machiavelli tells us:

> And the first opinion which one forms of a prince, and of his understanding, is by observing the men he has around him; and when they are capable and faithful he may always be considered wise, because he has known how to recognize the capable and to keep them faithful.

> –The Prince, Chapter XXII

Miranda manages the money for myself and directly or indirectly for several other associates, as well as any group funds. I had to acquaint her with the concept that a nobleman might employ a man-of-business or a King a Lord Exchequer, but in the end it is a matter of capability. I am a terrible financial manager; she is a good one. Therefore she manages the money.

In the end, our household shares a great deal but comes to our different understandings. For my part, I always reference James Hilton in Lost Horizon: "Moderation in all things ... even moderation."

I suspect it's unlikely that our household will ever feature prominently in the records of those keepers of M/s tradition such as the Carter-Johnson Leather Library or the Leather Archives & Museum. These are people who built the permissions that allow us to experiment, and we owe them a great debt. We are not the brave settlers who hewed their way into new lands with axe and brow sweat. We're the second generation, the shopkeepers, lawyers, bakers and bankers. Our mission is not to establish or carry the torch of some fictional or legendary Tradition, but to build a new tradition rooted in twenty-first century life and experience.

Summary

Over about a decade I failed to find a perfect plan for either power exchange relationships or the larger management of the "household" that will tend to form around any stable non-monogamous group that is engaged in power exchange. I've tried not to grossly misrepresent any trends, and obviously not every one of my associates would agree with every detail I have written here. Flexibility allows for differences, and pragmatism suggests that forcing acceptance of any belief would result in a smaller, less capable group of associates. What I think our joint endeavor has begun to establish is the sort of skillset and idea-base that makes a household possible.

As I worked and learned, I realized that power exchange, polyamory, and alternative sexuality are just parts of a larger social trend. The industrial age made the medieval model of marriage—a pragmatic compromise of the late Middle Ages—obsolete. From the late nineteenth century of Mary Wollenstonecroft through the Victorian era and the twentieth century, couples and groups struggled with new ways of living together. C.B. Wadström's *Plan for a Free Community*, the Oneida Community of the 1840s, and the Kerista commune of the late fifties and sixties which settled into the Haight, were all faltering attempts to discover the dynamics of new ways for humans to be together. Even if all abuse and ignorance which causes human beings to leave their families of birth and seek free associations were removed (and we hope someday they will be), we would still have a tendency to seek adult groups for affiliation.

In grade school I was taught that our primitive ancestors lived together in familial bands. The model of the "cave family" was an extended male family group, with grandfather still around and presiding white-bearded over sons, grandsons, and their spouses. It turns out that this picture was probably more reflective of medieval and nineteenth-century villages and farming culture than of primitive humans. In 2011, Arizona State University anthropologist Kim R. Hill and University of Missouri anthropologist Robert S. Walker looked at data from thirty-two living hunter-gatherer societies, according to a paper they published in *Science*. The surprising result was that only about ten percent of the adult members of a band were closely related.

While we cannot prove that "family of association" is the natural state of man, that certainly suggests it is not a recent or unnatural innovation.

The industrial and information eras are freeing us from many of the factors that tied Victorian and medieval agrarian peoples to a farmstead and extended family unit. There is almost certainly no "natural" or "correct" way for humans to live in associative groups. What we *can* provide is successful working models and skillsets that empower our associations of choice.

Our Archetypal Array
Raven Kaldera, with Joshua Tenpenny and Brandon Hardy

When I began soliciting essays for this book, I assumed that my own essay about M/s relationship styles would be tucked into one of the categories in this book. However, as I began to read them, I realized that I really wanted to talk about more than one of the archetypal roles that inspired us, and that we've integrated into our relationship. That meant that I was relegated to my own category of "eclectic", but perhaps that isn't so bad; my whole life is so eclectic that it might as well be a really unusual rummage sale.

Renaissance Manservant

Actually, this archetype extends itself well into the eighteenth century, although it had changed a great deal by Victorian times. Wealthy medieval households had many servants of varying ranks, but personal attendants really came into their own during the Renaissance, with the rise of a middle class that couldn't afford a whole household, but could pay one well-trained servant to cover all but the menial tasks. By Renaissance England, the personal attendant was sometimes referred to as a valet (the word is first found in writing in 1567), sometimes as a "serving-gentleman" or "waiting-gentleman", and sometimes just "my man" (e.g. Shakespeare's line "Romeo came not home last night; I spoke with his man..."). The female equivalent was the "serving-gentlewoman", "waiting-gentlewoman", or "maid", not to be confused with the later position of housemaid. Their jobs did include dressing their superior and looking after clothing, but they also encompassed being a traveling companion, carrying bags, taking messages, digging up dirt, making sure that their superior got fed, and many other tasks. Most importantly, their biggest job was to be "in waiting"—waiting for the next order, whatever that might be. They were a plucky, resourceful, respectful, and entertaining (if desired) sidekick who stuck to the side of their master or mistress, no matter where that road led.

You can check out Shakespeare's plays to see the blossoming of that archetype; there are upper-class masters and mistresses galore, each with their ingenious, capable, and quick-witted personal attendant. In fact, M/s practitioners may appreciate the loyal, competent, and often opinionated servant characters better than most modern readers will. In *A Place In The Story: Servants and Service in Shakespeare's Plays* (a book which I highly recommend), Linda Anderson writes: "…Modern critics want servants to be 'other' because it is hard for intellectuals to accept that virtue and intelligence may be weak and powerless. Furthermore, obedient servants—as most of Shakespeare's servant-characters are—may seem to us to be traitors to the working class; shouldn't they be rebelling, or at least protesting?"

Long ago, while browsing *Life In Elizabethan England: A Compendium of Common Knowledge*, written as a handbook for reenactors by Maggie Pierce Secara, I ran across her advice for those playing this specific kind of servant. She wrote: "A servant and master strive to do each other credit. As a lady of quality, it is unbecoming to your dignity to carry your own shopping basket. As that lady's servant, it is unbecoming to your dignity to let her." She then went on to write: "The good servant, like a good waiter, is attentive. The best servant is a little bit psychic. He is there when you need him but never hovers. He finds some virtuous occupation when you disappear. He is neither lewd nor vain, but maintains a respectable countenance, to the credit of his master. He is modest but never craven, humble but never base, candid but not insolent." At the time I didn't even know about consensual power dynamics—in fact, I couldn't even imagine that anyone would willingly put themselves in that position for life without pay—but the words struck home with me. I carried that thought for a long time, and it strongly affected how I would eventually construct my perfect power dynamic in my head. I also absorbed her words about my side of the dynamic as well: "The good master is proud but never despotic. He is patient, governing his household with fatherly care. He does not twist your sincere desire to serve into a sincere desire to punch him out. He lets you do your job. He maintains his superior station, as God has given it him, by honourable behavior, not by argument."

In practice, this means that my boys are expected to be able to manage the "charming companion" job on top of the "resourceful servant" job. Our public protocol is less formal but more subtle—less about being a silent servant and more about being exactly the companion I want, in exactly the specific ways I want it. My slaveboy Joshua once referred to it as "learning to be the perfect boyfriend"—someone who is always helpful, respectful, deferential (but not in an obviously obsequious way), and cheerfully wants to do whatever you want them to do. It passes in front of the public work I have to do in other demographics where they wouldn't understand M/s, and doesn't make me look bad in the eyes of vanilla people who would be made uncomfortable by a silent, withdrawn, very-submissive-acting slave.

Additionally, it's important to my ability to inhabit this role that my servants actually feel that I have some reason for being their superior beyond just our mutual agreement that this would be a cool thing. My superior status has to be based on more than just our mutual desire for a power dynamic and the fact that I'm a decent enough guy to make submitting to me reasonably safe. I am not their social superior by virtue of my class birth (as a noble would be), but they have to feel that there is some other reason that would make me, in some meaningful way, their superior even if they weren't in service to me. I absolutely don't expect that attitude and belief from anyone else in the world, and in fact I automatically assume otherwise from them; this is just something I need from my s-types to keep me on my own path of noblesse oblige.

Which brings us to my end of the deal. *Noblesse oblige* literally means "the obligations of the nobility", and as I understand it, this is honorable behavior. If one believes one's self to be superior, one should evince public behavior that is better than those one feels superior to. All the time. No exceptions. And, by the way, "public" means "where any other human being can see you, or will find out about it". The peasants get to be jerks to each other. I don't. I sometimes fail, but it is never acceptable, and I am always striving to hold to that goal. That's part of how I earn that special regard. It's also important to my servants that I show consistently better judgment in important matters than they do, so I'd better stay on my game and make sure I'm thinking deeply enough on each issue to make that happen.

Many s-types spend a great deal of time arguing about how their master is not actually "better" than they are as a person. They chose to serve them not because those masters or mistresses are naturally superior people, but out of love (or perhaps because that master or mistress was the person they happened to be monogamously married to when they decided M/s was important). However, I wanted a master who would be my superior in enough ways to really make a difference. I would not be comfortable being owned by someone who was not my superior; they have to be better than me in some significant way in order for the power dynamic to feel appropriate.

The most important part of the Renaissance manservant (or handmaiden) role, as I see it, is that the servant needs to have an independent perspective to contribute, but should not be contributing independent goals or agendas. This is because people in this role often end up being an advisor or confidante, and if they are asked their opinion, they should have a thoughtful one. Being with them is like being alone, in the sense that if the right amount of trust has developed in both directions, the master should not feel the need to have privacy from them or impress them, but can be entirely unself-conscious. I am to be a comfortable presence; it's not my place to give unsolicited comments or opinions. The more of a confidante I am, the more I should know about my master's favorite topics so that I can provide good conversation as part of the "charming companion" role. However, I am not owed the opportunity to be his confidante at any given time, nor is he obligated to give it to me. On the other hand, although I am expected to be deferential, I need only be as submissive as it takes to defer to him.

The only time when unsolicited commentary is (usually) welcome in this role is when I think he is about to commit a social error. This is because it's my job to help him look good, and it's been useful to learn numerous subtle and respectful ways to help him to not inadvertently be an ass in public. For my part, I generally act more conservatively and respectfully in public than he does when we're working this style, in contrast to the Superhero/sidekick style which we'll touch on next.

In this role-pair, there's generally little to no overlap in skills between master and servant, and that's fine. Our spheres of work are separate. My job is to do the stuff he doesn't do, and to be good at it. That's another hallmark of this style—there is no reason for the master to have anything but pride in the excellence of their servant's skills, and it is completely appropriate for the master to be dependent on the servant for many "support-staff" tasks. In fact, if the master attempts to do the servant's job in anything but an emergency, or feels some need to be independent from the servant, to me that suggests trust issues on the part of the master; perhaps they do not trust the servant to be there and do their job long-term. Interdependence is and has always been a key part of this style.

–Joshua, Raven's Alpha Boy

Superhero/Sidekick

Just to the left of the noble's servant is the superhero's sidekick. They are the same in many ways, but there is one major difference: the servant need only think that the noble's character is superior. The sidekick is there because they believe in the superhero's goals, ideals, and work in the world. They aren't satisfied with a leader whose reach stops at the doorstep. They want to change the world, but they know that on their own, nothing will ever happen, so they attach themselves to a force that is already doing that, and help it move even faster.

While one would expect that a good servant would want to be reliable and able to come through on orders, with this archetype there is a greater sense of peril if things go wrong. If Robin drops the rope when he and Batman are fleeing the scene over a wall, it's not just something that a reprimand can fix. Because the Superhero is generally doing something Bigger, something that extends outside the home and affects other people, the Sidekick may be given some responsibilities that are much more crucial than just getting dinner made. This can be frightening for an s-type who is not used to taking on such serious tasks, or who signed up for the bottom side of a power dynamic relationship because it promised a lack of such vital responsibilities in the first place. I remember one boy who left his master because the master became a titleholder, and the constant scrutiny—"You're a titleholder's boy, you'd better act like quality in public at all times or it will reflect poorly on your master!"—was too much pressure for him. I remember another who left her mistress because the lady's very fulfilling work for a non-profit agency seemed to engross her more than her slave did, and the slave resisted the expectation that she would put in volunteer labor for a cause she didn't care about.

On the top side of this dynamic, the master has to have some meaningful work that they do that is larger than the home base. They need a passion, and it's up to the would-be slave to make sure that this person's passion is one where they can honestly feel good about possibly playing second fiddle to it, and being a constant support for it.

> I recently read an article that mentioned how most people go through life continually searching for meaning and purpose, and I was suddenly so grateful for my own situation. Not only do I have meaning and purpose to my life in serving a worthy master as thoroughly and well as I possibly can, I also have the knowledge that my service to him supports his service to the world. As an activist and educator, I can see the positive impact he has on people, both directly and indirectly. I'm a small part of something much bigger, and this makes our relationship so much more meaningful than if I was just getting him drinks and polishing his boots.

> This aspect of our relationship manifests most strongly in our work traveling and educating together. Unlike the manservant role, there is often a large overlap in skillsets in this style—in fact, the skills may even be identical. One is the senior partner, and one is the junior partner. The exception is that the superhero is the one who sets the goals. There's a strong mentorship aspect to this relationship, but even if the two become peers in their skill level, the sidekick owes the superhero obedience for getting them to that point.

> In this style, it's acceptable for the Superhero to risk the sidekick, perhaps even put them in a little danger (so to speak). They don't need protection. They should be sturdy and resilient, an asset rather than a liability in risky situations. The Superhero is allowed to give them poorly specified goals—"Figure it out, just get it done!" and their assignments are not required to be reasonable, because the

superhero's own tasks are also often unreasonable. The motto, spoken or unspoken, is that everyone on this team is expected to go above and beyond. After all, you're trying to change the world! This isn't going happen by sitting around watching TV.

In my experience, this isn't a particularly submissive role, and there is more leeway for challenging decisions than in many other roles. Obedience is very important, because the work is so crucial, but the sidekick is not required to believe that the superhero is always right. The sidekick should, however, admire the superhero and look up to them. Having shared values and morals is important here, but the sidekick can be a little more petty or impulsive than the superhero, because the superhero keeps them in line. For that matter, I think that there's a slightly lower bar for emotional maturity than in other roles, especially if the master doesn't mind a mouthy sidekick, and this style can work well with Daddy/boy or other adult/adolescent styles.

It is interesting to me that both of these roles are not especially submissive, since after all, I am owned property. I can be—and I find a great deal of fulfillment in being—highly submissive and deferential, but our public role often demands otherwise, especially when we are educating non-M/s populations. A spunky sidekick is more useful to my master in these situations, where people would likely be uncomfortable with an excessively deferential or overtly submissive role. I'm also very private with my emotions, so it is a relief to rarely be asked to put the full depth of my surrender on public display.

–Joshua, Raven's Alpha Boy

Artist/Sculpture

I remember going to a gay male M/s support group for the first time, and the chosen activity was that everyone there (of whom only my slaveboy and I, along with an unaccompanied s-type, were the only ones who were actually practicing power dynamics at the time) was to couple up randomly and portray archetypes. These included Master/slave, but also trainer/pet and a few others. We were given a huge box of Legos to use as props. Joshua asked permission to go off with another man and be a dog for ten minutes; I granted it and he spent the next period fetching Legos with his mouth on all fours. I, in turn, was approached by a sincere but rather callow young man who wanted to experience "the Master/slave thing", if only for a few minutes.

I pointed to the Legos and told him to build me a ski lift. He looked at me blankly. I figured out quickly that he didn't have a lot of problem-solving skills, and I walked him verbally through the building of a ski lift (with grape-stem trees and popcorn snow from the snack table), not telling him what to do so much as asking leading questions and helping him through the process. At the end, he asked me what this had to do with a Master/slave relationship. I told him that if he was my slave, I'd be training him in problem-solving, and all the areas where he had trouble and needed some polishing. In fifteen minutes of being under me, he had learned plenty to take with him.

For some couples, helping the slave to improve as a human being is an altruistic act for the master; it makes them feel good about themselves to help others do better. For some, it's simple self-interest—they want to get the slave to the point where they can fulfill the master's desires, and that requires some reworking. But there's a third reason, and it's being an inveterate tinker, an artist for whom everything is a canvas (or wall) to paint, a piece of wood or stone or clay to sculpt, a piece someone's thrown away that could be perfectly serviceable and maybe even awesome with just a little work. Were I a mechanic, I'd be picking up old classic cars and rehabilitating them. The idea that something needs work doesn't put me off; it gets my creative juices flowing and my hands itch to start reworking it in the image of my inspiration. My boys are my works of art, my projects, which I constantly polish and tinker with. The fact that they are both greatly improved as people from when I got them, that's a nice side effect, but it's not my real motivation.

As a point of warning: This is a very objectifying style, and it may not be acceptable to an s-type who is reacts badly to objectification. I'm fortunate in that both of my boys strongly eroticize and take comfort from being objectified, so they respond very well to being my "things" that I tinker with. (I've jokingly referred to them as Thing 1 and Thing 2, for the Dr. Seuss fans out there. Although I am far too serious to be the Cat in the Hat.) However, some s-types feel humiliated (in a bad way) by objectification, so discuss things carefully before boarding this particular ship.

When I was in junior high, I saw a part of some documentary on TV about the history of tattooing. The portion I happened to watch talked about the practice of skinning the backs of dead people who had gotten particularly amazing ink work done there when alive, then preserving, stretching, and framing the skin. This was the start of both my dream to be someone's art materials when I died, as well as maybe being somebody's canvas while I was still around to enjoy it. Now I have happily started down this road with my Master.

Some people think that having a Master who wants to change me, who could not like me Exactly As I Am, is inherently a bad thing. While I have been in relationships where I have been made to feel horrible about who I am, this certainly isn't what's going on here. And quite honestly, if someone looked at who I am now and thought, "There's no room for improvement here," I'd be convinced that they were lying to me. I have no intention of stagnating or pretending I've reached some mythical state of perfection, just as I can value what I have worked to achieve thus far. He meets me on that middle ground and we go from there.

As far as my Master is concerned, wanting me and wanting to improve me aren't opposing sentiments. To the parts of him that are an artist, I'm appreciated as raw material. Like a chunk of stone I can be beautiful in my own right, but under the hands of an artist who truly knows how to work me, I can become something else altogether. And just like any medium, I have my limitations that only an artist skilled at their craft will know. You can't do with soapstone the exact same things you could do with marble or granite, and the slab you get usually has irregularities and faults to take into consideration. That is not a judgment call on the material, that's taking the reality of what one has to work with, and then putting in *the time and effort to mold it into a masterpiece (or Master's piece, for the fellow pun lovers out there).*

It is quite objectifying, though, which is a reasonable issue for many people, but objectification has been a good tool for me through many of my problems. As a transsexual cripple, I have numerous issues with my body. The very act of having an enjoyable interaction with someone on the basis of nothing but my body is very healing. Not only does it show me that my body is a vessel that can both provide and receive pleasure, it also shows that my body is something enjoyable in of itself, in a very tangible way. Things about my body that can often be deal-breakers or sources of interpersonal strife get an appraising look, accompanied by a statement such as, "Hm, I can work with that," instead of the usual reactions of shame or tolerance. These physical struggles become part of the artwork rather than oppositions to my ability to ever be valued. And as he molds me with these things in mind, I can find pride in his talent and beauty in the "me" he has shaped. I mean, I may not be a framed hunk of flesh, but it's still pretty great.

—Brandon, Raven's Omega Boy

Guru/Chela

While the full description of our M/s version of *gurubhakti*—devotion toward and service to one's spiritual teacher—can be found in the anthology *Sacred Power, Holy Surrender: Living a Spiritual Power Dynamic* (Alfred Press 2011), and while we can't cover every aspect of this relationship here, I will start by saying that the traditional (Hindu and other faiths) guru/chela relationship does not include sexual contact or emotional intimacy. In fact, those are considered to be detrimental to the roles of spiritual teacher and disciple. We, however, are living a form *of gurubhakti* in a way that does include some of both.

The word "guru" means "teacher", and specifically spiritual teacher. "Chela" means "student" today, but it once meant "servant" or "slave", as chelas were supposed to render a great deal of service to their gurus in return for their teaching. In some Hindu sects, carefully preparing the guru's ritually clean food is an honor, but it had to be done with a specific attitude of peace and mindfulness because it was thought that the food would absorb the energy of the preparer and server. Washing the dust off the guru's feet needed to be done in a similar way.

As Master Thomas discusses earlier in this book, a serious part of the Gurubhakti M/s model (or, for that matter, any spiritual model of M/s) is acknowledging the chain of command. The slave may be at the bottom of it, but the master is not at the top. He or she answers to a Higher—or perhaps Deeper—power, who keeps them on their path and pushes them to continually be more worthy of their position of spiritual leadership.

Part of the slave's job is to help the master in various spiritual ways to keep on their path and come to it more cleanly. This can be done by ritually "seeing" them as their higher self, and focusing on that— perhaps in a meditation while sitting at the master's feet. While this sounds cheesy, it does actually work. If the slave gets it right—not attempting to push the master in any direction, just sitting in the master's presence and meditating with all their might on them at their very best and highest self—it can suddenly give the master a boost of courage, confidence, and judgment to help on their path. I've found that this works—surprisingly enough—and it's interesting to think about how much power that actually gives my slave.

> *I actually got into conscious power-exchange relationships completely by accident. When I signed up to serve my Master, I was actually only looking for a guru. I had been taken under the motherly wing of the woman who tends to most of the worldly needs of the Swami at the local Vedanta Hindu temple. The service she was rendering spoke to me on a deep level, and I wanted to do what she did: gurubhakti. And although Vedantic Hinduism is chill with Jesus, I felt I was simply too Christian to follow this path and prayed for another way to pursue it. So, long story short, here I am serving a Northern Tradition Pagan shaman.*

> *A central part of my service from the beginning has been that his life is focused on doing spiritual work, and I am taking care of designated day-to-day tasks that would otherwise distract him. By enabling his spiritual work in this way, I am in turn doing my own.*

Then, as the M/s relationship started to form after months of this, I found that the vast majority of services I already rendered as his chela in the appropriately-detached spiritual way were complimented by services rendered as his submissive on a more personal level, and vice versa. One clear example is preparing his meals. From a service perspective, this is pretty straightforward: he wants food, I prepare it. When I started taking a little extra time to do floofy garnishes, it gave him reason to smile, so it became part of the service. But when looking at it from the perspective of a chela preparing food for their Guru, one finds a long tradition that focuses on the attitude and intent of the chela more than on the food itself. This mindfulness carries through and encourages the same attitude in the Guru. So the service of getting him food and the spiritually mindful attitude with which I do it go hand-in-hand, and even if they have different priorities, they share the one of bringing him some joy.

I find, though, that when I talk about kinkifying my spirituality, most minds go immediately to a sadomasochistic scene. There is certainly a wealth of potential there, but I find that by itself it doesn't scratch the itch for me. Whereas many spiritual practices with a cornerstone in BDSM focus on creating an Experience for the masochist/bottom/submissive, I find that even though this has its place at times for me as a means to an end, I am much more fulfilled by facilitating an experience for others through service, and my Master is certainly no exception. When we do our weekly ritual of my washing his feet, it is my responsibility to put everything together, chant appropriately, and clean up while he relaxes and makes himself open to the experience.

Even when he is facilitating a cathartic experience for me, I still prioritize finding a way to make it enjoyable for him. We gravitate towards his favorite ways to hurt me, and heavily take into consideration what strikes his fancy that day. I tell him how I am most likely to break, as well as what emotional and physical points are notably tender, so that he has the option of ending it quickly or drawing it out as painfully long as he wants. The involvement of orgasm of any kind is completely up to him. Often he'll change things up in the moment because I have provided information, not a script, *so I am under no illusion that I actually have any control over the scene nor that I have any important knowledge of what is going to happen. The final call is his, as it is with everything we do, but it does mean that I have done all in my power (well, in the power he allows me) to make the things he does for his spiritual work easier, especially if that thing involves me.*

It has also helped that the realization of non-duality is a large common goal he and I both hold, and we're pretty set up for exploring it. He is driven to take control while I am driven to surrender; both his spiritual path and body require meat to be a staple of his diet while I have been a vegetarian by choice since I was four years old; he is Pagan while I am Christian ... and none of these are more spiritually valid, enlightened, or better than the other. They are simply different, and don't have to be at odds. In fact, they can even work together very well. This builds into another shared goal—one that many people consider to be the goal of the Guru/chela relationship—which is for the chela to be able to see that the Divine Spark they worship in their Guru exists in them as well. Even if our personal trappings are so very different, one day I hope to achieve the realization that just as I view so many of his actions as beautifully lit by that Spark, mine and everyone else's are lit in that same way.

–Brandon, Raven's Omega Boy

Of course, we don't generally announce that we are slipping from one style to another; it happens more organically than that. Both boys understand that specific events require certain styles—a kink conference, a church picnic, a puja to Shiva, or fixing breakfast will each gravitate the boys to the correct styles. More usually they look to me for cues, or they just ask: *How do you want me to be, Sir?* I'm a versatile person who wears a lot of hats, and I need them to be just as versatile in order to keep up with me and serve me most effectively. In its own way, being skillfully eclectic is as much a discipline as being dedicated to one single style all the time.

We are what we repeatedly do.
Excellence, then, is not an act, but a habit.
–Aristotle

About the Editor

Raven Kaldera is a queer FTM transgendered intersexual shaman, as well as a pervert and slave-owner. He is the author of too many books to list here, including *Dark Moon Rising: Pagan BDSM And The Ordeal Path* and *Power Circuits: Polyamory In A Power Dynamic*. He and his beautiful and useful slaveboy Joshua have been teaching and presenting workshops regularly for many years to the BDSM, Neo-Pagan, Sex/Spirituality, transgender, and a few other communities. He sees his physical challenges as just another obstacle to overcome in his quest to change the world whenever possible. His slaveboy Joshua refers to himself as "a wholly owned subsidiary of the vast enterprise that is Raven Kaldera." *'Tis an ill wind that blows no minds.*

www.ingramcontent.com/pod-product-compliance
Lightning Source LLC
Chambersburg PA
CBHW020606270326
41927CB00005B/205